Why have some interstate crises escalated to war when others have not? Are there patterns of behavior that war-prone disputes share in common? What are the most effective strategies to employ in managing crises? These are some of the questions considered by Russell Leng as he examines the behavior of nations in forty militarized crises occurring between 1816 and 1980. Leng considers the conditions under which crises are more or less likely to escalate to war or be resolved peacefully, and compares the descriptive and prescriptive validity of two competing perspectives on conflict behavior: classical realism, and the psychological approaches of behavioral scientists. The investigation employs a mass of empirical data on the structure of crises, and on the actions and interactions of the crises participants, to develop models of crisis escalation, and to test hypotheses regarding the relationship between the crisis structure and the influence strategies and tactics of the participants in determining crisis outcomes. The empirical results are compared with research findings from a wide range of studies, not only from quantitative studies of international conflict, but also from social psychology, game theory, and case studies.

The author concludes that elements of both the realist and psychological perspectives are necessary for an adequate understanding of interstate crisis behavior, and that the most effective approach to crisis bargaining combines each perspective in a firm-but-flexible "reciprocating" strategy. The epilogue presents a provocative critique of the bargaining strategies pursued by the United States and Iraq during the Gulf Crisis of 1990–1991.

CAMBRIDGE STUDIES IN INTERNATIONAL RELATIONS: 28

INTERSTATE CRISIS BEHAVIOR 1816–1980

Cambridge Studies in International Relations is a joint initiative of Cambridge University Press and the British International Studies Association (BISA). The series will include a wide range of material, from undergraduate textbooks and surveys to research-based monographs and collaborative volumes. The aim of the series is to publish the best new scholarship in International Studies from Europe, North America and the rest of the world.

CAMBRIDGE STUDIES IN INTERNATIONAL RELATIONS

INTERSTATE CRISIS BEHAVIOR, 1816–1980: REALISM VERSUS RECIPROCITY

RUSSELL J. LENG

Department of Political Science, Middlebury College

CAMBRIDGE
UNIVERSITY PRESS

Published by the Press Syndicate of the University of Cambridge
The Pitt Building, Trumpington Street, Cambridge CB2 1RP
40 West 20th Street, New York, NY 10011–4211, USA
10 Stamford Road, Oakleigh, Victoria 3166, Australia

First published 1993

Printed in Great Britain at the University Press, Cambridge

A catalogue record for this book is available from the British Library

Library of Congress cataloguing in publication data

Leng, Russell J.
Interstate crisis behavior, 1816–1980: realism vs. reciprocity / Russell J. Leng.
   p.   cm. – (Cambridge studies in international relations; 28)
Includes bibliographical references.
ISBN 0 521 39141 5
1. War. 2. World politics – 19th century. 3. World politics – 20th century. 4. Military
history – 19th century. 5. Military history – 20th century. I. Title. II. Series.
U21.2.L39   1993
327.1′6 – dc20   92–32370CIP

ISBN 0 521 39141 5 hardback

CE

To the memory of my father,
Percival K. Leng, Jr.

CONTENTS

ix

FIGURES

TABLES

PREFACE

The research for this book began twenty-two years ago, during a leave spent at the University of Michigan. Following a brief correspondence, I had managed to attach myself to David Singer's Correlates of War (COW) Project. Singer had launched what has since become the largest data-based research project on the problem of war, and in 1970 he and his associates were deeply engaged in generating aggregate data on the onset, magnitude, and severity of all wars since the Congress of Vienna, and on the attributes of the international system and its member states during the same period. Missing from the COW project, however, was any attempt to generate data on the behavior of states in the crises that preceded the wars in order to identify differences in the patterns of action between those crises that ended in war, and those that were resolved peacefully. When I mentioned to Singer that it seemed odd that such a promising predictor of the outbreak of war was not included, he seized upon my innocence regarding the data generation problems such an effort entailed, and suggested that I immediately begin working on that part of the project. That effort has been my major scholarly preoccupation ever since.

Over the next two decades I completed a number of articles dealing with interstate crisis behavior, all of which made use of the data that had been generated up to that time. This book goes back over some of the ground covered in those earlier studies, but with the larger sample of forty crises, and the advantage of the insights gained from the research conducted in the intervening years. Thus all of the chapters represent new analyses conducted with a larger sample of cases, and, in several instances, new research techniques. Nonetheless, this study in no way claims to represent the last word on the subject of crisis behavior. The sample of forty crises is still relatively small. The quantitative analyses are used to provide an empirically based argument for an approach to crisis bargaining that combines the insights that can be drawn from realist and behavioral perspectives on crisis behavior. The quality of that argument, and the robustness of the empirical findings on which it is based, ultimately are dependent on the degree to which they are replicated in other studies.

The book is written in a manner intended to make it accessible to any serious student of international affairs. The analyses of crisis behavior employ quantitative data, but with the possible exception of the log linear analysis described in Chapter 6, readers with only an elementary background in statistics should encounter no difficulty in understanding the techniques employed.

The Behavioral Correlates of War project has been something of a cottage industry in comparison with efforts like the larger Correlates of War project. I teach at an undergraduate liberal arts college, so that, aside from occasional summer visits by graduate students from Michigan, my immediate working colleagues most often have been undergraduates who have aided in the data generation. This sort of effort naturally suffers from certain inefficiencies, but it has offered me the rewards – as well as the frustrations – of being directly engaged in every aspect of the research project, including all aspects of the data generation, computer programming, and data analysis. This is not to say that I have not benefited from the assistance and advice of colleagues and associates with greater expertise. Professor John Emerson, of the Middlebury mathematics department, has provided invaluable advice and assistance with statistical questions on many occasions. James Krupp and Thomas Copeland from Academic Computing at Middlebury, and undergraduates like John Emerson, Jr., and, most recently, Ding Chun, have been the main authors of the computing programs. The project's greatest debt, however, goes to a long line of undergraduate coders, who have spent countless hours recording and coding events.

When I think of those people who should be acknowledged for helping to bring this project to fruition, I think first of the early encouragement of my mother and father, and my uncle, Leonard Tennyson, who was particularly influential in kindling my interest in studying and writing about world affairs. My work on the BCOW project, and much of my scholarly career, owe an enormous debt to David Singer, who has been a valued colleague and friend ever since I invited myself to Ann Arbor in 1970. I also owe intellectual debts to Charles Gochman, Robert Goodsell, Christopher Lenhardt, James Ray, Steven Walker, and Hugh Wheeler, who have collaborated with me in different phases of the project. Portions of the book have benefited from the comments of colleagues, particularly, Murray Dry, Patrick James, Yossi Shain, and Allison Stanger.

The project throughout has benefited from several grants from the

National Science Foundation, including a recent grant for the completion of the research for this book, National Science Foundation Grant no. 8818927, and continuing support from Middlebury College, including a leave of absence to write the manuscript. None of this would have been possible without the continuing patience and support of my wife, Cilla, who, on different occasions, has served as a coder, computer programmer, and editor, as well as attending to more important things.

1 REALIST AND PSYCHOLOGICAL PERSPECTIVES

The problem of war lies at the heart of the study of international relations. We continue to study war in the hope that greater knowledge will help us to eliminate it, yet, in the face of its continuing recurrence, we must admit to knowing too little about war's causes, and less about its prevention.

One of the things we do know is that almost all wars are preceded by militarized crises, that is, disputes in which the conflict between the two sides has escalated to a level where both sides have indicated a willingness to go to war to achieve, or to defend, their interests. What I will call a "militarized interstate crisis" is the last stop on the road to war, the station at which questions of war and peace hang in the balance. How states respond to militarized crises, and how they ought to respond if they wish to protect their vital interests without the costs of war, are questions that have been asked about specific crises since the advent of the modern state system, at the Congress of Vienna, in 1816.

The first question is descriptive. We do not have much empirically based information on how states – not particular states, but states in general – tend to behave in crises. We need to know more about their central tendencies. There also is a predictive component to the question. To ask how states behave in crises leads to more specific questions regarding the conditions under which particular patterns of behavior are most likely to occur. The second question is prescriptive. We want to gain a better understanding not only of how states behave in crises, but what types of behavior are more or less likely to lead to success or failure. This book explores these questions by looking at some of the key attributes of the participants and their behavior in a sample of forty interstate crises occurring in the period between 1816 and 1980. Throughout the analysis in succeeding chapters, we will consider the relative descriptive and prescriptive validity of two competing theoretical perspectives: classical realism, with an extension of its precepts to crisis bargaining by conflict strategists, and a psychological

1

perspective on crisis behavior that has grown out of research by behavioral scientists.

The key assumptions of these two perspectives are discussed in the second half of this chapter. Chapter 2 describes the methodological approach employed in conducting the analysis of the forty crises. The substantive analysis begins in Chapter 3, with a consideration of the relationship between the crisis structure, which is defined as the intersection of the perceived interests and war-fighting capabilities of the two sides, and crisis outcomes. Chapter 4 considers the potential effects of the escalatory process on the actions of the participants. After examining the relationships among the crisis structure, patterns of escalation (or deescalation), and crisis outcomes, in Chapter 5, we will turn to a more microscopic look at the influence tactics and strategies employed by the crisis participants in their efforts to influence each other's behavior. Chapter 6 is devoted to a consideration of the relationship between particular varieties of influence attempts and the responses of their recipients. Chapter 7 examines the relative effectiveness of different types of influence strategies, and Chapter 8 takes a closer look at the use, and effectiveness, of what I have labeled Reciprocating influence strategies, that is, strategies combining firmness and flexibility.

Which influence strategies and tactics foreign-policy-makers will consider most appropriate in the course of an evolving crisis are dependent to some degree on their views regarding what is most likely to be effective under the circumstances, and that view depends, to a large extent, on their beliefs regarding the nature of interstate conflict.[1] National leaders, like the rest of us, act according to theories about the nature of the environment in which they must operate. While the particulars of the political beliefs of foreign-policy-makers are bound to vary across time and states, most contemporary international relations scholars would agree that the dominant overall perspective is that of realpolitik.[2] This investigation begins with the assumption that, however policy-makers may actually *behave* in interstate crises, over the past century and three-quarters, they have shared a perspective on crisis behavior that is consistent with realpolitik, that is, that interstate conflict is driven by considerations of interests and power. The dominance of realpolitik has grown out of an historically established tradition that finds its theoretical expression in the works of classical realist thinkers, of whom the most influential modern exponent has been Hans Morgenthau (1946, 1960). The precepts of Morgenthau, and other classical realist thinkers, have been extended to prescriptive theories of conflict bargaining by theorists, such as

2

Kahn (1962, 1965) and Schelling (1960, 1966), whom I will label "conflict strategists," after Schelling's influential work, *Strategy of Conflict* (1960).[3]

The descriptive validity of the behavioral assumptions of classical realism, along with the bargaining prescriptions of the conflict strategists, have been challenged by experimental research on interpersonal bargaining, as well as by empirical studies of crisis behavior by behavioral scientists. Besides questioning whether statesmen behave according to the basic precepts of realism, these studies suggest that following the prescriptions of conflict strategists may lead to disastrous consequences. The remainder of this chapter is devoted to a discussion of the principal assumptions of classical realists and conflict strategists, and the challenge to these assumptions presented by seemingly contradictory findings from behavioral research.

The realist perspective

Classical realism assumes different forms in the hands of different scholars, so much so that it lacks the precision that we would normally associate with a formal theory;[4] nevertheless, there are certain assumptions that form a coherent and internally consistent image of the essence of international politics and international conflict in particular.[5] Realists claim that these shared assumptions have led to a tradition of statesmanship which has produced an "astounding continuity" (Morgenthau, 1960:6)[6] in the foreign policies of disparate states. Understand how other statesmen *really* think and act, Morgenthau advises us, and you will understand how to act effectively in "a world where power counts."

Realist assumptions

An understanding of the realist perspective begins with the assumptions of classical realist theory. Classical realism conceives of political action as a manifestation of an ongoing struggle for power among individuals, a view that has its roots in a pessimistic view of human relations. Nowhere is it stated more succinctly than in Thucydides' account of the words of Athenian ambassadors addressing the magistrates of the tiny Island of Melos about the surrender that will be necessary for the Melians to spare their city and its inhabitants from the dreadful consequences of an Athenian invasion:

> But out of those things which both of us do really think, let us go through with that which is feasible; both you and we knowing, that

3

in human disputation justice is then only agreed on when the necessity is equal; whereas they that have odds of power exact as much as
they can, and the weak yield to such conditions as they can get.
(Thucydides [431–411 BC] 1975:V, 89)

This, as Michael Walzer (1977, ch. 1) puts it, is "interest talk." In the
course of disputes, men do not think and act according to ethical
constraints, but in accordance with their interests, and their ability to
obtain those interests is a function of their relative power. "The main
signpost that helps political realism to find its way through the land-
scape of international politics is the concept of interest defined in
terms of power" (Morgenthau, 1960:5).

At the heart of classical realism lies a pessimistic view of human
nature. The most infamous realist account of human nature occurs in
Machiavelli's *The Prince* ([1513] 1964:145–6), when he makes the case
that, if one has to choose between being loved and feared, it is better to
be feared. To a desire for power and a fear of the power of others,
Hobbes ([1651] 1958:106) adds pride, or a desire for personal glory: "So
that in nature we find three principal causes of quarrel: first, competition; secondly, diffidence; thirdly, glory. The first makes men
invade for gain, the second for safety, and the third for reputation."

Hobbes's ([1651] 1958:80) view of man as driven by "a perpetual and
restless desire for power after power that ceaseth only in death," is
echoed by Morgenthau (1946:168) when he writes that "man is born to
seek power." The realist theologian Reinhold Niebuhr (1944) views the
biological drive for power as spiritualized in human self-love and
pride. Writing in reference to the role played by pride in relations
among states, Aron (1966:366) has observed that "the difficulty of
peace has more to do with man's humanity than his animality."[7]
Politics raises the interpersonal struggle for power to another level.
The nexus of political action is the domination of one person by
another. "Politics is a struggle for power over men, and whatever its
ultimate aim may be, power is its immediate goal and the modes of
acquiring, maintaining, and demonstrating it determine the technique
of political action" (Morgenthau, 1946:195).

Morgenthau argues that, in the modern world, the individual power
drive has been controlled and redirected by the state. The state has
become the most exalted object of loyalty on the part of the individual
and the most effective organization for the exercise of power over the
individual. The individual ego, with all its flaws, is redirected to the
state. Moreover, while the state is ideologically and physically more
powerful than its citizens, it is free from restraint from above. The
result is not a suppression of the power drive, but a quantitative and

4

qualitative extension of it. In an anarchic international system, with no higher authority to place limits on the behavior of sovereign states, only the balancing power of other self-interested states can blunt the power drive of individual members. "In a world where power counts," writes Morgenthau, "no nation pursuing a rational policy has a choice between renouncing and wanting power ... (1946:200)" Morgenthau's admonition is an echo of Thucydides' account of the cause of the Peloponnesian Wars: "the growth of the Athenian power; which putting the Lacedaemonians into fear, necessitated the war" (1975:42). Viewed from a classical realist perspective, power is a relational concept, and power relations between states are essentially zero-sum.

Thus, classical realism begins at the individual level with a pessimistic view of human nature that describes politics as a continuing struggle for power. The individual drive for power is redirected by the state, which acts without any higher constraints in an anarchic system. Some contemporary realist thinkers, who have been described as "structural realists," or "neorealists," have moved away from classical realism's emphasis on a pessimistic view of human nature to focus primarily on the anarchic conditions of the international system. Notable among these theorists is Waltz (1959:232), who argues that "wars occur because there is nothing to prevent them," at least, nothing other than the balancing power of other states.[8] Viewed from this perspective, the central problem of international relations is that of achieving cooperation in an anarchic, but increasingly interdependent, world (see Keohane, 1989).

The realist's world is statecentric, with security concerns taking precedence over all other interests. At their best, relations among competing states are based on reciprocal exchange through careful diplomacy. At their worst, their relations are based on deterrence and war. War is, in Clausewitz's ([1832] 1966:I:I:24) oft quoted words: "a mere continuation of policy by other means." It is a necessary and normal activity of states concerned with maintaining their security and extending their power. In such a world, the sole regulatory device is the balance of power, exercised through the prudent application of political power. Prudence – the weighing of the consequences of state actions – becomes the supreme virtue in international politics. Prudence entails knowing the limits of one's power, and of rationally calculating the costs and risks of action in terms of interests at stake. As a normative guide, prudence represents no more than the exercise of commonsense within a realist perspective. It is a situational ethic, but one judges the likely outcome in a given situation according to realist assumptions regarding the motivations and actions of states, and one judges the quality of the outcome according to its conformity with realist values. A prudent policy is a rational policy insofar as rationality can be defined as acting in accordance with the best interests of the state.

In international politics, where national leaders must make subjective choices with limited and ambiguous information, *rationality* is best understood in an instrumental sense (Riker and Ordeshook, 1973:16–19; Zagare, 1987:10–11). Instrumental rationality does not require omniscience, but it does assume that the actions taken by states represent the conscious choices of national decision-makers, and that, in making those choices, the decision-makers are able to evaluate and order predicted outcomes. To these two assumptions, classical realists would add a third: that the decision-makers make these choices based on a calculation of national interests in terms of their relative power. "We assume that statesmen think and act in terms of interest defined as power, and the evidence of history bears that assumption out," writes Morgenthau (1960:5). Whatever the ultimate objectives may be, the immediate objective of foreign policy must be to maintain, demonstrate, or extend the power of the state, because power is the means to all other objectives in the international arena. The statement has prescriptive as well as descriptive implications. This, the realists tell us, is how statesmen do think and act, and, in a world where power counts, it is how statesmen *should* think and act. In fact, it is the prescriptive element that is stressed by classical realism. Realists are well aware of deviations from this prescription in the foreign policies of some particular states, which they regard as misguided, at best.

The conflict strategists

If classical realism continues to have validity in describing state behavior and in providing prescriptive guidance to national decision-makers, then it would appear to be most applicable in militarized interstate crises where security is immediately at stake. It can be argued that, regardless of the complexities of networks of communication and influence that may drive policy in other situations, in militarized crises the state acts as an integrated unit through the official foreign-policy-making body. There may be debate and coalition-building within that body (see Allison, 1971; Snyder and Diesing, 1977), but the debate will be over the national interest in terms of security and power. Other issues, realists would argue, are secondary.

By the same token, the view of politics as a struggle for power is

6

most compelling in situations in which each party must consider the consequences of a war with the other. If these assumptions are linked to the rationality assumption described above, then one ought to be able to predict the behavior of states in crises based on each state's policy-makers' perceptions of the state's power relative to that of the adversary, and on the interests at stake. Snyder and Diesing (1977) refer to the intersection of the perceptions of comparative power and interests for the two parties as the *structure* of the crisis. They argue, in the realist tradition, that the behavior of the participants is dependent on their perceptions of the structure of the crisis.

If perceptions of relative power and motivation are presumed to be the key variables influencing the behavior of states in crises, then it ought to be possible to develop a prescriptive theory of crisis bargaining, that is, an effective theory of influence. Schelling (1960:4) has described such a theory as a "strategy of conflict," a theory of "intelligent, sophisticated conflict behavior – of successful behavior." Schelling (1960, 1966) has been one of the most influential theorists among a group of scholars (Burns, 1961; Kissinger, 1957; Kahn, 1962, 1965) who have extended classical realism to bargaining in interstate disputes, particularly crises. Although there is considerable variance among these "conflict strategists," they share a perspective that views crisis bargaining as an expression of the power struggle in action. Effective crisis bargaining becomes dependent on exploiting the other party's fear of war through the skillful use of threats and punishments, and on demonstrating one's own willingness to accept the risk of war to achieve one's objectives. Bargaining power becomes a "function of perceived comparative resolve" (Snyder and Diesing, 1977:190).

This is not to say that these theorists are reckless proponents of power politics. Theorists such as Schelling and Kissinger are well aware that interstate conflicts are not necessarily zero-sum situations, and that prudence requires considerations of the possibilities of accommodation, as well as coercion in crisis bargaining.[9] These writers also recognize the need to use care in the exploitation of the threat of force, and the need to allow states that are forced into submission to save face. Nevertheless, the emphasis is on the skillful use of the techniques of coercion, or what Schelling (1960:5) refers to as the "exploitation of potential force." In this respect, the view of crisis bargaining held by conflict strategists resembles Clausewitz's view of war, with its emphasis on the calculated exploitation of force in an uncertain, game-like, environment (see Clausewitz [1832] 1966:I:I:18–21). One of their principal critics, in fact, has labelled these theorists the "neo-Clausewitzians" (Rapoport, 1968:60).

7

When crisis bargaining is viewed from this perspective, success is achieved through the exploitation of the other party's fear of war, and through the demonstration of one's own determination to accept the consequences of war. Success is a function of a credible demonstration of resolve, that is, of a willingness to accept the costs and risks of war to achieve one's objectives. A consequence of accepting these assumptions is to view crisis bargaining, in Kahn's (1965:16) words, as a "competition in risk-taking." The realist paradox is that one must prepare for war to maintain peace; the conflict strategists' extension of the paradox is that one must credibly threaten war to avoid it, and escalate a crisis to end it.

Realism's paradoxes

There are more specific paradoxes within classical realist theory that create difficulties for researchers attempting to test its validity. Two of these paradoxes raise important questions for the investigation at hand. The first lies in the relationship between rational and nonrational behavior. As I noted at the beginning of the discussion of classical realism's assumptions, realists emphasized the influence of nonrational elements on human motivation and action. Moreover, they are well aware of the influence that nonrational thinking has had on the foreign policies of particular states. For example, Clausewitz [1832] 1966:I:I:3), who urges statesmen to view war as an instrument of policy, notes that one of the two major causes of war is "instinctive hostility ... even the most civilized nations may burn with passionate hatred of each other."

Realists argue that the best way to understand foreign policy is through a rational reconstruction of what a cooly calculating statesman, motivated by considerations of the national interest in terms of power, would do under the circumstances (see Morgenthau, 1960:5). But, if the struggle for power has its roots in nonrational impulses, why should we not expect nonrational impulses to confound what realists would consider rational policy-making? And, if realists admit that statesmen frequently do behave in a nonrational manner, where does that leave the theory? The descriptive answer to these questions appears to be that what realism describes as a rational foreign policy is how realists think *successful* statesmen behave. The descriptive answer obviously has prescriptive implications. If you want to be successful (1) you should think and act in terms of interest defined as power, and (2) you should assume that other statesmen think and act in the same way. The focus on a calculated pursuit of power rejects consideration

8

of the confounding effects of other variables – a sense of what is fair, or equitable, feelings of hostility a concern for personal honor, or emotional reactions to stress – on what is assumed to be a rational calculation of security interests and power on the part of the other party.

Another paradox surfaces in conjunction with the conflict strategists' emphasis on exploiting the other side's fear of war. If crisis bargaining power can be properly described as a function of perceived comparative resolve, the realist admonition to demonstrate power places a high premium on credibly demonstrating a willingness to accept a high risk of war. But the prescription makes sense only if the other party is both rational, in the realist sense of that term, and more cautious than the party following the prescribed influence strategy. The problematic quality of the first assumption was mentioned above, but it is consistent with the basic tenets of realism. The second assumption presents a different sort of problem. Statesmen are urged to assume that their adversaries will follow the same realist precepts that they themselves should follow, but to assume that those same adversaries will be less willing to accept the risks that they, themselves, are urged to accept. The rationale for expecting the other party to be less risk acceptant is not presented, but it is critical to the effectiveness of the bargaining prescription. Since the same advice is available to both parties, it would not be unreasonable to expect both parties to follow the same strategy, with potentially disastrous results.

In fact, the appropriateness of the crisis bargaining prescriptions of the conflict strategists is dependent on two key assumptions regarding the crisis behavior of the other party: (1) the other party will respond to coercive influence attempts in a rational manner, by calculating its moves in terms of the national interest defined as power; and (2) the other party is less risk-acceptant, that is, there is an asymmetry in the willingness to risk war, which favors the influencer. Much of the work of those who challenge the applicability of the realist perspective to crisis behavior, begins by questioning the validity of those two assumptions.

Summary

Classical realism assumes that political action is the manifestation of an ongoing struggle for power, a struggle that has its roots in human nature. Politics consists of the pursuit of interests defined as power. At the international level, the realist views states as unitary actors who place security concerns above all other interests. Order is

9

preserved through the balance of power, both at the level of the international system, and in dyadic relations between particular states. Prudence, the weighing of the consequences of state actions in terms of one's power interests, is the only normative constraint. Policy-making is assumed to be instrumentally rational: statesmen make their decisions based on a calculation of interests in terms of their per-ceptions of the relative power of their states. Although realists do not argue that all national decision-makers follow the precepts of realism all of the time, they argue that those who do are more likely to be successful.

Successful crisis bargaining requires that state leaders base their decisions on a hard-headed calculation of interests in terms of power, and that they assume that the leaders of other states think and act in the same way. Working from realist assumptions, conflict strategists argue that it is possible to develop a prescriptive theory of successful crisis bargaining. A successful influence strategy is viewed as depen-dent on exploiting the other party's fear of war, through threats and punishments, and credibly demonstrating resolve through a willing-ness to accept a high risk of war to achieve one's objectives.

As a guide to bargaining in interstate crises, there are three problem-atic realist assumptions. The first is that crisis bargaining should be viewed primarily in competitive terms, so that an integrative solu-tion,[10] that is, a solution in which the two parties work cooperatively to achieve a mutually beneficial outcome, as opposed to a compromise, is not possible. The second problematic assumption lies in classical real-ism's emphasis on the nonrational components of the power struggle on the one hand, and policy prescriptions, by both classical realists and conflict strategists, based on assumptions of rational behavior, on the other. The third problematic assumption appears in the conflict strategists' implied assumption of asymmetry in motivation favoring the party following their prescriptions.

A psychological perspective

International relations scholars often make a dichotomous distinction between realism and idealism, in theory between thinkers like Clausewitz and Kant, and in practice between statesmen like Winston Churchill and Woodrow Wilson. The division between the two perspectives occurs with regard to such issues as the perfectibility of humankind, the moral standards of international behavior, the power of international institutions, and the appropriate use of force in interstate relations. Those critics of realism, whom we will be considering in the course of this investigation, however, challenge the realist perspective at a more pragmatic level. The question at issue is not the morality of states, or the perfectibility of humankind, but the accuracy of realism as a descriptive theory of interstate conflict, and the validity of the conflict strategists' prescriptions for crisis bargaining. The challenge comes not from a competing philosophical tradition, but from the research findings of contemporary social scientists who have studied interpersonal and interstate conflict from the perspective of behavioral science.

The critiques of the view of conflict behavior held by classical realists and, particularly, by conflict strategists, that will be discussed in this section do not challenge the realist view of an anarchic, statecentric, international system, in which states pursue policies directed at serving their interests. Nor do they necessarily challenge the importance of considerations of security and political independence in calculating state interests. The challenge is directed more at the classical realist assumption of state action as dictated by a competitive power struggle, and the conflict strategists' view of conflict behavior as a calculated, rational, activity, in which the most effective bargaining techniques are based on the exploitation of the other side's fear of war.

The classical realist focus on the power struggle as the nexus of interstate relations encourages a purely competitive view of crisis bargaining. A number of students of diplomacy and negotiation question the wisdom of that approach. As Zartman and Berman (1982:12) put it, the objective of negotiation is not to "win," but the "transformation of a zero-sum situation and attitudes into positive-sum solutions and approaches." Some of these critiques (Rapoport, 1960; Osgood, 1962; Zartman and Berman, 1982; Pruitt and Rubin, 1986) have suggested ways in which conflicts may be transformed to allow for integrative solutions. Most of the critiques of realist approaches, however, have focused on the dysfunctional consequences of accepting the conflict strategists' other two problematic assumptions: the explicit assumption of rational crisis decision-making and the implicit assumption of asymmetry in resolve. Criticisms of the rationality assumption tend to focus either on the cognitive limitations facing national decision-makers in crisis, that is, on those factors that encourage them to misperceive, or misinterpret, the capabilities, motivations, and actions of the other party, or on those psychological factors that motivate national decision-makers to respond to crises in a nonrational manner.

The implied assumption of asymmetry in resolve is also challenged from two different directions. On the one hand, there are the logical

11

consequences of a symmetrically escalating confrontation between two parties who are each bent on demonstrating greater resolve. On the other hand, there is the competing influence of a tradition of reciprocity in international relations that encourages tit-for-tat behavior, that is, of responding in kind to efforts at coercion.

I will say a bit about each of these challenges to realism, particularly as realism appears in the prescriptions of conflict strategists, and then discuss how they may be interrelated to form a critique of some of classical realism's descriptive assumptions, and the prescriptions of conflict strategists.

Rational and nonrational behavior

Cognitive limitations and misperception. Realists are well aware of the difficulties facing decision-makers as they attempt to estimate the comparative capabilities of other states, and the intentions behind their actions. Nevertheless, as a descriptive theory, realism accounts for this problem only by treating it as something to be avoided.

It can be argued, however, that misperception is not a problem that can be avoided easily in international politics. Simon's (1957) pioneering work on "bounded rationality," has been followed by a number of studies demonstrating the cognitive limits of memory and calculating ability on the part of human decision-makers. Added to these endemic limitations are those problems peculiar to interstate relations, and, particularly, decision-making during crises. In a case study of two post-World War II diplomatic crises in relations between two friendly allies, the United States and Britain, Neustadt (1970:56) describes their interactions as representative of a pattern "woven from four strands: muddled perceptions, stifled communications, disappointed expectations, paranoid reactions."

Jervis (1976) has pointed out the unusually high noise to signal ratio in interstate relations, where information is likely to be incomplete and ambiguous, and where national decision-makers are likely to be politically and psychologically committed to maintaining certain views regarding the character and intentions of other states. Some researchers (see Holsti, 1989; Lebow, 1981) have found the problem to be exacerbated when decision-makers must endure the high stress associated with performing when the stakes are high, under severe time constraints, and often with little sleep, that is endemic in decision-making in militarized crises.

Empirical evidence of these problems appeared initially in the Stanford study of the behavior of national leaders of the Dual Alliance and

12

Triple Entente states in the crisis preceding World War I (North, Brody, and Holsti, 1964). The Stanford researchers found that the decision-making in the 1914 crisis was far removed from the cool and careful calculations prescribed by realism. As the crisis escalated, the participants – particularly those within the Dual Alliance – increasingly overestimated the hostility of the other side. These misperceptions, the authors argued, fueled the conflict spiral that was observed in the escalating threats and counter-threats of the two sides.

The Stanford study was one of the earliest of a number of empirical studies that have reported evidence that crisis decision-making can be a far from rational process. These studies have produced numerous examples of serious misperceptions of intentions, intolerance for ambiguity, restricted search for alternative bargaining strategies, insensitivity to the other side's perspective, stereotypical thinking, and erratic behavior.[11] The jury is still out regarding the overall capacity of national decision-makers to make rational decisions in crises (see Oneal, 1988; Brecher, 1993). Brecher's (1993) careful study of ten twentieth-century crises, in particular, yields evidence that challenges the notion that the high stress associated with militarized crises leads to dysfunctional decision-making. Nevertheless, the cognitive problems suggested by researchers like Jervis (1976) and Holsti (1989) raise important questions in light of the continuing prominence, not only of realism *per se*, but also of the use of rational choice models as the preferred methodological approach to the study of crisis decision-making.

Psychological reactance. Besides illustrating the cognitive limitations of decision-making in crises, the Stanford research demonstrates the potentially confounding influence of psychological variables on predictions of crisis behavior that are based on assumptions of rational choice. The assumption that the other party will respond in a rational, reasonable, manner to coercive inducements lies at the heart of the prescriptions of realists and conflict strategists. In preliminary studies of influence attempts and responses in interstate crises (Leng, 1980; 1984), however, I found a strong tendency on the part of states to react in a defiant manner to attempts at coercion, particularly military coercion. Just why this is so is not apparent from the data, but there are suggestive explanations in the work of social psychologists focusing on interpersonal relations.

The psychological reactions of individuals to conflictual situations have yielded a wide range of findings in social psychology. One of the earliest of these efforts produced the "frustration-aggression" theory of Dollard and his associates (1939), which argued that individuals

13

were likely to respond in an aggressive manner to situations or actions that thwarted, or threatened to thwart, goal attainment. Two decades later, in a study of social power relations, French and Raven (1959) found individuals to be strongly motivated to resist any coercive efforts to obtain compliance, especially if the coercion is perceived to be illegitimate.

An intriguing psychological explanation, in light of the centrality of the sovereignty principle and the realist emphasis on a power drive as the motivating force in international relations, appears in Brehm's (1966) theory of "psychological reactance." The theory, which is set at the level of interpersonal relations, begins with the assumption that, for any given individual, there are a set of behaviors in which he or she can engage freely. When one of these "free behaviors" is threatened the individual experiences "psychological reactance." Psychological reactance is a motivational state directed toward maintaining and exercising the threatened freedom, by whatever methods are available, including aggressive defiance. The magnitude of reactance, according to Brehm (1966:ch. 1), is a direct function of (1) the importance of the threatened behavior; (2) the proportion of freedom threatened or eliminated; and (3) the magnitude of the threat. Two other psychological responses to the threat to the individual's freedom, which have been found in subsequent studies, also are of interest, given our particular concern with interstate crisis behavior. One is that once a freedom is threatened, it becomes more attractive to its holder (Brehm and Brehm, 1981:108). The other finding is that the individual receiving the threat is likely to become hostile toward the threatening agent (Worchal, 1974).

These theories, and the experimental findings that have provided support for their validity, are grounded on the observation of interpersonal relations, not interstate conflict. Nevertheless, as we have seen above, at the heart of realist thinking is the notion that relations among states are an extension of the power drive at the individual level. Moreover, the struggle for power is directly related to the freedom of the individual actor. Morgenthau (1946:101) puts it in Rousseauian language, "Man is born a slave, but everywhere he aspires to being a master." Whether or not we accept that component of realist theory, few among us would challenge the notion that foreign policy decisions ultimately are made by individuals who are subject to the same psychological pressures as individuals in other, less elevated, circumstances. In fact, an argument can be made that "psychological reactance" might prove to be an even more powerful influence on behavior in relations among sovereign states.

14

Given the international norm of sovereignty, which assumes freedom of action on the part of all states, it can be argued that threats to the freedom of states would be likely to produce greater resistance than threats to the freedom of individuals, who face a variety of constraints on their behavior, which are imposed by higher authorities. Furthermore, the values that states hold most dear – their "vital interests" – are related directly to their power and freedom: territorial sovereignty and political independence. In an interstate crisis, there is a direct relationship between the importance of the issues at stake and the degree of behavioral freedom that is threatened.

The other variable that is said to contribute to the magnitude of psychological reactance is the magnitude of the threat itself. This is consistent with the finding of French and Raven (1959) that individuals tend to react aggressively to attempts at coercion, particularly when the coercion is viewed as illegitimate. Some evidence of this pattern in interstate crises appeared in the Leng (1980) study of influence attempts and responses. In relations among sovereign states, *all* attempts at coercion are viewed as illegitimate.[12] With that in mind, there also would be good reason to expect Worchal's (1974) finding that individuals become hostile toward those who threaten their freedom to hold in interstate relations as well. Taken together, these possibilities raise troubling questions about the logic of the realist admonition to demonstrate power and its extension into the conflict strategists' prescriptions for the "exploitation of potential force" (Schelling:1960:9).

By taking a close look at patterns of influence attempts and responses in Chapters 6 through 8, we ought to be able to reach some conclusions regarding the relative validity of the rationality assumptions held by the conflict strategists as opposed to the psychological reactions found in the interpersonal experiments of social psychologists.

Symmetry and reciprocity

Symmetry and the conflict spiral. As I noted in the discussion of realism's ambiguities above, a second problematic aspect, which appears in the prescriptions of the conflict strategists, is associated with their emphasis on a credible demonstration of resolve as the key to successful conflict bargaining. If bargaining is viewed as a competition in risk-taking, so that it is generally assumed that the best means of achieving one's objectives is through a firm demonstration of resolve in the form of credible threats, what happens when both

15

parties are following the same coercive bargaining strategy? After all, the same advice and tactics are available to both sides. If they are evenly matched in determination, and both follow the same escalating coercive strategy, the conflict is likely to spiral out of control. The situation is exacerbated because the prescription for success encourages *bluffing*.[13] As the parties employ bluffs in attempts to cause the other side to overestimate their willingness to risk war, the effect is to encourage the other side to overestimate hostile intentions as well, and to raise the stakes of the conflict as each side attempts to out-bluff the other. If bargaining is viewed as a competition in risk-taking, so that it is generally assumed that the best means of achieving one's objectives is through a firm demonstration of resolve in the form of credible threats, what happens when both parties are following the same coercive bargaining strategy? If they are evenly matched in determination, and follow both the same escalating coercive strategy, the conflict is likely to spiral out of control.

As more coercive tactics are employed by both parties, and tensions mount, the stakes, in terms of each side's prestige and reputation for resolve, grow as well. The higher stakes encourage a stronger commitment to stay the course, and to employ more coercive bargaining tactics. At the same time, the coercive tactics encourage greater hostility between the two parties. The link between the escalation in conflict and the rise in political stakes creates a situation that goes beyond the usual conception of social entrapment (Brockner and Rubin, 1985:121–25).[14] In an escalating crisis, the conflict escalates beyond the point at which its costs and risks can no longer be justified by the initial stakes, not just because so much already has been committed to the effort and there is the hope of success lying just around the corner, but also because the political stakes now *are* much higher. A well-known example of this phenomenon at work was the continued escalation of the United States commitment to the war in Vietnam in the 1960s. Presidents Johnson and Nixon found themselves justifying the continuing American commitment to the war on the basis of the cumulative commitment of preceding American presidents, as well as the costs in money and lives. For Johnson and Nixon, the stakes *had* grown higher. The escalation became a justification for continuing to escalate.

The escalation of a dispute can cause what Pruitt and Rubin (1986:92–96) describe as "structural changes" in the relations between the two sides. Each party's attitude toward the other side becomes increasingly negative and aggressive; the dispute becomes viewed more in zero-sum terms; as the two sides become more polarized, existing safeguards against the outbreak of violence, such as preceding attitudes of mutual interdependence and friendship, are eroded; and there is a reduction in the perceived available options. The escalatory process can lead to what Rapoport (1960) has described as a "fight." The two parties begin by employing what they perceive as defensive strategies to preserve their interests, but the escalatory tactics employed cause the objectives to change from serving the original interests at issue to defeating, and, eventually, to punishing, the other side. The competitiveness reaches a level at which each party measures success, not according to its own interests, but according to the difference between its outcome and that for the other side. As each side commits more energies and emotions to winning, the conflict escalates almost automatically; the two parties become "locked-in" to a pattern of rising tit-for-tat coercive exchanges. North, Brody, and Holsti (1964) found evidence of such a pattern of spiraling conflict in the pre-World War I crisis. At the height of the crisis, Germany's Kaiser Wilhelm is reported to have exclaimed: "If we are to bleed to death, England shall at least lose India" (Holsti, North, and Brody, 1968:137).

But, whether, or when, escalating crises more generally are likely to spiral out of control remains an open question. An early look at this phenomenon by the author (Leng and Goodsell, 1974), albeit with a very small sample of cases, yielded mixed results. We will take a closer look at this question in Chapters 4 and 5. After describing the escalatory process in Chapter 4, we will turn to its relationship to the issues at stake and the perceived comparative capabilities of the two sides, in Chapter 5.

Reciprocity and escalation. Besides the psychological variables affecting behavior during an escalating crisis, recent empirical research has uncovered another pattern in conflict behavior, which is related to the ancient norm of reciprocity in human relations.

Reciprocity is the most easily grasped norm for cooperative behavior in any system of self-help, whether it be a primitive community or the interstate system (Masters, 1969; Gouldner, 1960). The notion has particular appeal in the interstate system because of the presumed sovereign equality of its members. As such, the reciprocity norm lies at the heart of much of international law and the practice of diplomacy. Evidence of the prevalence of reciprocating, or "tit-for-tat," behavior between states has appeared in a number of empirical studies of interstate relations generally (Gamson and Modigliani, 1971; Ward, 1982; Goldstein and Freeman, 1990) and in crisis bargaining in particular (Leng and Goodsell, 1974; Snyder and Diesing, 1977; Leng and Wheeler, 1979).

If states do tend to reciprocate each other's cooperative and conflictual behavior in crises, then not only is the efficacy of a crisis influence strategy based on escalating coercive inducements placed in doubt, but the conflict strategists' assumption that it is not possible to move away from contentious bargaining to find an integrative solution to the dispute is open to challenge. That is, if states are prone to respond in kind to both coercive and cooperative initiatives, we would expect an influence strategy based on coercive moves to encourage something like the conflict spiral described above, and for properly employed cooperative initiatives to yield responses in kind. In fact, evidence of both of these phenomena have been suggested by recent studies employing Prisoner's Dilemma games in computer tournaments (Axelrod, 1984) and in interpersonal bargaining experiments (Esser and Komorita, 1975; Komorita, Hilty, and Parks, 1991), as well as empirical studies of interstate crisis bargaining (Leng and Wheeler, 1979). Stronger evidence of the *effectiveness* of bargaining strategies based on reciprocity would raise serious questions about the prescriptive advice of conflict strategists. We will take a closer look at this question when we consider the relative effectiveness of "Bullying" and "Reciprocating" bargaining strategies in Chapters 7 and 8.

Summary

Challenges to the realist perspective raise questions about the validity of assuming that crisis bargaining is unalterably contentious, that policy-makers will respond to coercive influence tactics in a rational manner, and that the prescriptions of the conflict strategists will lead to effective bargaining tactics and strategies in disputes between adversaries evenly matched in motivation. In rejecting the necessity of assuming that crisis bargaining must be purely competitive, critics, of the realist perspective suggest the possibility of moving to mutually cooperative behavior to a degree that challenges the classical realist assumption of international politics as an unalterable struggle for power. In questioning the rationality of crisis decision-making, researchers taking a psychological perspective cite the cognitive limitations of national decision-makers confronting a dynamic and ambiguous situation with limited and, often, unreliable information, as well as noting the influence of psychological and political pressures to respond in a nonrational manner to stressful situations and threatening behavior. Some studies have noted psychological influences, beyond those related to the power drive, that are likely to confound rational responses to coercive influence attempts.

These challenges also raise questions about the validity of the conflict bargaining prescriptions of the conflict strategists, who begin with the assumptions of classical realism. Brehm's (1966) theory of psychological reactance is of particular interest in this regard, because it questions the efficacy of escalating coercive bargaining strategies. Other critics question the implied assumption of asymmetry in motivation, which lies behind the prescriptions of conflict strategists. Findings indicating a tendency on the part of states to respond in kind to influence attempts suggest the dangers of the spiraling tit-for-tat escalation observable in a "Fight" on the one hand, and the possibilities of building on reciprocal responses to move to mutually accommodative bargaining, on the other. Studies indicating the presence of a high degree of reciprocity in interstate relations, including crises, suggest both the dangers associated with tit-for-tat responses to coercive influence tactics, and the possibilities of moving to cooperative settlements through influence strategies based on reciprocity.

In the introductory chapter of a psychological study of normative constraints on war, Michael Walzer (1977) began by noting that "realism is the issue." This investigation proceeds from the assumption that statesmen share a realist perspective on the nature of interstate relations in general, and of conflict behavior in particular. The issue is the validity of that perspective – both as a description of how states behave in crises, and as prescriptive advice regarding how they should behave if they wish to best serve their interests. Realism has been attacked on both of those grounds by researchers who have approached the study of crisis behavior from a psychological perspective. The substantive investigation that follows in Chapters 3 through 8 attempts to provide an answer to the issue of realism in militarized interstate crises. But, before plunging into the investigation itself, it is necessary to describe the approach to be taken. Chapter 2 outlines the conceptual and methodological assumptions, the manner in which data were generated, and the analytic techniques employed in the investigation.

2 METHODOLOGY

The analyses in succeeding chapters seek answers to two general questions. (1) Have the actions of states in militarized crises been consistent with what would be predicted from a realist perspective? (2) When states in militarized crises have followed the prescriptions of classical realists and conflict strategists, have they been more successful? This chapter describes and defends the research methods employed in seeking answers to these questions. It begins by describing the methodology of the Behavioral Correlates of War (BCOW) project within the context of contemporary research on conflict behavior. Then key concepts are defined; the data generation process is described; and the approach to analysis is described and defended. Readers who are less interested in the "nuts and blots" of empirical research may wish to skip certain sections of this chapter, particularly the detailed discussion of the data generation in the sections entitled "An overview of the data," and the "BCOW typology and the coding scheme."

Research on crisis behavior and the BCOW project

The research findings on interstate conflict behavior that are discussed in this book are drawn primarily from four methodological approaches: (1) qualitative case studies; (2) game theory; (3) interpersonal experiments in bargaining; and (4) quantitative studies employing events data. The BCOW project falls into the last category, but, in order to place it in perspective methodologically, it may be useful to start with a brief description of each of the other three approaches.

Qualitative case studies

Qualitative case studies remain the most widely used approach to the study of international crises. The case study approach consists of a close examination of the available written record of the crisis, or crises, of interest, which is informed by the insights of a scholar familiar with the political and historical background of the case, or cases, being studied. The finished work may range from a richly detailed account of a single crisis, to the application of a theoretical framework to a number of cases, as in Snyder and Diesing's (1977) study of thirteen historical crises. The detailed and contextually rich examination of particular crises allows for a grasp of the subtleties and nuances of bargaining and diplomacy that is difficult to achieve through other techniques. A number of the insights regarding crisis behavior that appear in this book have been drawn from qualitative case studies, particularly the work of Snyder and Diesing (1977).

There are drawbacks to the case study approach, which are inevitable trade-offs to the gains in detail and subtlety. A thorough examination of each case is so time consuming that the researcher is forced to suggest generalizations from one, or just a few cases. There are, to be sure, lessons to be learned from particular crises. The issue is the extent to which they are generalizable to other crises. One response to this problem is to undertake a larger number of case studies in a standardized manner that allows comparisons across cases. George (1979) has referred to this systematic approach as "structured, focused, comparison." Although the authors do not employ the particular structure suggested by George, Snyder and Diesing's (1977) study is a good example of the application of a single theoretical framework to a comparative study of several cases.

Critics of qualitative case studies note that they lack the scientific attributes of random selection, operational definitions, and objective testing, which are necessary to generate replicable and cumulative findings. The subjectivity involved in any qualitative study, regardless of how structured it may be, encourages the researcher to find what he or she expects to find. In sum, there are trade-offs between the subtleties and nuances that can be gained from an imaginative intuitive interpretation of events, and the requirements of scientific objectivity.

Game theory

Additional insights into crisis bargaining can be found in the rational choice models of game theorists. Game theory employs deductive mathematical models in which the bargaining strategies of competing players are reduced to the utilities associated with specific outcomes. The utility of each strategy choice is dependent on the intersection of that player's strategy with the strategy chosen by the other player, so that each player's best strategy is dependent on the strategy chosen by the other player. The solution to a game is based on finding an equilibrium, that is, an outcome in which neither player has an incentive to choose a different strategy.

The researcher determines the utilities and the rules for the play of the game. Traditionally, the moves are made simultaneously, with each player having complete knowledge of the utilities, in this case the preference orderings, of the other side. But, there are numerous variations in games of strategy, depending on the number of players, the number of strategy choices for each player, the outcome utilities, and the rules of play. Some of the most carefully researched games are analogous to situations faced in interstate conflicts. The most notable example is Prisoner's Dilemma, which is described at the beginning of Chapter 7. Moreover, recent variations in the rules of play, particularly the innovations of Brams and Wittmann (1981) in developing games in which moves are made sequentially by players basing their strategies on calculations that extend beyond one move, have made the dynamics of games more immediately applicable to interstate crisis bargaining.

Methodologically, game theory is at the opposite pole from qualitative studies. Richness of detail and nuance are sacrificed in favor of parsimony, mathematical elegance, and logical rigor. Game theoretic studies related to crisis bargaining first appeared in the 1960s, most notably in the suggestive work of Schelling (1960, 1966). They have been continued in the formal and fully executed models of theorists such as Brams (1985), Zagare (1987), and Powell (1988). It requires a leap in one's imagination to draw conclusions about real world crisis behavior from the elegantly simple mathematical models of game theory, and the assumption of rational choice has been the subject of continuing theoretical debate. The approach, nevertheless, has provided intriguing and provocative hypotheses regarding crisis bargaining more generally, and the relative effectiveness of different types of influence strategies in particular. The work of Axelrod (1984) has been particularly influential in drawing attention to the efficacy of bargaining strategies based on tit-for-tat in the repetitive play of Prisoner's Dilemma games, an issue to which we will return in Chapters 7 and 8.

Controlled bargaining experiments

Many of the interpersonal bargaining experiments conducted by social psychologists have been constructed from situations modeled by game theorists, such as Prisoner's Dilemma games. In contradistinction to the emphasis on rational choice in game theory, these studies underline the psychological component of bargaining behavior.

These experiments take place in a controlled laboratory environment, in which human subjects, most often university students, bargain over small amounts of money, or other token prizes. Here too, a creative leap is required to apply the findings from these experiments to interstate crises, in which national decision-makers bargain over issues immediately affecting the security of their nations. Nevertheless, these experiments have yielded fruitful analogies to the bargaining problems facing foreign policy decision-makers, including some intriguing and provocative findings. The work of theorists, such as Rapoport (1960), and Pruitt and Rubin (1986) on escalation, of Esser and Komorita (1975) on reciprocity in bargaining, and of Brehm (1966) on psychological reactance, have been particularly useful in suggesting avenues to explore in this investigation.

Quantitative studies: event data research

Attempts to apply the operational techniques of scientific research directly to the behavior of states in real world crises are of relatively recent origin. One of the earliest quantitative studies dealing with crisis behavior *per se* appeared in 1964, with the Stanford (North *et al.*, 1964) study of the pre-World War I crisis. The Stanford researchers employed content analysis to examine the stream of communications between members of the Triple Entente and Dual Alliance in an effort to measure the role of psychological and perceptual variables, particularly perceptions of hostility, in the escalation of the crisis to war.

The content analysis employed in the Stanford study laid the groundwork of a number of new schemes designed to generate machine readable data on interstate conflict behavior in a simpler and more efficient manner. The approach employed in these schemes, which fall under the general rubric of "event data" research, consists of extracting descriptions of the actions taken by states, or by other international actors, from written records in the press and diplomatic histories, and then coding these descriptions into machine readable form for aggregate analyses. The actions then are categorized, and/or scaled, along dimensions of interest, such as the escalation or deescalation of hostile behavior over the course of a crisis. This approach has the advantage of combining descriptions of real world crises with the rigor and replicability of operational procedures.

Event data research is not without its practical and theoretical

23

problems, however. The coding of international events presents serious problems in attaining valid and reliable data (see Howell, 1983; McClelland, 1983; Leng, 1987b). Critics of the approach argue that forcing interstate actions and communications into a pre-set category of actions creates data that cannot adequately represent the subtle distinctions and nuances that are a critical component of crisis bargaining. Others point out that the generalizations that can be achieved through the use of statistical techniques are often difficult to apply to individual cases, which contain their own idiosyncratic qualities. If it is difficult to generalize from a single, or even several case studies, it also is difficult to apply the general relationships found in quantitative studies to specific cases. The response to these objections is that the objective of quantitative studies is to identify those variables that exert a salient influence on the behavior of states across a wide range of cases, so that the variations that occur within individual cases can be seen within the context of more generalizable patterns of behavior. Viewed from this perspective, the findings from qualitative case studies and events data research can complement each other.[1]

The Behavioral Correlates of War project. The research reported in succeeding chapters falls into the category of events data research. The Behavioral Correlates of War (BCOW) project was begun by the author in the spring of 1970, as a component of the Correlates of War (COW) project, under the direction of J. David Singer, at the University of Michigan. The COW project is a large research effort, which, until that time, had been devoted to generating quantitative data on the attributes of wars and on a number of systemic and state attributes presumed to be associated with the outbreak, magnitude, and intensity of war. The BCOW project initiated the effort to generate data on the behavior of states in militarized disputes and crises.

The BCOW typology, which was developed by Leng and Singer, borrowed from earlier efforts to describe small group interaction by Bales (1951), Blau (1964), and Homans (1961), as well as other event data schemes, most notably McClelland's (1968) World Event/ Interaction Survey (WEIS), and Corson's (1971) East–West Interaction project.

In light of the absence of any widely accepted theory of interstate conflict behavior, the BCOW typology was designed to be "multi-theoretical," to allow for the testing of a number of different theories. This was in keeping with the self-consciously multitheoretical and inductive approach to examining alternative explanations of war that had been adopted by the Correlates of War project. The construction of the BCOW typology, nonetheless, proceeded from certain *a priori*

24

assumptions. One assumption was that there has been considerable homogeneity in the political beliefs and decision rules of foreign-policy-makers across nations and decades over the past century and two-thirds. Specifically, we assumed that the key variables to which policy-makers historically have directed their attention in the course of militarized interstate crises are those variables identified as significant by realists.

Besides the focus on those variables identified as most significant by realists, the BCOW typology was designed to capture the most salient elements of interstate bargaining behavior. This component of the construction of the typology was influenced by the work of conflict strategists, particularly Schelling (1960), as well as by a theoretical model of internation influence suggested by Singer (1963). The objective has been to obtain quantitative descriptions of the actions and interactions of states in crises that would yield data allowing us to come as close as possible to the detailed description of conflict bargaining afforded by qualitative case studies, without losing the advantages in reliability and replicability that come from operationally defined procedures.

Overview of the BCOW data

The behavioral data employed in this study consists of the actions of participants in a sample of forty militarized interstate crises (MICs) occurring between 1816 and 1980.

Militarized interstate crises

A militarized interstate crisis falls near the upper end of a ladder of increasing belligerence that extends from (1) an interstate dispute, to (2) a militarized interstate dispute, to (3) a militarized interstate crisis, to (4) an interstate war. The distinctions among these levels of belligerence are based on variations in the observed dispute behavior of the participants.

Interstate disputes are contentions with at least one member of the interstate system, as defined by Small and Singer (1982:47), on each side, in which neither side threatens or uses military force. At a higher level of belligerence, a *militarized* interstate dispute is identified by the overt threat, display, or use of military force by at least one of the participants. This distinguishes those disputes in which the threat of war becomes overt as reaching a new level of severity.

A militarized interstate dispute escalates to the level of a militarized

25

interstate *crisis* when the threat, display, or use of force is reciprocated by a member of the interstate system on the other side. Thus, for an MID to escalate to an MIC, it is necessary that a military challenge by one side be resisted with a counter-threat, display, or use of force from the other side. This criterion distinguishes crises from those disputes in which, for example, one state reacts forcefully to a perceived transgression by another, and the matter is quickly resolved with an apology from the transgressor, or through a clarification of a misunderstanding. The rationale for this distinction is based on the assumption that a dangerously high probability of war occurs when one side threatens force and the other side responds in kind. Definitions of interstate crises vary considerably among researchers, but there is a consensus that a necessary distinguishing attribute is a dangerously high probability of war (Bell, 1971; Snyder and Diesing, 1977; Brecher, 1977). States can find themselves embroiled in such situations for many reasons, but certainly there must be a perception that the interests at stake are high enough to signal a willingness to risk war to defend them.

Thus, the operational indicator of the mutual perception of a dangerously high probability of war is the presence of a threat of force, display of force, or use of force by parties on both sides of the dispute. Out of a population of 965 MIDs occurring between 1816 and 1976, 593 (62 percent) qualify as MICs.[2] This appears to be a reasonable distinguishing criterion. Among those cases qualifying as MICs, there are significantly higher ($p = 0.001$) scores along three salient dimensions: (1) the number of dispute-connected fatalities; (2) the peak level of hostility displayed by the first party to threaten force; and (3) the duration of the dispute from the first threat of force to its termination.

Different researchers have suggested a number of other potential distinguishing characteristics of crises. Two of the conditions most frequently mentioned are unusually intense interaction (McClelland, 1961; Zinnes, Zinnes, and McClure, 1972), and a sense of time pressure (Hermann, 1972; Brecher, 1977). Devising operational definitions of these concepts raises several difficult questions, beginning with what actions, taken when, and by whom, should be included, and ending with the issue of determining a threshold to distinguish between "normal" and "unusually intense" interaction. In the absence of any convincing *a priori* reasons to add these criteria, we will consider a reciprocated threat, display, or use of military force to be a sufficient threshold indicator of the presence of an MIC.

One other criterion has been added to the selection of cases for this investigation. Since an objective of this study is to search for behavioral

26

patterns in the actions and interactions of the states involved in MICs, only those cases in which there are at least fifty interactions between the two sides have been included. This criterion is based on practical considerations related to the purposes of this study; it is not a necessary attribute for classification of an MIC.

Crisis boundaries. An MIC begins with a precipitant event, an action that challenges, or changes, the status quo to such an extent that another actor responds with an explicit threat, display or use of force.[3] Precipitants include at least one of the following attributes: (1) an explicit threat, display, or use of force; (2) a challenge to the strategic interests of the target; or (3) a serious affront to the prestige of the target state. When the precipitant includes the threat, display, or use of force, it also qualifies as the *challenge* that identifies the dispute as a militarized dispute. If the challenge is resisted by the other side with a threat, display, or use of force, the dispute qualifies as an MIC. Actions identified as specific precipitants are based on the accounts of diplomatic historians, and the judgment of the author. Threats, displays, and uses of force are identified from the BCOW data described below.

There are two steps to the identification of when an MIC ends. The first step is to distinguish between those crises that end in war and those that do not. The outbreak of war changes the status of the dispute from that of an MIC to an international war. The Correlates of War (Small and Singer, 1982) criteria are used to identify the onset of war, which serves as the termination date for the MIC. In those cases that do not escalate to war, a second distinction is made between those MICs that end in a diplomatic settlement, and those cases that end in a stalemate. Settlements are identified by the presence of a treaty or other written agreement, by an exchange of letters, or by an explicit verbal understanding (see Maoz, 1982). If no settlement is reached, an MIC is presumed to have ended in a stalemate if no new threats, displays, or uses of force occur for six months.

Crisis participants. Some of the crises in the sample are essentially dyadic. The Fashoda crisis of 1898, for example, was a dispute between France and Britain over colonial influence in the Sudan. But other cases involve several states. The crisis preceding the First World War, for example, could be treated as several dyadic disputes: Serbia vs. Austria, Austria vs. Russia, Russia vs. Germany, Germany vs. France, and Germany vs. Britain, or as a single conflict between two sides: The Triple Entente plus Serbia vs. the Dual Alliance. An argument for disaggregating a crisis into several dyadic disputes can be made on the grounds that different actors enter and exit the dispute at different times, that they are involved to different degrees, and that their

27

motives and actions vary according to the parties with whom they are interacting on the other side.

On the other hand, the actions of each party, on each side, are likely to affect all of the crisis participants. In the pre-World War I crisis, the Austrian decision to issue its July 23 ultimatum to Serbia was influenced by guarantees of support from Germany, and the Serbian response to the ultimatum was influenced by indications of Russian support for Serbia against Austria. If we are interested in predicting the crisis outcome from the actions of the participants, we cannot detach particular pairs of participants from the overall dispute. This can be true even in disputes that appear to be essentially dyadic in nature. The Agadir crisis of 1911, for example, grew out of an ongoing dispute between Germany and France over the extent of French influence in Morocco. For the most part, this was a dyadic dispute between the two main participants; however, an inflammatory speech by Lloyd George of Great Britain, who intervened on France's behalf, appears to have been very influential in the escalation of the crisis. The British also played a role in persuading the French to attend an international conference to settle the issue. The evolution and outcome of this essentially dyadic dispute was strongly influenced by the participation of a third party, Great Britain. In these, and other cases involving several participants, all of those states that were directly involved in the dispute have been included as participants on one side or the other, with the analysis directed to the behavior of the two sides.[4]

To qualify as an MIC, a dispute must have a member of the interstate system as a participant on each side. There are, however, a number of other international actors that may exert a strong influence over the evolution and outcomes of disputes, and they are included as crisis participants. The Cyprus crisis of 1963–64, for example, began with clashes between Greek and Turkish Cypriots who continued to play a strong role in the evolution and outcome of the consequent interstate crisis between Greece and Turkey. The United Nations also is included, because the UN Security Council played a mediating role. In general, subnational, intergovernmental, and transnational actors have been included as crisis participants whenever they appear as active participants.

Sample selection. When the BCOW project was launched in 1970, no reliable list of the populations of MICs existed. The long-term solution to that problem was to construct the list of candidates that now appear in the MID data set (Gochman and Maoz, 1984), but the construction of the list of all MIDs has constituted a major data generation effort in its own right. Because of our desire to move ahead with the generation of BCOW data, we created a tentative list of the population of cases drawn from five sources. The list of crises ending in war consisted of those cases appearing on the Singer and Small (1972) list of interstate wars, which was later up-dated by Small and Singer (1982). A list of nonwar cases was generated from Langer's *Encyclopedia of World History* (1968), which was supplemented for the post-World War II period by qualifying cases drawn from Butterworth (1976).[5]

The sample of forty cases was stratified to include a representative number of cases from three diplomatic eras: (1) from the Congress of Vienna in 1816 through World War I; (2) the interwar period from 1918 through World War II; and (3) the post-World War II era, 1946–80. The three periods represent differences that are significant from a classical realist perspective: the traditional balance of power system of the nineteenth century; the experiment with parliamentary diplomacy in the League of Nations and the rise of the ideological states in the interwar period; and the emergence of a bipolar system, the dawn of the atomic and nuclear age, and the entrance of newly independent states on the world stage after World War II. The distribution of cases across the three eras is proportional to that appearing in the population of militarized interstate disputes (MIDs) compiled by the COW project (Gochman and Maoz, 1984:592). The sample also has been stratified to include a relatively even balance between crises ending in war and those that ended peacefully.[6]

Although the sample of cases is considerably larger than those used in comparative qualitative studies, it is relatively small given the potential population of MICs.[7] The size of the sample is partly a function of the time-consuming effort required to generate microscopic data on the behavior of states in crises, and the realities of available funding for data generation, but it also provides certain advantages in an investigation of this sort. The smaller number of cases allows the researcher to obtain greater familiarity with the details of each case, so that the analysis of the crises is informed by more than a mechanical process of counting, weighting, and statistically analyzing the coded data. Consequently, although the research is primarily quantitative, it is informed by a qualitative understanding of each case in the sample. A list of the forty cases appearing in the sample appears in Table 2.1.

The BCOW typology and coding scheme

The investigation focuses on the actions and interactions of the participants as they attempt to influence the behavior of each other

29

Table 2.1. *Sample of interstate crises, 1816–1980*

Name	Side A	Side B	Date
1. Pastry War	France	Mexico	Mar. 2, 1838 – Mar. 9, 1839
2. Crimean War	Russia France England	Turkey	Apr. 19, 1853 – Mar. 31, 1854
3. 2nd Schleswig-Holstein War	Prussia Austria-Hungary	Denmark	Mar. 30, 1863 – Feb. 1, 1864
4. Russo-Turkish War	Russia	Turkey	May 13, 1876 – Apr. 12, 1877
5. British-Russian Crisis	Britain	Russia	May 6, 1877 – May 30, 1878
6. British-Portuguese Crisis	Britain	Portugal	Aug. 19, 1889 – Jan. 12, 1890
7. Spanish-American War	Spain	US	Feb. 15, 1898 – Apr. 21, 1898
8. Fashoda Crisis	Britain	France	July 10, 1898 – Dec. 4, 1898
9. 1st Moroccan Crisis	France	Germany	Mar. 3, 1905 – Mar. 31, 1906
10. 2nd Central American War	Honduras Salvador	Nicaragua	Dec. 1, 1906 – Mar. 2, 1907
11. Bosnian Crisis	Austria-Hungary Germany	Serbia Russia Turkey	Oct. 6, 1908 – Mar. 31, 1909
12. 2nd Moroccan crisis	France Britain	Germany	May 21, 1911 – Nov. 4, 1911
13. 1st Balkan War	Serbia Bulgaria Greece	Turkey	Mar. 13, 1912 – Oct. 18, 1913
14. 2nd Balkan War	Bulgaria	Romania Greece Serbia	Feb. 20, 1913 – June 30, 1913
15. Pre-World War I	Austria-Hungary Germany	Serbia Russia France Britain	June 28, 1914 – Aug. 4, 1914
16. Teschen Crisis	Czechoslovakia	Poland	Dec. 10, 1918 – July 28, 1920
17. Chaco Dispute	Bolivia	Paraguay	Feb. 25, 1927 – May 1, 1930
18. Chaco War	Bolivia	Paraguay	June 15, 1931 – June 15, 1932
19. Manchurian War	Japan	China	June 27, 1931 – Dec. 19, 1931
20. Italo-Ethiopian War	Ethiopia	Italy	Nov. 22, 1934 – Oct. 3, 1935
21. Rhineland Crisis	France Belgium Britain	Germany	Mar. 7, 1936 – Oct. 31, 1936
22. Anschluss Crisis	Austria	Germany	Feb. 12, 1938 – Mar. 12, 1938
23. Munich Crisis	Czechoslovakia Britain France	Germany	Feb. 20, 1938 – Sept. 30, 1938
24. Polish–Lithuanian Crisis	Lithuania	Poland	Mar. 12, 1938 – Mar. 31, 1938
25. Danzig Crisis (Pre-WWII)	Germany	Poland Britain	Oct. 24, 1938 – Sept. 1, 1939
26. Italo-French Crisis	Italy Germany	France	Nov. 30, 1938 – Sept. 3, 1939
27. 1st Kashmir War	India	Pakistan	Oct. 22, 1947 – Jan. 1, 1949
28. Berlin Blockade	Britain France US	USSR	June 7, 1948 – May 12, 1949

Table 2.1 (*cont.*)

Name	Side A	Side B	Date
29. Trieste Crisis	Italy	Yugoslavia	July 16, 1953 – Oct. 5, 1954
30. Suez Crisis	Egypt France Israel	Britain	July 26, 1956 – Nov. 2, 1956
31. Honduran Border Dispute	Honduras	Nicaragua	Feb. 2, 1957 – July 21, 1957
32. Sino-Indian Border Dispute	China	India	Oct. 18, 1958 – Apr. 19, 1960
33. Bizerte Dispute	France	Tunisia	July 8, 1961 – Sept. 29, 1961
34. Cuban Missile Crisis	US	USSR Cuba	Sept. 4, 1962 – Nov. 20, 1962
35. Cyprus Crisis	Greece Greece Cyprus	Turkey Turkey Cyprus	Nov. 30, 1963 – Sept. 15, 1964
36. 2nd Kashmir War	India	Pakistan	Dec. 21, 1964 – Aug. 5, 1965
37. Rann of Kutch	India	Pakistan	Mar. 20, 1965 – June 30, 1965
38. Cod War	Britain	Iceland	July 15, 1975 – June 1, 1976
39. Beagle Channel Dispute	Argentina	Chile	Apr. 19, 1977 – Jan. 18, 1979
40. Sino-Vietnam War	China	Vietnam	Nov. 25, 1977 – Feb. 17, 1979

over the course of the crisis. The actions of the participants must be identified and categorized in a manner that enables us to describe them according to attributes of interest. I noted above that we began the BCOW project with an effort to produce a typology of inter-national actions that would be as multitheoretical as possible, in order to be able to test a variety of theories of crisis behavior, but that also would identify variables of interest to policy-makers working from a realist perspective. Simply put, the BCOW typology is designed to extract actions to answer the Lasswellian questions: who is doing what to whom? when? where? and how?

Data sources

The data to answer these questions is drawn primarily from the accounts of journalists and diplomatic historians, including, as a minimum, the reporting of events in the daily *New York Times* and at least two narrative accounts by historians or political scientists.[8] In some instances, as many as five different accounts have been used; however, the number of additional events found drops of sharply as each additional source is added. Before the actual coding of events is begun, a master verbal chronology is constructed from the narrative accounts.

Coding scheme

The description of each action begins with the date on which the action occurred, the actor, the target of the action, where the action

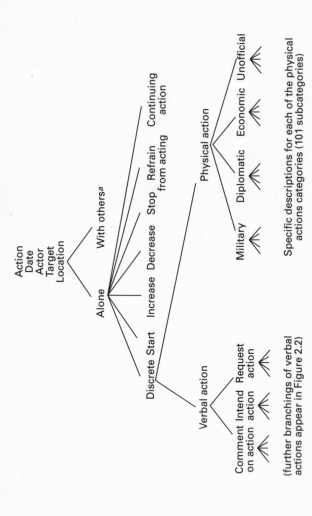

Figure 2.1 BCOW typology: hierarchial choice tree

Note: *a* We present the subcategorization for the left-most branch of the tree only, when the subcategorization is the same for all branches, to save space.

occurred, whether the actor was acting unilaterally or with another state, and the "tempo" of the action. The last descriptor, the tempo, first identifies whether the action is a verbal communication, or a physical deed. In cases where the action is a physical deed, the tempo descriptor indicates whether the action begins and ends on the same day, or if it continues beyond one day. If the physical action continues beyond one day, then the tempo descriptor indicates whether, on the day in question, the action is beginning, increasing in tempo, decreasing in tempo, or stopping. The tempo descriptor allows us to track physical behavior, such as negotiations, or military alerts, from start to finish, while noting increases or decreases in intensity along the way.

The next step is to describe the specific attributes of the action. The typology, at this point, is designed in the form of the hierarchical choice tree depicted in Figure 2.1. The first branching distinguishes between physical actions and verbal communications. Physical actions are categorized according to the resource that the actor brings to bear – military, economic, diplomatic, or unofficial. Then each of these categories branches into more specific descriptions of the act. Examples of the diplomatic action types are: Consult, Negotiate, Declare Neutrality, Change the Status of Diplomatic Relations. The military types include actions such as: Alert, Blockade, Clash, Show-of-Force, and Military Assistance. Examples of the actions in the economic categories include Economic Assistance, Change in Trade Relations, Freeze Assets, and Economic Intrusion. The "unofficial" category refers to actions that are not overtly conducted by the government, such as Anti-foreign Demonstration, Sabotage, or Hostage-taking. There are 101 different subcategories of physical actions (see Leng and Singer, 1987:App. B).

The coding procedure for verbal communications is a bit more complicated. Our interest in crisis bargaining requires that the coding of these actions be extended to include a full description of *how* these actions are communicated to the target, as well as describing *what* is communicated. We begin by branching into three general verbal categories: (1) comments on actions or situations; (2) requests or demands for action (or inaction) by the target; and (3) intentions, that is, statements indicating that under certain conditions, the actor intends to take certain action.

Once the verbal type has been identified, we describe *how* the action was communicated. In the case of a comment on action, we first indicate whether the actor is commenting on a past action or situation, or on a possible future action or situation. Then we indicate whether the comment is official or unofficial, and whether it indicates approval,

33

disapproval, is neutral, or is a denial that the action has taken place (or will take place). If the verbal action is a request, we indicate whether there are any conditions, or inducements that the requestor has attached to the demand, whether there is a time limit for compliance with the demand, and how specific the actor is regarding the action to be taken. If the verbal action falls into the intend action category, that is, a threat or a promise, then the conditions attached to the intended action – action or inaction by the target, action by some third party, or unconditional – are described, along with whether a time has been specified for when the action would be taken, and whether the action to be taken is specific, or vaguely stated.

These detailed descriptions of how verbal actions are communicated are crucial to the analysis of crisis bargaining. Requests and intended actions form the component parts of *influence attempts* – demands accompanied by inducements in the form of some combination of threats, punishments, promises, and rewards. For example, if a request is accompanied by an intend action in the form of a threat indicating that a specific action will be taken if the target does not act within twenty-four hours, conflict strategists would argue that the specific commitment to action would make it a more credible inducement than if the actor simply indicated that, if the situation worsened, it would have to consider taking some unspecified action. The first example would be coded as an intended action, with the action to be taken conditional upon target inaction, with a specified deadline for compliance to avoid the action, and the negative action to be taken, in the event of noncompliance by the deadline specified. The second example would be coded as: an intended action, with the action conditional on unspecified circumstances, with no specified time limit for compliance, and the action to be taken, in the case of noncompliance, unspecified. The first example might be described as an ultimatum; the second would be more likely to be described as a warning. These distinctions, obviously, are of importance to any analysis of the effectiveness of different types of threats or promises.

Consider, for example, the content of the message received by the United States from the Soviet Union at the height of the Alert crisis during the Yom Kippur war of 1973, when the USSR's Brezhnev demanded that the United States join the USSR in fielding a peace-keeping force in the Sinai to separate Egyptian and Israeli troops: "It is necessary to act here without delay. I will say it straight that if you find it impossible to act jointly with us in this matter, we should be faced with the necessity urgently to consider the question of taking appropriate steps unilaterally" (Kissinger, 1982:583). The message was received by US Secretary of State, Henry Kissinger, who later described it as "in effect, an ultimatum" (Kissinger, 1982:583). Should Brezhnev's influence attempt be classified as an ultimatum? It says that, should the United States not act as requested, the Soviet Union would be forced to "consider" the "question" of taking some unspecified action at some unspecified date. Other observers might describe the action as a warning. The BCOW coding scheme avoids such terms in favor of describing the action according to its attributes. It would appear in the coded data as a demand accompanied by an intended action. The request would be described as conditional upon the same action by the USSR, with the time unspecified, and the requested action – the joint peacekeeping force – specified. The intended action accompanying the demand would be taken on the condition of inaction by the US. The action would be taken unilaterally by the USSR, but the type of action, and the time when it would be initiated, are unspecified.

This approach to describing verbal actions avoids lumping together a wide range of behaviorally different types of actions to which different observers might attach different labels. If we were to rely simply on the label attached to the action by one commentator or another – and different commentators tend to choose different labels – we would not be able to make important distinctions according to potentially salient attributes, such as, the conditions attached, specificity of the action, the type of action requested, whether or not there is a deadline for compliance, and the type of action threatened or promised. As we shall see in Chapter 6, these distinctions are important to the examination of the association between different attributes of influence attempts and responses to influence attempts.

After describing *how* the verbal statement is communicated, the next step in the coding process is to identify *what* is requested, intended, or is being commented upon. The branching of the choice tree for verbal actions appears in Figure 2.2.

To describe the action commented upon, requested, or intended, we fully code that action in the same manner as the verbal action coded up to that point. The general descriptors – date (if specified), actor, target, location, alone or with others, and tempo – are all described. Then, once again, the action is identified as physical or verbal. If the action commented upon, requested, or intended is a physical action, then that action is fully coded in the manner described for physical actions, to complete the description of the action. In the case of US action demanded by Brezhnev, for example, the date is unspecified, the actor is the US, the targets are the Egyptians and

35

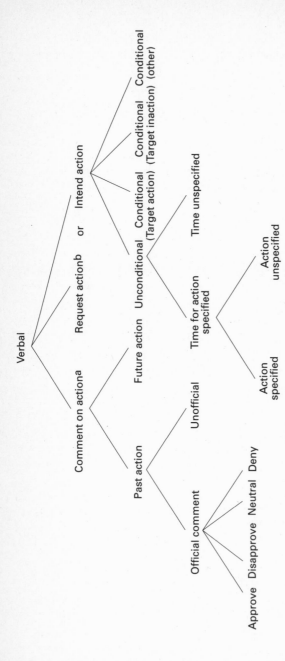

Figure 2.2   BCOW verbal action subcategories

Notes: *a* We present the subcategorization for the left-most branches of the tree only, when the subcategorization is the same for all branches

b The branching for Intend Action and Request Action are the same. They refer to the action intended by the actor in intended actions and to the action requested of the target in requested actions.

After reaching the final branching, the coder returns to the start of the choice tree (Figure 2.1) and fully describes the action commented upon, intended, or requested by the actor.

Israelis, the location is the Sinai, the action is to be taken with others (the USSR); the tempo is "start," and the action description is a "Peacekeeping Force." A complication arises, however, in the case of verbal actions referring to other verbal actions. In these instances, the description proceeds through the full coding of *how* the verbal action commented upon, requested, or intended was, or would be, communicated before describing *what* would be communicated. This complication would have arisen, for example, if Brezhnev demanded that the United States demand that Israel observe the cease-fire.

The coding of verbal actions, which I have just described, adds a degree of complexity to the BCOW typology that does not exist in other extant event data typologies. But, along with the ongoing description of the tempo of physical actions, it adds a degree of richness to the description of events that goes well beyond that obtained in other event data coding schemes. Most important for our purposes, it allows us to examine closely the sequence of influence attempts and responses that comprise crisis bargaining.

The interested reader can find a detailed description of the BCOW typology and coding procedures in the *User's Manual* (Leng, 1987a), which also contains brief narrative accounts of the crises included in this investigation. Detailed instructions for employing the BCOW typology to code events appear in the most recent edition of the *Coder's Manual* (Leng, 1991).

Intercoder reliability

The BCOW project has placed its strongest emphasis on obtaining a high degree of validity in describing international actions. To obtain a relatively high degree of reliability with such a complex coding scheme, however, requires extensive training and monitoring of coders. Intercoder reliability tests run for fourteen pairs of coders using more recent editions of the *Coder's Manual* (Leng, 1991) have yielded a mean score of 0.94, using Scott's *pi* (Holsti, 1969:140–46).[9]

Analyzing the data

The substantive analysis in the following chapters falls into two basic analytic perspectives. Chapters 3 through 5 present a macroscopic examination of the crisis structure, patterns of behavior, and crisis outcomes. Chapters 6 through 8 take a more microscopic look at crisis bargaining. The analytic approaches employed in each of these efforts is described briefly in the next two sections.

The crisis structure, behavior patterns, and outcomes

One purpose of this investigation is descriptive. We do not have very much empirically based information on how nations – not particular nations, but nations in general – behave in crises; but the primary purpose is predictive. Chapter 3 examines the extent to which it is possible to predict whether or not crises will end in war based on the attributes of the crisis structure, defined as the intersection of the perceived comparative war-fighting capabilities and interests at stake for each side. Chapter 4 begins by categorizing crises into four basic behavioral types, according to patterns of reciprocity and of escalation or deescalation. Then it moves to a consideration of the extent to which crisis outcomes may be predicted from the behavioral types. Chapter 5 explores associations among all three variables: the crisis structure, the behavior of the participants, and crisis outcomes.

Typing and weighting actions. The indicators of variations in behavioral patterns of reciprocity and escalation are extracted from time series of the actions of participants on each side of the crisis. Each action is first classified according to whether its *immediate impact* on the target is positive, negative, or neutral. A promise of economic aid, for example, would have a positive impact, a threat to withdraw aid would have a negative impact, and a request for aid would have a neutral impact. Then each of the positive and negative actions is weighted according to the degree of accommodation or coercion associated with that type of action. The weights, which run from 3 to −3, are based on a scale developed by Rubin and Hill (1973) and modified to fit the BCOW typology. A disapproving verbal comment, for example, would receive a score of −1, whereas a military attack would receive a score of −3.

The weighted actions for each actor are then aggregated at seven-day intervals over the course of the crisis, to obtain weekly scores of the level of hostility or cooperation for each actor.[10] These scores form the basis for the behavioral analyses appearing in Chapters 4 and 5.

Influence attempt-response sequences

While the analyses in Chapters 4 and 5 are concerned with patterns of escalation, those in Chapters 6 through 8 focus on crisis bargaining. The primary units of analysis in these chapters are influence attempt-response sequences. Chapter 6 focuses on the responses associated with different types of influence attempts; Chapters 7 and 8 explore the relationships among overall influence strategies, the crisis structure, and crisis outcomes.

In these later chapters, crisis behavior is viewed as a sequence of influence attempts and responses. The influence attempt is assumed to be the central component of the bargaining process – the means by which each side communicates its desires and intentions to the other. Each influence attempt consists of a request, or demand, that may or may not be accompanied by one or more inducements. Requests represent one of the categories of verbal actions (threats or promises), physical actions (displays, punishments, rewards), or a combination of verbal and/or physical actions, including positive, negative, and "carrot-and-stick" inducements. The target's responses are measured according to the extent to which it complies with the actor's request. The target may comply with the request, placate the actor with an alternative accommodative response, ignore the request, respond with defiance in the form of a threat and/or punishment, or offer a mixed response combining defiance and some accommodation. Chapter 6 examines the immediate responses to variations in influence attempts, that is, variations in *how* they are communicated – the conditions for carrying out inducements, the specificity of inducements, etc. – as well as *what* types of actions are requested, threatened, or promised.

Influence attempts may be thought of as the tactical moves that form discrete components of an overall *influence strategy*, through which the actor attempts to persuade, or coerce, the target to comply with the actor's demands. Chapters 7 and 8 explore the relative effectiveness of different types of influence strategies.

Some caveats

The focus on the crisis structure and the observable behavior of the participants as predictors of the evolution and outcomes of MICs is consistent with a realist perspective on conflict behavior. Classical realists and conflict strategists, as well as researchers who ascribe to the psychological approaches described in Chapter 1, assume that the actions of each side are chosen to influence the behavior of the other side. Our focus on the observable behavior of states means that the foreign-policy-making process is treated as a black box. There is no attempt to conduct an examination of how choices of bargaining strategies and responses may be influenced by the type of decision unit, the role conceptions of policy-makers, bureaucratic politics, organizational structures, or the personal qualities of national leaders. This omission reflects our interest in observing whether or not states choose policies that are consistent with a realist perspective, as opposed to examining how those policies are chosen. Nonetheless, the

39

absence of a consideration of how choices are made weakens any attempts to explain why states choose particular bargaining strategies over others, or why they react to the actions of other states in one way, rather than another. The perceptions of the interests at stake, of relative capabilities, and of the best bargaining strategies to pursue are often the subject of debate within governments and can change over the course of the crisis as one or another faction within the government gains ascendency.

A similar criticism can be directed at the assumption that states in militarized crises choose their actions either to influence the other side, or to respond to moves by the other side. Although that assumption is consistent with the two perspectives that are being examined, it omits any consideration of domestic politics. The alleged effects of domestic politics on the behavior of states in crises are frequently cited by diplomatic historians. To cite a few examples in our sample: pressure from slavophiles is alleged to have been influential in encouraging the Russian government to go to war with Turkey in 1877; the "yellow journalism" of the Hearst papers is credited with creating public pressure for an aggressive American policy toward Spain in 1897; and public memories of World War I are said to have created pressure on the governments of Britain and France to avoid war over the Munich crisis of 1938. To the extent that these pressures exerted a significant influence on the policies of the states in question, they weaken the descriptive validity of either the realist or psychological perspectives presented in Chapter 1. In that respect, the absence of any consideration of the role of domestic politics limits the completeness of any explanation of crisis bargaining that we will be able to present, and it places a heavier burden on the predictor variables that are examined in this study.

Finally, this study does not examine the possible differences that might occur in crisis behavior resulting from variations in the structure of the international system. The omission results from the author's view that the dyadic relationship between the crisis participants exert a considerably more salient influence on their behavior than the structure of the larger international system.[11]

Epistemology

Perception and behavior. The relationship between behavior and perception is an ongoing issue in the study of interstate behavior, and it becomes particularly salient in the analysis of action-response sequences. One cannot argue with the view that policy-makers must act upon their perceptions of reality, and that those perceptions include subjective estimates of the capabilities and intentions of the other party. The issue concerns the best way in which to obtain the most accurate possible indicators of those perceptions. One approach is through the explicit written statements of the participants, which may appear in memoranda, communications, or personal journals written at the time, or in memoirs written after the fact. The difficulties with this approach, beyond the practical issue of undertaking such a prohibitively time-consuming and expensive enterprise, is that on the spot comments are rare and difficult to find, and that memoirs are notoriously self-serving and unreliable. Writing from the perspective of several decades of professional experience, Harold Nicolson (1946:19) wrote that "most documents are composed after the event and all too frequently they are designed, and even falsified, in the hope of giving to what was a chance or empirical decision the appearance of prescience, wisdom and intent."

Consider, for example, the comment in Kissinger's (1982) memoirs quoted above, which indicates that he considered Brezhnev's influence attempt in the 1973 Alert crisis to constitute "in effect, an ultimatum." The United States reacted to Brezhnev's statement by placing its military forces on a high state of alert (DEFCON III), and sending a firm "carrot-and-stick" response back to Brezhnev. At the time, Nixon and Kissinger were criticized for overreacting, and for doing so in order to draw attention away from Nixon's domestic problems, specifically the Watergate scandal. Kissinger's memoirs provide a rationalization for his actions in that situation, as in others. That is not to say that he did not perceive Brezhnev's action as an ultimatum at the time; we have no way of knowing whether he did or did not. But we do know what was in Brezhnev's statement, what physical actions accompanied it, and how the United States responded to the Soviet statements and deeds.

What we are seeking to understand in this study is how states generally interact over the course of a crisis. If states most often respond in particular ways to particular types of influence attempts, then it is reasonable to assume that those influence attempts were perceived in a particular manner in most instances. If, for example, Brezhnev's action in 1973 is classified as a warning, accompanied by a physical threat of force, and the United States response is stronger than one usually finds associated with actions of that sort, then it represents an exception that may be explained by Kissinger's perception of the action as "in effect, an ultimatum," or as partially a reaction to domestic considerations, or some other combination of

41

variables. If, on the other hand, the United States response is typical of how states respond to such "warnings," then Kissinger's statement in his memoirs may be hyperbole. The epistemological argument here is that the most valid basis on which to conduct a study of interstate crisis behavior lies in the observation and description of the actual behavior of the participants. The extent to which that observation will bring us closer to an explanation of why states behave in certain ways in certain circumstances is dependent on the extent to which we can find consistent patterns of action in those circumstances.

Approach to analysis. The analytic approach that we will be employing is descriptive and correlational. It begins by identifying those variables that are considered most salient from a realist perspective and then tests their associations with the most relevant dependent variables. In the tradition of the Correlates of War project (Singer, 1969; 1976), the analysis begins with simple bivariate tests of association and moves to multivariate relationships. The bivariate associations are examined before moving to multivariate analyses because of my conviction that it is important to gain a good understanding of the relationships among variables in lower dimensions in order to understand their interactions in high dimensions.

The statistical analysis is correlational. If we find that variable A covaries with variable B, we can say whether the association between the two is, or is not, consistent with what would be predicted from a realist perspective. If the covariance between A and B is consistent with a realist perspective, we can observe its associations with different crisis outcomes to say whether or not the states in the sample generally have been successful when they have acted in accordance with that particular component of the realist prescription. But, based on the correlational findings alone, we cannot say *why* states – even the states in the sample – do, or do not, act in a manner consistent with the realist perspective, or why they are more, or less, successful when they do. The jump from observed associations to explanations of why those associations exist requires subjective inference in any social science research, where so many different variables can interact in different ways to influence behavior. I noted above that two potentially influential variables – domestic politics and bureaucratic politics – are missing from this study, and the reader probably can think of other candidates he or she would deem worthy of inclusion. In this investigation, we are limited by the number of cases and the categorical level of the data, but, even if it were possible to add several additional predictor variables, and we were able to generate data from a sufficient number of cases to test all the possible interaction between them, we still would be left with an incomplete picture. Social processes are too complex and indeterminate to consider all potential relationships. With this limitation in mind, I have tried to emphasize the tentative nature of any "findings" resulting from this investigation by describing them as "suggestive" of particular relationships, or "supportive" of one view or another.

On the other hand, the descriptive and correlational findings are likely to be more consistent with one explanation than another. In that sense, the findings from the data can offer evidence that strengthens, or weakens, one argument or another. When we find that those variables identified as most important by realists are associated with each other in a manner consistent with classical realist theory, then the burden of the argument falls on critics of realism to show why states would behave in such a manner if they were not following realist precepts. By the same token, when we find, as we do on several occasions, that states behave in a manner contrary to the predictions of conflict strategists, the burden of the argument falls on those who would defend the bargaining predictions and prescriptions of conflict strategists. Explanations consistent with the correlational findings will not be the last word on the subject, but the empirical evidence will require those who would challenge them to offer a plausible alternative explanation of how such associations could occur.

Statistical techniques

The statistical techniques available to this investigation are limited by the categorical level of the data, and, in those analyses in which the variables of interest are the attributes of crises, or of crisis participants, by the relatively small number of cases. Consequently, most of the analyses employ relatively simple statistical techniques, primarily cross-tubular analysis and bivariate tests of statistical significance and association. An exception occurs in Chapter 6, where our focus on individual influence attempts and responses provides a sufficient number of observations to generate a log linear model.

The constraints imposed by the relatively small sample of crises and the categorical level of the data offer advantages as well as disadvantages. The small sample – not to mention the time devoted to generating it – allows the researcher to become intimately familiar with the data in a way that is not possible in very large samples. As I have worked on this project over the past two decades, I have become more and more convinced that an intimate familiarity with the data may be the most important prerequisite to successful quantitative research.

43

Although the choice of relatively simple statistical techniques has been made out of necessity, it offers certain advantages to the reader. Not only are the techniques themselves more accessible to the untrained reader, but the analysis is presented in tables that allow the reader to undertake a closer inspection of the data than is possible with summary statistics from complex multivariate models.

Concluding remarks

The research that follows is in the tradition of the Correlates of War project in a number of respects: the selection of variables consistent with a realist perspective, the time and effort devoted to obtaining valid and reliable data, the focus on the observable behavior of states, and the use of correlational analysis. It also shares the COW project's concern with policy relevant questions related to issues of war and peace, with a strong bias in favor of the latter. The ultimate test of the relative value of the realist perspective and its extension to crisis bargaining by conflict strategists is the extent to which their prescriptions contribute to effective diplomacy. In that respect, the author shares Morgenthau's (1960:539) view that "diplomacy that ends in war has failed in its primary objective: the promotion of the national interest by peaceful means."

3 THE CRISIS STRUCTURE AND WAR

The essence of classical realism is summarized in Morgenthau's (1960:5) dictum that "statesmen think and act in terms of interest defined as power, and the evidence of history bears that out." If Morgenthau is correct, then we should find that the outcomes of crises are strongly associated with the intersection of the perceived interests and comparative capabilities of the two sides.

Within the context of a militarized crisis, power can be defined as the capacity to influence the behavior of other states. From a realist perspective, the most critical measure of power is the state's comparative war-fighting capability. Realists would argue that the amount of risk that a state should be willing to take to demonstrate its resolve to achieve, or to maintain, its interests is dependent on the balance between those interests and the consequences of war. The weight of the first is a function of the extent to which security interests are at stake; the weight of the second is based on the state's utility for war, which is dependent on the war-fighting capabilities of its side *vis-à-vis* those of the adversary.

Perceived interests and comparative capabilities may be viewed as the two most critical components of the *crisis structure*. Which of the two – capabilities or interests – exerts a stronger influence on foreign policy behavior has been the subject of debate. For some realists (Blainey, 1973; Lebow, 1981), perceptions of comparative war-fighting capabilities are the critical variable. They argue that states perceiving themselves as militarily superior will be more risk acceptant, because the prospect of war exerts less of a restraining influence. Others (Waltz, 1967; Osgood and Tucker, 1967; George and Smoke, 1974) have suggested that the interests at stake may be a more potent determinant of behavior. But, while analysts may disagree on which of these factors exerts a more potent influence on crisis behavior, the realist prescription is clear: statesmen should base their actions on a calculation of both factors.

Snyder and Diesing (1977:ch. 2) have presented a theoretical model of the crisis structure that is consistent with a realist perspective. In Snyder and Diesing's model, the interests at stake and the actor's perception of its capabilities determine the actor's preference ordering with regard to four possible crisis outcomes: a diplomatic victory, compromise, war, or submission to the demands of the other side. (A fifth possibility, which is not included in Snyder and Diesing's typology, is a stalemate without a settlement.) How a state will behave in a crisis is dependent on its preference ordering of outcomes. For example, a state that prefers war over submission is less likely to yield to coercive influence attempts than a state that would rather submit than face the costs of war.

Each party's understanding of the crisis structure is based on its perception of the intersection of the outcome preference orderings of the two sides. Snyder and Diesing view the bargaining that takes place during a crisis as a process in which each party attempts to gain an accurate perception of the crisis structure. Once each party obtains what it considers a clear understanding of the actual crisis structure, the dispute should move to resolution, either through a peaceful settlement, or the resort to war.

Snyder and Diesing's conception of the crisis structure is of particular interest in this study, because it presents a logical and coherent extension of the classical realism to crisis behavior. It also highlights the critical role of the intersection of the interests and capabilities of the two parties in determining the crisis structure and its presumed relationship to crisis behavior. Assuming that there is some observable association between the crisis structure and crisis outcomes, we can posit at least three potential relationships. The first is a simple direct causal linkage: national leaders decide to go to war, or to accept the best possible peaceful settlement, based on their perceptions of the crisis structure. A second possibility is that the crisis structure encourages patterns of behavior that determine the crisis outcome. A third possibility is that both the crisis structure, and the behavior that it has encouraged, exert potent influences on crisis outcomes. The crisis structure is a key consideration in decisions regarding whether or not to accept the costs and risks of war, but those decisions also are influenced by the dynamics of the interactions of the two sides and their psychological and political effects. Each of the three possibilities is considered in the next three chapters. This chapter examines potential bivariate associations between the crisis structure and crisis outcomes. Chapter 4 examines the associations between crisis behavior and crisis outcomes, and Chapter 5 considers the most likely relationships among the three variables.

There is a subjective element to the putative relationship between the crisis structure and crisis behavior. How states actually behave is dependent on how the crisis structure is *perceived* by the statesmen carrying out the policies of their states. Although realists prescribe action based on an objective calculation of the crisis structure, and the assumption of a similar calculation by the other side, they recognize the difficulties involved in making that judgment (see Morgenthau, 1946, 1960; Blainey, 1973). Therefore, the examination of the association between the crisis structure and crisis outcomes focuses on the participants' *perceptions* of the interests at stake and the relative capabilities of the two sides, as opposed to objective measures of interests or military capabilities.

The crisis structure

Capabilities

From a realist perspective, a national leader's consideration of the crisis structure begins with the balance in capabilities, specifically, usable military capabilities. To put it another way, a state's utility for war can be viewed as an increasing function of the probability and ease of winning the war – its *perceived comparative war-fighting capability*. This view has been stated most directly by Blainey (1973:ch. 7), who argues that the outbreak of war is a function of optimism by both sides regarding its outcome, and a failure in the measurement of its relative war-fighting capabilities by at least one side.

While realists place a careful calculation of relative power at the top of a statesman's duties, most recognize the near impossibility of achieving reliable estimates. Morgenthau (1960:153) argues that the task "resolves itself into a series of hunches." Blainey (1973:123) offers a list of seven factors that ought to be considered, but most of those factors require subjective judgments, such as estimating the adversary's degree of national unity, or the quality of its leadership.

No one would argue with the view that statesmen must act on their perceptions of reality, and few would dispute the notion that those perceptions are subjective at best. Consider one of the most notorious cases in our sample: the Munich crisis of 1938–39. The British, in deciding to accept a face-saving way out of the crisis, based their judgment on an overestimation of Germany's military strength. Within Germany there was considerable disagreement over the relative military power of the two sides, with Hitler's more optimistic view prevailing over the pessimism of his military staff (see Richardson,

47

1988: Weinberg, 1988). The crisis behavior of the two sides was based on these judgments, not on what might have been the objective military balance between the two sides. A more recent candidate, which is discussed in the Epilogue, is suggested by the actions and statements of Saddam Hussein preceding the Persian Gulf War of 1991.

To be consistent with the realist view, and with what seems to be the most practical approach to the relationship between comparative capability and behavior, we have developed a three-place ranking of each state's estimate of the most likely outcome of a war: (1) the state enjoys the military capability to achieve an easy military victory; (2) its military capabilities are roughly equal to those of the other side, so that a war would be potentially costly, and its outcome would be uncertain; (3) the state would be virtually certain to suffer a decisive defeat at the hands of a militarily stronger adversary.

The capability indicators have been drawn from the accounts of diplomatic historians that were used for the generation of the behavioral data. This approach has been chosen over employing objective indicators, such as the Correlates of War capability data, in order to obtain descriptions of the *perceptions* of policy-makers.

Interests at stake

Among the interests at stake in a crisis, a distinction can be made between tangible military, political, and economic interests, and intangible, or reputational concerns. Realism presumes a hierarchy of tangible interests, with vital security interests – territorial integrity and political independence – in the first rank. These are followed by other security interests, which are presumed by realists to take precedence over other political, economic, or ideological concerns.

Tangible interests. Metternich once said that "the first of all interests is independence" (Kissinger, 1964:42). In an interstate system based on the sovereignty principle, independence and territorial integrity are presumed to represent the most "vital" interests of states. This view is codified in Article 2(4) of the United Nations Charter, which outlaws the "threat or use of force against the territorial integrity or political independence of any state." As Walzer (1977:61–62) puts it, in the view of the international community, "these are rights worth dying for." From a realist perspective, they represent the core of what is meant by the "national interest."

A second distinction can be made between those interests which are related directly to the military security of a state, and other interests. A distinguishing component of realism is its assumption of a hierarchy of interests, with security concerns taking precedence over all other interests. Some recent evidence for the descriptive validity of this assumption has been found by Brecher and James (1986:64–68) in their study of crises occurring since World War I.

Other political, economic, or ideological interests are assumed to be of less salience. The interests falling into this category include: lesser political issues, such as colonial disputes, the rights and security of citizens abroad, or border disputes; economic concerns, including control over third party resources, trade issues, or nationalization of property; or religious or ideological issues. As in the case of the capability indicator, there is a three category ranking of tangible interests at stake: (1) vital security interests; (2) security interests short of vital interests; and (3) other tangible interests.

The accounts of diplomatic historians that were used to generate the behavioral data have provided the primary source for the indicators of tangible interests at stake, as they have for the capability indicators.

Intangible interests. The three place ranking of interests includes only tangible interests. But, the drive for power, which lies at the heart of classical realist theorizing, is often expressed in biological or psychological terms: Morgenthau's (1946) "lust for power," Aron's (1966) "pride," or Niebuhr's (1944) "will to power." The difficulty with including these values in any ranking of interests, however, is that they should be present in *all* crises, with their relative potency a function of the virtually unmeasurable psychological state of respective policy-makers. This component of realism, which stresses the psychological side of the competition for power, introduces a constant into the structural equation that suggests that all crises should be characterized by predominantly coercive bargaining, but it does not indicate when we should expect to find variations in behavior.[1]

Reputation for resolve. The most important reputational interest, from a realist perspective, is a state's "reputation for resolve," which represents a state's reputation for standing firm and accepting the risk of war to achieve its objectives (see Snyder and Diesing, 1977:185). Appearing weak, or irresolute, is presumed to weaken the state's image of power in succeeding crises, as well as weakening the personal reputation of the national leader identified with the irresolute performance.[2]

In much the same manner as the drive for power, the concern for a state's reputation for resolve is present in *all* crises. To the extent that structural differences might affect the relative potency of a national leader's concern for the state's – and his or her own – reputation for resolve, a good candidate would be the state's power status relative to

49

that of the adversary. In an earlier study (Leng, 1980), which included findings that states tended to react more belligerently to threats from status equals, than from either more powerful or less powerful states, I speculated that there may be an underlying norm of *equity* in relations among sovereign states. States may be willing to tolerate or ignore threats from weaker powers, with little risk to their reputation for resolve; prudence may dictate that they yield to overwhelmingly more powerful adversaries, but they may feel that they cannot afford to submit to threats from status equals.

Two hypotheses emerge from the foregoing discussion. (1) The high degree of visibility, high stakes, and contentiousness of a militarized crisis should cause a concern for a state's reputation for resolve to be a major consideration in *any* crisis, thereby increasing the level of belligerency and the likelihood that the crisis will end in war. (2) The stakes, with regard to a state's reputation for resolve, are highest when it is engaged in a confrontation with a status equal. The first of these hypotheses simply adds a constant that suggests that the stakes will be high in all crises. To the extent that it has an influence on our analyses, it should dampen the differences in crises outcomes that we would expect to find based on tangible interests alone. The second hypothesis, however, suggests a third structural variable that may encourage behavior that is not entirely consistent with considerations of war-fighting capabilities, that is, a state's power *status, vis-à-vis* the other side in a crisis, may be inconsistent with its perceived comparative war-fighting capability.

Probably the most meaningful distinction with regard to the question of power status is that between *major* and *minor* powers.[3] Minor powers may believe that they can yield to the demands of major powers with no great loss in their reputations for resolve, while major powers similarly may believe that they can afford to ignore or appease minor powers. On the other hand, neither major nor minor powers are likely to assume that they can yield to states of their own rank without suffering reputational costs. If this hypothesis is correct, we should find crises escalating to war most often when the contending parties are of equal power status.

Identifying which states qualify as major powers contains an obvious element of subjectivity, which makes any classification scheme problematic. The most widely accepted list, however, is that employed by the Correlates of War project. According to the Correlates of War criteria (Small and Singer, 1982:44–45), the major powers have comprised: Austria-Hungary (1816–1918), Britain (1816–present), China (1950–present), France (1816–1940, 1945–present), Italy (1860–1943),

Japan (1895–1945), Prussia/Germany (1816–1918, 1925–45), Russia/ Soviet Union (1816–1917, 1922–91), and the United States (1899– present).

Reputation for reliability. Another reputational variable of interest is an actor's concern with its reputation for reliability, especially a credible demonstration of loyalty to its allies. During the Vietnam War, American presidents frequently made this argument to defend America's military commitment to South Vietnamese government.

Formal alliance ties represent the most visible commitments to assist another state in protecting its interests. But a concern for a state's reputation for reliability in keeping its commitments can be expressed in a variety of ways in an ongoing crisis, depending on how the committed state views its own interests. Alliance partners wishing to avoid war – or the embarrassment of reneging on a commitment to come to the aid of its ally – may persuade an ally to yield to an adversary's demands, as the British and French persuded Czechoslovakia to yield to Germany in the Munich crisis of 1938–39. On the other hand, an alliance partner may encourage the outbreak of war by providing an ally with a promise of unconditional support, as in the "blank check" that Germany offered to Austria in the 1914 crisis.

Some recent empirical studies (Siverson and King, 1979; Huth and Russett, 1984) have found a positive relationship between alliance commitments and the entrance of states into wars in which their alliance partners have been engaged. These findings suggest that alliances contribute to the expansion of wars already begun, but they do not enlighten us as to the most likely contribution of alliances to the outbreak of war, or to its avoidance. An extensive review of the alliance literature by Vasquez (1987) finds little evidence of an association between alliance membership and war-proneness, a finding that is consistent with a recent study by Wayman (1991). None of these studies, however, has focused directly on the relationship between alliance ties and war-proneness in crises.

A three-category distinction will be employed as an operational measure of the extent to which a state's reputation for reliability is at stake: (1) crises in which the actor was the only directly involved state on its side; (2) crises in which it was collaborating with or assisting other states, but had no formal alliance commitments to aid them in the case of a war with a disputant on the other side; and (3) crises in which participant states had formal commitments to assist militarily another participant state in the event of war with a disputant on the other side.[4] The reputational stakes for reliability would be highest in the third case and lowest in the first. In generating data for this

Table 3.1. *Perceived capability, interests, and reliability*

Crisis name	Actor	Target	Target's relative capability	Target's interests at stake	Target's interest + capability: motivation	Target's reliability reputation score
Pastry	France	Mexico	1	2	3	1
	Mexico	France	3	1	4	1
Crimean War	Russia	Turkey, France, Britain	2	3	5	2
	Turkey, France, Britain	Russia	3	2	5	1
2nd Schleswig-Holstein	Prussia, Austria	Denmark	2	2	4	1
	Denmark	Prussia, Austria	3	2	5	3
Russo-Turkish	Russia	Turkey	1	3	4	1
	Turkey	Russia	3	2	5	1
British–Russian	Britain	Russia	1	2	3	1
	Russia	Britain	3	2	5	1
British–Portuguese	Britain	Portugal	1	2	3	1
	Portugal	Britain	3	2	5	1
Fashoda	Britain	France	1	2	3	1
	France	Britain	3	2	5	1
Spanish–American	Spain	US	2	2	4	1
	US	Spain	2	2	4	1
1st Moroccan	France	Germany	2	1	3	1
	Germany	France	2	1	3	1
2nd Central American	Honduras	Nicaragua	3	2	5	2
	Nicaragua	Honduras	2	3	5	2
Bosnian	Austria, Germany	Russia, Serbia, Turkey	1	2	3	2
	Russia, Serbia, Turkey	Austria, Germany	3	2	5	3
Agadir	France, Britain	Germany	2	1	3	1
	Germany	France, Britain	2	1	3	2
1st Balkan	Serbia, Bulgaria, Greece	Turkey	1	3	4	1
	Turkey	Greece, Serbia, Bulgaria	3	2	5	3

Conflict	Side A	Side B				
2nd Balkan	Bulgaria	Serbia, Romania, Greece	3	2	5	2
Pre-WWI	Serbia, Romania, Greece	Bulgaria	3	2	5	1
	Austria, Germany	Serbia, Russia, France Britain	2	2	4	3
Teschen	Czechoslovakia	Poland	2	2	4	1
Chaco Dispute	Bolivia	Paraguay	1	2	3	1
	Paraguay	Bolivia	3	2	5	1
Chaco War	Bolivia	Paraguay	2	2	4	1
	Paraguay	Bolivia	2	2	4	1
Manchurian	China	Japan	2	2	4	1
	Japan	China	3	2	5	1
Italo-Ethiopian	Ethiopia	Italy	1	3	4	1
	Italy	Ethiopia	3	2	5	1
Rhineland	Britain, France, Belgium	Germany	1	3	4	1
	Germany	Britain, France, Belgium	1	2	3	3
Anschluss	Austria	Germany	2	2	4	1
	Germany	Austria	3	3	5	1
Munich	Czechoslovakia, Britain, France	Germany	1	2	4	3
	Germany	Czechoslovakia, Britain, France	2	3	4	3
Polish–Lithuanian	Lithuania	Poland	3	2	5	3
	Poland	Lithuania	1	2	3	1
Danzig	Germany	Britain, Poland	2	3	5	1
	Britain, Poland	Germany	3	2	5	2
Italo-French	Italy	France	3	1	4	1
	France	Italy	1	1	2	1
1st Kashmir	India	Pakistan	2	3	5	2
	Pakistan	India	2	3	5	1
Berlin Blockade	US, Britain, France	USSR	2	2	4	1

Table 3.1. (*cont.*)

Crisis name	Actor	Target	Target's relative capability	Target's interests at stake	Target's interest + capability: motivation	Target's reliability reputation score
Trieste	USSR	US, Britain, France	2	2	4	2
	Italy	Yugoslavia	2	1	3	1
	Yugoslavia	Italy	2	1	3	1
Suez	Egypt	Britain, France, Israel	3	2	5	2
	Britain, France, Israel	Egypt	2	2	4	1
Honduran Border	Honduras	Nicaragua	2	1	3	1
	Nicaragua	Honduras	2	1	3	1
Sino-Indian	China	India	2	2	4	1
	India	China	2	2	4	1
Bizerte	France	Tunisia	1	2	3	1
	Tunisia	France	3	1	4	1
Cuban Missile	US	USSR, Cuba	2	2	4	2
	USSR, Cuba	US	2	2	4	1
Cyprus	Greece, Greek-Cypriot	Turkey, Turkish-Cypriot	2	2	4	2
	Turkey, Turkish-Cypriot	Greece, Greek-Cypriot	2	2	4	2
2nd Kashmir	India	Pakistan	3	2	5	1
	Pakistan	India	2	2	4	1
Rann of Kutch	India	Pakistan	3	2	5	1
	Pakistan	India	2	2	4	1
Cod War	Britain	Iceland	1	2	3	1
	Iceland	Britain	3	2	5	1
Beagle Channel	Chile	Argentina	2	2	4	1
	Argentina	Chile	2	2	4	1
Sino-Vietnam	China	Vietnam	2	2	4	1
	Vietnam	China	3	2	5	1

indicator, we combined the judgments of diplomatic historians with the Correlates of War alliance data (Small and Singer, 1969).

The scores for the structural variables, for each of the participants, in each crisis, appear in Table 3.1.

Crisis structure and war

If foreign policy decisions are based solely on a rational calculation of interests in terms of power, then the interaction of the participants serves as a communication process that allows each party to gain a fuller understanding of the structure of the crisis (see Snyder and Diesing, 1977). Viewed from this perspective, foreign policy decisions to go to war, or to accept a peaceful settlement, are based on each participant's perception of the structure of the crisis. With that possibility in mind, we will explore the bivariate relationship between the crisis structure and war, or nonwar, outcomes, before turning to a consideration of the relationship between the crisis structure and crisis behavior.

Perceived comparative capability and war

A pure theory of power politics perspective assumes that the struggle for power encourages states to go to war whenever they believe that they have a chance to win at reasonable cost. This perspective was once described as "pure realism" by Carr (1939), who noted that it strips classical realism down to its essential elements. Interstate politics are viewed as a naked power struggle in which states seize opportunities to expand their power whenever they arise. The perspective surfaces in the writings of classical realists such as Clausewitz, or Bismarck, who once wrote: "As soon as it was proved to me that it was in the interests of a healthy and well-conceived Prussian policy, I would see our troops fire on French, Russian, English, or Austrians with equal satisfaction" (Crankshaw, 1981). The same view surfaces, in less dramatic form, in the contemporary theorizing of Blainey (1973), who sees war as a function of at least one side's optimism regarding the outcome for its side. Blainey argues that the outbreak of war is a consequence of a failure, by at least one side, in the measurement of its war-fighting capabilities. If the capabilities of the parties are uneven, the only rational policy for the weaker side is to yield; if the parties are relatively evenly matched, it would be a mistake for either side to accept the costs and risks associated with a long, hard war.[5] According to this thesis, crises are most likely to end in war when one side

55

believes that it can win a war easily, and the other side believes that it has at least a good fighting chance.

The conditions that develop over the course of a crisis may add to the weight of a pure power politics perspective. It can be argued that, once states have reached a level of conflict in which they are threatening war, the stakes are, *ipso facto*, already very high for both parties. The initial stakes had to be high for the conflict to escalate to the level of a militarized crisis in the first place, and the escalation of conflict over the course of the crisis creates high reputational stakes of its own, particularly with regard to a state's reputation for resolve. Therefore, with the stakes very high in *all* crises, it could be argued that decisions with regard to whether or not a state should go to war will be based primarily on comparative war-fighting capabilities.

Findings from empirical studies of the relationship between comparative capabilities and war have been mixed (see Sullivan, 1990; Levy, 1989), although most studies (see Bremer, 1992; Gochman, 1990; Wayman, Singer, and Goertz, 1983; Karsten, Howell, and Allen, 1984) find little, or no direct relationship between comparative capabilities and war. These studies, however, have been limited to the relationship between objective physical capabilities, as measured by the researcher, as opposed to each side's perception of its comparative war-fighting capabilities.

Proceeding from a power politics perspective, the intersection of the perceived capabilities of the two sides can be classified into one of three categories, based on the hypothesized likelihood that the crisis will end in war. (1) Crises are most likely to escalate to war when both sides expect to win easily, or when one side expects to win easily and the other believes it has at least an even chance. (2) Crises are less likely to end in war when both parties believe that they are relatively evenly matched. (3) Crises are least likely to end in war when either side expects a potential war to end in a defeat. The bivariate associations between degrees of comparative capability and war outcomes, for the crises in the sample, appear in Table 3.2.

Table 3.2 exhibits a striking difference between those cases in which a power politics model would predict war to be most likely and the other two categories. Crises ended in war eight out of nine times when either: both sides believed that they could achieve an easy victory in war; or, when one side believed that it could win easily and the other side believed that the two sides were evenly matched. On the other hand, there is little difference between those cases in which both parties assumed that they were relatively evenly matched, and those cases in which one side believed that it would lose. War occurs

Table 3.2. *Capability perception and war*

Capabilities (States A and B)		War	Nonwar	Total
A = Win easily	B = Win easily	1(1.00)	0(0.00)	1(1.00)
A = Win easily	B = Even	7(0.88)	1(0.12)	8(1.00)
A = Even	B = Even	5(0.31)	11(0.69)	16(1.00)
A = Win or even	B = Lose	4(0.27)	11(0.73)	15(1.00)
A = Lose	B = Lose	0(0.00)	0(0.00)	0(0.00)
Total		17(0.42)	23(0.58)	40(1.00)

Note: Numbers represent frequency counts with percentages in parentheses.

between one-quarter and one-third of the time in both cases. Thus, the associations in Table 3.2 are consistent with a power politics perspective in indicating that crises are most likely to end in war when the opposing sides are most confident about their war-fighting capabilities. These instances account for less than one-quarter of the cases in the sample, but they do include slightly over half of the cases ending in war. The remaining cases in Table 3.2, however, suggest that confidence in one's war-fighting capabilities is neither a sufficient nor a necessary prerequisite to deciding to go to war. Other variables must be influencing those decisions as well. The most prominent candidate, from a realist perspective, would be the interests at stake.

Tangible interests and war

Some realists (Waltz, 1967; Osgood and Tucker, 1967), along with other theorists (Jervis, 1984) have argued that an edge in motivation can out-weigh a perceived capability advantage. Contrary to the pure power politics model, this view argues that statesmen may decide to enter wars even though they view the probability of success as low, provided that the stakes, in terms of either the gains from a victory, or the costs of yielding to the demands of the other side, are high enough. One does not have to look far for candidates, beginning with Thucydides' account of the Melian response to the challenge from the Athenians and extending to more recent wars in Vietnam and Afghanistan. There also has been more recent empirical evidence of a positive relationship between the interests at stake and the likelihood of crises escalating to war. Brecher and Wilkenfeld (1987:216) have found evidence in a study of interstate crises occuring between 1928 and 1980 to suggest that crises are more likely to end in war when the parties "basic values" are threatened.

We can examine the bivariate association between the interests at stake and the likelihood of a crisis in the sample escalating to war by

Table 3.3. *Tangible interests and war*

Comparative interests (States A and B)		War	Nonwar	Total
A = Vital	B = Security	7(0.87)	1(0.13)	8(1.00)
A = Security	B = Security	10(0.40)	15(0.60)	25(1.00)
Either A or B = No Security		0(0.00)	7(1.00)	7(1.00)
Total		17(0.42)	23(0.58)	40(1.00)

Note: Numbers represent frequency counts with percentages in parentheses.

employing the three level ranking of interests at stake that was mentioned above. Based on that categorization we can hypothesize that (1)
crises are most likely to escalate to war when both sides have high
interests at stake, including vital interests for at least one side; (2) they
are less likely to end in war if neither side has vital interests at stake;
and (3) they are least likely to end in war if either side has no security
interests at stake. The associations between tangible interests and war
appear in Table 3.3.

The associations in Table 3.3 suggest that one can do very well in
predicting war or nonwar outcomes based solely on the degree of
tangible interests at stake, provided that the stakes are either (1) very
high for one side and high for the other, or (2) there are no security
issues at stake for at least one of the two sides. War occurred in seven
of the eight cases in which vital interests were at stake for at least one
side and the other side had lesser security interests at stake; war did
not break out in any of the seven instances in which at least one side
did not have any security interests at stake. Table 3.3 also indicates that
those cases in which both sides had nonvital security interests at stake
are the least predictable. These cases comprised over half of the crises
in the sample.

Reputational interests and war

Tests of the two reputational variables that might confound
the effects of tangible interests on crisis outcomes – concern for power
status and reputation for reliability – yielded no significant bivariate
associations that would contradict the descriptive validity of realism
suggested by the associations above. Tests of the relationships between
power status and war outcomes indicate that the outbreak of war is
least likely in major power crises. War occurred in only three of twelve
major power crises, as opposed to war outcomes in eight of fifteen
minor power crises, and in six of thirteen crises between major and

minor powers. These associations are consistent with Morgenthau's (1960:ch. 31) argument that more experienced states are better able to manage crises than less experienced minor powers.

This finding is intriguing given the results of a recent empirical study by Bremer (1992), which considered the relationship between dyadic power combinations and the outbreak of war, within a given observation year, for the full population of states in a comparable time period (1816–65). Bremer found that wars occurred with the *greatest* frequency in major-power–major-power dyadic combinations. Bremer's findings, however, do not necessarily contradict those found within the sample. Because major powers are more likely to be active in a wide range of international disputes, they may be more likely to become engaged in crises in the first place, or to enter wars that are already underway. In other words, major powers may be better at managing crises than avoiding them in the first place.

No significant relationship can be observed between alliance ties and a greater or lesser likelihood of crises ending in wars, a finding that is consistent with related empirical studies finding no significant relationship between alliance commitments and war-proneness. The lack of any significant relationship is also consistent with a realist perspective, which would predict that the interactions among allies that result from such commitments would be likely to vary according to the interests at stake and the comparative capability calculations of the participants. That is, they would consult their national interests, of which a reputation for reliability would be only one consideration, and a minor one, in comparison with the tangible interests at stake. When the lack of any significant positive relationship between these two reputational variables and war is compared to the impressive associations between perceived tangible interests and crisis outcomes, the results support the descriptive validity of the classical realist view of the most salient interests for national decision-makers.

Capability, interests, and war

Based on the bivariate associations between perceived comparative capabilities and war, and between tangible interests and war, it appears that the crises in the sample were most likely to end in war when either (1) one side estimated that it had the military capability to win easily and the other side estimated that it had, at least, a fighting chance, or (2) one side had vital interests at stake and the other side had other security interests at stake. Having found some support for the influence of each of these variables, the next step is to consider their combined association with war or peaceful outcomes to crisis.

Most realists adopt the commonsensical view that statesmen attempt to balance the costs and risks of war and the interests at stake in deciding whether to go to war, or to accept the best possible peaceful alternative, and there is some empirical evidence to support its validity. Buena de Mesquita's (1981) study of wars since 1816 employs a rational choice model based on the assumption that national leaders decide whether or not to go to war based on a rational calculation of the costs and benefits of victory or defeat, weighted according to the probability of the occurrence of one or the other. Although the persuasiveness of his findings is weakened somewhat by the indirectness of some critical indicators, Buena de Mesquita has obtained impressive statistical support for a rational utility model combining interests and capabilities.[6]

The approach to considering the association between perceived comparative capabilities and interests, and war outcomes that will be employed here, is less elegant than Buena de Mesquita's, but it offers the advantage of empirical directness. In the preceding analyses, for each of the two variables, capabilities and interests, the intersection of the structural scores for the two sides to the dispute was ranked according to a realist prediction of its association with war. For each variable, there are three ranks of predicted war outcomes: (1) most likely to end in war; (2) less likely to end in war; and (3) least likely to end in war. For example, for the capability variable, the first rank – crises predicted to be most likely to end in war – contained those cases in which one side expected to win a war easily and the other side believed that it had an even chance of prevailing.

An examination of the association between the *combined* capability and interest indicators with war, or nonwar, outcomes, requires us to consider each possible pairing of the outcome predictions for each of the two structural variables. There are nine possible permutations, beginning with a pair in which the intersection of interest scores for the two sides and the intersection of capability scores for the two sides are both predicted to have the highest association with war outcomes, and ending with the pair in which both are predicted to have the lowest association with war. Working from a realist perspective, we expect those cases that fall into the highest rank for both variables to be the most likely to end in war, and those cases that rank lowest for both variables to be least likely to end in war. It is more difficult, however, to state an hypothesized association with war outcomes for those cases in which the paired ranks disagree, for instance, those cases that rank

Table 3.4. *Combined capability and interest scores with war*

Scores	I=H C=H	I=H C=M	I=H C=L	I=M C=H	I=M C=M	I=M C=L	I=L C=H	I=L C=M	I=L C=L	Total
War	2	1	4	7	3	0	0	0	0	17
Nonwar	0	0	1	1	7	7	0	4	3	23

Note: I = Intersection of interest scores of the two sides. C = Intersection of the combined capability scores of the two sides. H = Highest rank in predicted association with war outcomes, M = Middle rank, L = Lowest rank.

highest on the predicted association between the intersection of the two sides' capability scores and war, and lowest on the intersection of the two sides' interest scores and war, or vice versa. On the other hand, a closer look at these cases may give us a better sense of the relative potency of considerations of comparative military capabilities and the interests at stake in influencing the escalation of crises. The associations between these combined structural relationships and war outcomes are depicted in Table 3.4.

In Table 3.4, I refers to the intersection of the interest scores of the two sides, and C refers to the intersection of capability scores of the two sides. H, M, and L refer to the ranking of those scores with regard to the predicted probability of war. H represents the highest predicted probability of war, M represents the middle rank, and L represents the lowest rank. Thus, column 1 includes those cases in which the intersection of both the interest scores of the two sides and the intersection of the capability scores of the two sides fall into the category predicted to have the highest association with war outcomes.

The number of categories relative to the size of the sample yields relatively small frequency counts within categories; nevertheless, Table 3.4 reveals some interesting associations. The capability-interest combinations with the strongest association with war appear in columns 1 and 4 of Table 3.4. These associations indicate that wars are most likely to occur when the capability relationship is one in which one of the parties believes it can win easily in the event of war, and the other side believes it has at least an even chance, *and* when security interests are at stake for both parties. Under these circumstances war occurs nine out of ten times. This association is consistent with a realist perspective based on an interactive relationship between capabilities and interests, in which security interests take precedence over other interests. The Polish-Danzig crisis preceding World War II in Europe is typical of this pattern. Germany expected a decisive military victory; Britain, France, and Poland expected a long war with a less predictable outcome. Both sides had security interests at stake, in fact, vital interests in the case of Poland.

A realist perspective that attempts to balance considerations of security interests and power also is supported by the associations appearing in column 3. The four of five cases in column 3 that ended in war offer an explanation for the earlier finding, in Table 3.2, that there were four crises in the sample that ended in war, despite the fact that one of the parties expected to be defeated. From a pure power politics perspective, this should not happen. The weaker side should yield to the stronger rather than accept the costs of a losing war. Column 3 of Table 3.4 offers a straightforward explanation for this anomaly in the decisive military advantage perceived by the stronger side coupled with vital interests at stake for the weaker side. Consider the four cases in column 3 that ended in war: the Russo-Turkish crisis of 1876–78, the First Balkan crisis of 1912, the Manchurian crisis of 1932, and the Italo-Ethiopian crisis of 1934–35. In all four of those crises, the weaker side – Turkey in the Russo-Turkish crisis, Turkey in the First Balkan crisis, China in the Manchurian crisis, and Ethiopia in the Italo-Ethiopian crisis – had vital interests at stake. These also were all instances in which the stronger side expected an easy military victory, so there was less reason for the stronger side to moderate its demands, or to accept a compromise solution. The situation faced by the weaker side in each of these cases, in fact, is distressingly similar to that faced by the Melians in the account presented by Thucydides. The Athenians demanded that the hopelessly over-matched Melians sacrifice their political independence to avoid the terrible consequences of an Athenian invasion. The Melians too, decided to fight. A third interesting relationship appears in columns 8 and 9, which indicate that war was avoided in all those cases in which *either* side had no security interests at stake. Since there are no cases in the sample (column 7), in which this coincided with a capability combination predicting the highest likelihood of war, it is unclear whether the lower stakes are a sufficient condition for avoiding war. It adds, however, to the impressions from other findings that variations in the tangible interests at stake in crises do make a significant difference in determining their outcomes. The likelihood of war does not appear to be a function of capability alone; nor does it appear that differences in tangible interests at stake become meaningless in light of the serious reputational interests at stake in all crises.

Finally, column 5 of Table 3.4 suggests the most unpredictable situation: when the stakes are security interests short of vital interests, and the two sides see themselves as evenly matched in terms of

Table 3.5. *Combined capabilities, interests, and war*

Capability,	Interest	War	Nonwar	Total
Cap. = High	Int. = H or M	9(0.90)	1(0.10)	10(1.00)
Cap. = M or L	Int. = High	8(0.35)	15(0.65)	23(1.00)
Cap. = H, M, or L	Int. = Low	0(0.00)	7(1.00)	7(1.00)
Total		17(0.42)	23(0.58)	40(1.00)

Notes: Cap. = Intersection perceived comparative capabilities for two sides, Int. = Intersection of tangible interests for two sides. H = Highest predicted probability of a war outcome, M = Middle rank, L = Lowest predicted probability of a war outcome. Numbers represent frequency counts with percentages in parentheses.

military capability. War occurs in three of the ten instances falling into this category.

The associations in Table 3.4 suggest an interactive relationship between capability and interests that is associated with the likelihood that crises will end in war. While the associations in Table 3.4 are not consistent with a power politics model in the most narrow sense, to the extent to which they suggest a causal relationship between the crisis structure and war, that relationship is quite consistent with a classical realist perspective. These relationships can be depicted most simply by collapsing Table 3.4 to a simple three-by-two table, as in Table 3.5.

The associations in row 1 of Table 3.5 tell us that, insofar as there is a relationship between the crisis structure and war, a crisis is most likely to end in war when one of the parties believes that it can win a war relatively easily, the other side believes that it has at least an even chance, and both parties have vital interests, or other immediate security interests, at stake. In fact, among the crises in the sample, under these conditions, war occurred in nine of ten instances.

Row 2 of Table 3.5 tells us that eight of the twenty-three crises in the sample ended in war in those cases in which there were vital interests, or other security interests at stake for both sides, but, either both parties believed that they were evenly matched in war-fighting capabilities, or one of the parties believed that it would be defeated. This is the least predictable situation, although we do know from Table 3.3 above, that four of the eight instances in which war occurred were cases in which the stronger side felt confident of victory in war, and the weaker side expected to be defeated, *but* the weaker side had vital interests at stake.

The relationship between the level of interests at stake and the likelihood of war also is apparent in row 3 of Table 3.5. These are cases in which the comparative capabilities of the two sides were the same as those in row 2, but neither side had vital interests or other security interests at stake. None of these seven crises ended in war.

The overall relationship in tables 3.4 and 3.5 yields a standardized *lambda-y* (Goodman and Kruskal, 1954) score of 0.64, which indicates that predicting the likelihood of the onset of war based on the combined capability-interest category yields a 64 percent reduction in error over a random guess.

Conclusion

The chapter began by quoting Morgenthau's (1960:5) assertion that the realist assumption that statesmen "think and act in terms of interest defined as power" is supported by historical evidence. Morgenthau's claim is not challenged by the findings from the historical crises analyzed in this chapter. There is impressive evidence to indicate that there is a positive association between the crisis structure and crisis outcomes, and that the most important components of the crisis structure are the tangible interests at stake and each side's perception of its comparative war-fighting capabilities. According to the precepts of classical realism, war is most likely to occur when the security stakes are high and both parties are optimistic regarding their chances if a war should occur.

Among the interests at stake, we found that the most important, in terms of predicting the crisis outcome, are security interests, and the most important security interests are political independence and territorial sovereignty. Reputational interests, to the extent that we were able to employ operational indicators of their variation from one crisis to another in a manner distinct from the effects of the interactions of the participants, did not appear to be significantly related to the likelihood of crises ending in war.

We also found a positive relationship between optimistic perceptions of comparative war-fighting capabilities and the outbreak of war. Wars occurred most frequently when one side believed that it could win easily and the other side believed that it had at least an even chance of winning.

Combining the capability and interest measures produced the most impressive results. When one side believed it could prevail easily in a war and the other thought that it had an even chance, and both parties had security interests at stake, the crisis escalated to war in nine of ten cases, a finding that is consistent with a realist view of conflict behavior based on a careful calculation of interests and power.

On the other hand, we found that, even if the parties viewed

64

themselves as unevenly matched in war-fighting capabilities, if the weaker side had vital interests at stake, the crisis was likely to escalate to war anyway. Such a finding is consistent with the arguments of analysts who depart from the pure power politics model in arguing that interests may be a more potent influence on state behavior than comparative capability. In fact, our studies suggest that a particularly dangerous combination occurs when a party confident of its superior fighting ability confronts a weaker party with vital interests at stake. It is a finding that has intriguing implications in light of recent wars pitting superpowers against Third World states. Finally, there is some cause for optimism in the evidence that war was avoided in all of the crises in which there were no security interests at stake for either party.

Realist predictions of the relationship between structural attributes and war or nonwar outcomes allow us to improve our predictive accuracy by 64 percent over a random selection. Nevertheless, these findings are just a beginning. Twenty-three of the forty crises in the sample fall into an intermediate category where the combination of interests and comparative capabilities yields moderate scores and weak predictions. Why did eight of these cases end in war, while the other fifteen did not? The structural scores alone do not help us answer that question. Moreover, in those more extreme cases in which the structural scores successfully predicted the outcome of the crisis, what was the relationship between the structural variables and the behavior of the participants? Did the structural conditions encourage certain patterns of escalatory behavior that led to war? Or did national decision-makers reach their war–nonwar decisions independent of their preceding interactions with the other side? The next two chapters take a closer look at these questions.

4 PATTERNS OF BEHAVIOR

As his narrative account of the diplomatic confrontation at the Congress of Vienna approached a climax, Harold Nicolson (1946:166) paused to warn the reader of the dangers of over-rationalizing events in their reconstruction: "The structure of an international crisis is organic rather than artificial; however much one may seek to detach and mount the specimens for purposes of exposition, it must never be forgotten that at the time they were part of the thought, feeling and action of sentient human beings, exposed to all the impulses and fallibility of human nature."

Nicolson's warning is worth bearing in mind as we begin this chapter, for we will be embarking on an investigation that begins with an effort in taxonomy: the classification of crises by behavioral types. The underlying assumption in such an undertaking is that, however much human feeling and thought may influence the direction of a crisis, it can be classified as a distinct behavioral type that shares features in common with a number of similar episodes involving different policy-makers from different states in different diplomatic eras.

There are two behavioral dimensions of particular interest to our study: (1) the degree of escalation in the mix of cooperative and conflictive behavior of each side, and (2) the degree of reciprocity exhibited in the interactions of the participants. These two dimensions are chosen because discussions of patterns of escalation and reciprocity have played such a prominent role in the critique of the prescriptions of conflict strategists. If those critiques are correct, we should find some evidence of their validity in the relationship between crisis outcomes and patterns of escalation and reciprocity in the behavior of the participants.

This chapter begins with the construction of operational measures of escalation and reciprocity. Then the forty crises in the sample are classified into four basic types according to the degree of escalation and reciprocity exhibited in each. After exploring the patterns of

behavior appearing in each of the four types, along with some interesting variants, we will turn to a consideration of the association between
the behavioral type and crisis outcomes.

Escalation

The discussion of escalation in Chapter 1 contrasts the realist
assumption of the ability of national policy-makers to make rational
and prudent decisions as the crisis escalates in intensity, with the
psychological approach's focus on the effects of confounding cognitive
and emotional factors that may be exacerbated by the escalation of the
crisis.

Realist perspective

From a realist perspective, the escalation of the crisis can be
seen as a process combining probing, signaling, and influence (Snyder
and Diesing, 1977:ch. 2). The probing consists of obtaining feedback
from influence attempts to discover the other side's resistance point, or
minimum disposition to reach a settlement. Coercive influence
attempts also are used to signal resolve, and to influence the other side
to lower its resistance to one's demands. Both sides are engaged in the
same process, so that, when the resistance points of the two sides are
clearly understood by each side, the crisis should reach a turning-point
and, in the case of two prudent adversaries, move to a settlement.
Viewed from this perspective, crises escalate to war only if one side
miscalculates its comparative war-fighting power, the resolve of the
other side, or both.

Snyder and Diesing's image of the escalation process is very much
like the ritualized escalation in displays of strength and hostility
observed by students of animal behavior. As the conflict escalates, each
animal gains more information regarding the relative strength and
resolve of its adversary, until one of the spiders, coral fish, or stags,
realizes that it is at a disadvantage and flees (see Archer and Huntingford, 1993).[1] The decision as to whether or not to escalate to fierce
fighting is based on comparative fighting capabilities and the interests
at stake. In models such as these, whether applied to animals, humans,
or states, the rising escalation can be viewed as a learning curve in
which each party obtains more and more information regarding the
motivation and comparative war-fighting capabilities of the other. A
fierce fight, in the case of stags, or a war, in the case of states, occurs
when one party misreads the structure of the dispute, but the decision-

making process is rational and calculated, with the feedback obtained during the escalation of the dispute adding to the information available to the two sides.

Psychological perspective

This image of dispute escalation can be contrasted with a psychological perspective that focuses on factors likely to confound rational decision-making and encourage the conflict to spiral out of control. Among the factors discussed in Chapter 1 were: (1) the cognitive limitations on decision-making in interstate crises, where information is incomplete and ambiguous, and the other side may be bluffing; (2) the deleterious emotional effects of stress; (3) the "competition in risk-taking" that results from adversaries who are each intent on demonstrating their superior resolve; and (4) the effects of considerations of pride, concern for reputation, or psychological reactance to threats to freedom, all of which encourage responding to coercion in kind.

If we return to the comparison between crisis escalation and the escalation of animal fights, one significant difference can be observed in the abruptness with which animal fights end when one of the disputants realizes that it is over-matched. The weaker, or less motivated, party immediately turns and flees – the equivalent of submission to the other party. That happens less often in interpersonal disputes, and it is even rarer on interstate crises. One of the most important differences between humans and lower animals can be seen in our ability to reflect on ourselves and our condition, and to be aware of how our actions may be perceived by others. These reflections produce those peculiarly human stakes that are present in interpersonal and interstate disputes: considerations of pride, honor, and reputation, particularly a state's concern with its reputation for resolve. These psychological concerns have a political dimension as well. Statesmen are concerned with the image in which they, personally, are held by their constituents, as well their state's reputation in the eyes of other statesmen. The same argument can be made with regard to the application of a theory of psychological reactance to coercive threats (see Brehm, 1966). In a world of sovereign states, threats to freedom have political implications as well. The prestige and resolve of the state – not to mention the political survival of its government – are threatened. The potential influence of these psycho-political factors provides a plausible argument for why the behavior of states in crises may not be consistent with what we would expect to find based solely on a rational calculation of war-fighting capabilities and interests.

Operational measures of escalation

The process of generating an operational indicator of escalation begins with classifying and weighting each of the actions of the crisis participants. Beginning with the precipitant action that initiated the crisis, and extending to the termination of the crisis, the actions of each side are classified as cooperative, conflictive, or neutral, according to the expected immediate effect of the action on the target state. Then each action is weighted according to a six-point scale, ranging from a score of 3 for the most conflictive category to a -3 for the most cooperative. A military attack, for example, is assigned a score of 3, a verbal threat of force a score of 2, and a protest a score of 1.[2] Then the scores are summed within seven-day intervals to provide the hostility scores for each side at each seven-day interval over the course of the crisis.

A description of the overall pattern of escalation, for each side, in each crisis, is obtained through time series of the hostility scores of the participants on each side. A summary measure of the overall degree of escalation for each crisis is obtained by combining measures of the rate of escalation or deescalation and the mean level of hostility over the course of the crisis. There are two components of interest in the summary measure of escalation: (1) the mean magnitude of escalation, and (2) the rate of escalation, or deescalation.

Magnitude of escalation. The mean magnitude of escalation is an indicator of the overall level of hostility exhibited in the actions of participants on the two sides over the course of the crisis. In computing a summary score for the magnitude of escalation, it is important to distinguish between short upward spikes of conflictive actions, and an extended period of highly conflictive activity unrelieved by any movement toward greater cooperation. The simplest means of obtaining such a measure is by calculating the mean magnitude of hostility represented by the weekly observations of the mix of weighted conflictive and cooperative actions for the participants on each side. The mean scores for the two sides are then summed to provide a measure of the magnitude of escalation for the crisis. Crisis behavior tends to be predominantly conflictual, so mean hostility scores are likely to be higher when there are a greater number of participants in any given crisis. This, however, is consistent with a measure intended as a summary indicator of the overall magnitude of crisis escalation.

69

Rate of escalation. The second escalation indicator is the rapidity with which the conflictive behavior of the participants increases over the course of the crisis, or, conversely, the extent to which it is relieved by deescalatory cooperative behavior. This can be described by the direction and magnitude of the slope in the mix of cooperation and conflict over the course of the crisis.

There are three steps to computing the measure of the rate of escalation. (1) An indicator of the rate of escalation for each side from one seven-day interval to the next is obtained by computing first differences from the time series of hostility scores for each side over the course of the crisis. (2) Then the mean score of each differenced series is computed, and (3) the signed mean scores for the two sides are summed to produce a single rate of escalation score for the crisis. The signed scores are used to allow a canceling effect if one side is moving toward predominantly more conflictive behavior at the same time as the other side is moving to more cooperative behavior. This procedure yields a summary measure that is unaffected by the number of observations, and is not dominated by the presence of dramatic, but short, upward or downward spikes.

Escalation score. The magnitude and rate of escalation scores are standardized and summed to produce a single *escalation* score for each crisis. The combined scores are then rank ordered. Those crises falling above the median are classified as high in escalation and those falling below the median are classified as low in escalation.

Reciprocity

The second behavioral attribute of interest is the degree of reciprocity in the interactions of the crisis participants, that is, the extent to which the parties on each side respond to actions of the parties of the other side in kind and magnitude.[3] Reciprocity has functioned as a norm in human relations since ancient times, and in the interstate system, where there exists no established central authority to maintain order, or authoritatively to judge those who commit transgressions, reciprocity provides the guiding norm for cooperation and the yardstick for applying sanctions against transgressions. The norm that has provided the foundation for much of international law and the practice of diplomacy can be stated very simply: respond in kind and in proportion to the actions received from the other party.

The tendency of parties in interstate conflicts to reciprocate each other's behavior has been observed in a wide variety of circumstances, including arms races, US–Soviet relations, and interstate crises. There is also growing evidence that reciprocating, or tit-for-tat, bargaining strategies are associated with success, not only in Prisoner's Dilemma games (Axelrod, 1984), but in real world crises as well (Leng and Wheeler, 1979; Leng, 1984), including instances of extended deterrence (Huth, 1988).

Within a crisis, a high degree of reciprocity can indicate the presence of either a "vicious circle" (Pruitt, 1969:393) of spiraling conflict where the two sides become "locked-in" to mutually reinforcing coercive actions, to generate what Rapoport (1960) has fittingly described as a "fight." Or, it may indicate the presence of a "benevolent circle" of mutually reinforcing accommodative moves leading to a cooperative settlement of the dispute. Evidence of either of these patterns of high reciprocity has been cited by critics of the realist perspective as evidence of either the dangerous escalatory effects of coercive bargaining tactics (reciprocity in conflictive actions), or the efficacy of adopting a more accommodative approach (reciprocity in cooperative actions).

Operational measures of reciprocity

A pattern of reciprocal action is like that of a ballroom dance, say a foxtrot, in the sense that the partners move together at the same tempo and in the same direction. In this regard, there are two important behavioral dimensions to reciprocity: (1) the *distance* between the behavior patterns of the two sides, and (2) the degree of congruity in the *direction* in which each is moving at a particular time in the crisis, that is, toward a more conflictive or more cooperative mix of behavior.

A high degree of reciprocity obtains when the distance between the two sides is small and they are moving in the same direction. It is not unusual, for example, to observe a pattern of crisis behavior in which both sides exhibit an upward trend of rising hostility, but one party maintains a substantially higher level of hostility over the entire course of the crisis. The actions are reciprocal in type, but not in magnitude. The dancers are moving in the same direction, but they are not close enough to be dancing together.

Distance. Conceptually, we think of a high distance score as indicating that one side is pursuing *consistently* more conflictive behavior than the other over the course of the crisis. Therefore, we want an indicator of distance that reflects the degree of consistency with regard to which party is exhibiting more conflictive behavior, as well as the overall distance between the hostility levels of the two parties.

There are four steps to the construction of an operational indicator of distance. (1) The weighted values of cooperative and conflictive actions, aggregated for each side at weekly intervals, are computed in the manner described above to obtain an hostility score for each side. (2) At each interval, the aggregate hostility score of side B is subtracted from that of side A to obtain the distance score for that interval. (3) The *signed* distance scores at each interval are summed. In this case, the signed values are used to insure that the mean score reflects the degree of consistency with regard to which party has the higher hostility scores. If the hostility levels of the two sides shift from one interval to the next, so that, at interval i, state A has the higher hostility score, and at interval $i + 1$, state B has the higher hostility score, the use of the signed interval distance scores in summing the scores over the course of the crisis will have a canceling effect, rather than augmenting the total distance score. (4) The mean distance score is computed from the summed interval distance scores.

This procedure allows us to obtain a summary measure that is consistent with the conceptual notion of distance. The higher the mean distance score, the further apart the two sides are in the mix of cooperative and conflictive actions.

Direction. The direction indicator measures the extent to which changes in the mix of cooperative and conflictive actions of the two parties occur in the same direction at the same time. That is, are the parties both becoming more contentious or more accommodative, or are they moving in opposite directions?

There are four steps to obtaining the direction measure. (1) First differences are computed for the weekly hostility scores for each side to provide weekly indicators of the movement of each side toward greater or lesser contentiousness. (2) The differenced scores for side B are subtracted from those for side A at each interval, beginning with the second interval. These scores provide a measure of the extent to which the parties have, or have not, moved together over the preceding seven days. (3) The interval direction scores are converted to absolute scores, which are summed over the course of the crisis. Absolute scores are used in this case to avoid the canceling effects of summing positive and negative interval scores. (4) The mean direction score is computed from the sum of the absolute scores. The higher the direction score, the greater the angle at which the two parties are moving away from each other.

Reciprocity. The combined reciprocity score for each crisis is obtained by standardizing and summing the mean distance and direction scores and then taking the reciprocal of that score in order to obtain a measure in which a high score is equivalent to a high degree of reciprocity. The combined scores are then rank ordered. Those crises falling above the median are classified as high in reciprocity and those falling below the median are classified as low in reciprocity.[4]

A caveat. The summary measures of escalation and reciprocity allow us to categorize the crises into types according to their scores on the summary measures. In doing so, however, we run the risks of oversimplification and arbitrariness. The danger of oversimplifiction is a function of the variety of behavioral patterns that can occur within a crisis. Certain patterns of behavior, which can be significant in the evolution of a crisis, may be masked by summary statistics. The most prominent of these cases occurs when a crisis begins with a long lull in activity, and then suddenly escalates at a rapid rate in its final phase. The two phases tend to balance each other out and produce a moderate overall escalation score. With this problem in mind, I have eliminated long periods of complete inactivity occurring at the beginning of crises from the calculations of reciprocity and escalation. To give the reader an appreciation of the other varieties of patterns of escalation and deescalation that can occur, graphical displays of variations in behavior patterns are exhibited in the next section.

The arbitrariness problem arises when one attempts to classify the particular crises according to the relative degree of escalation or reciprocity, that is, as "high" or "low" on these measures. The extreme cases present no problem, but where does one draw the boundary line between high and low?[5] Any choice is, to some extent, arbitrary, and the problem is exacerbated because we are dealing with a sample, rather than the full population of militarized crises. After experimenting with several different approaches, I have selected the median as the dividing line. The break-points for the median are consistent with an intuitive reading of the degree of escalation and reciprocity in the crises in the sample; and the use of the median offers the advantage of yielding an even proportion of cases in both categories. One minor adjustment has been made to obtain a more reasonable break-point between the high and low escalation scores. The boundary between high and low escalation scores has been moved up one rank beyond the median, because of a more significant difference between the 21st and 22nd ranks than between the 20th and 21st. The actual median occurs at a reasonable break-point in the reciprocity cases. Overall, the median appears to be a reasonable dividing line; nevertheless, there is no escape from the fact that the boundaries between the categories are arbitrary and that the categorization of cases that are close to the boundary lines is problematic.

A list of the standardized scores for the indicators of reciprocity and escalation for the sample of forty crises appears in Appendix 1.

Behavioral types

Each of the crises in the sample can be classified according to one of four behavioral types, based on the categorization of its reciprocity and escalation scores as high or low.[6] The four types are: (1) A Fight, which has high scores on both dimensions; (2) Standoff, which has a low reciprocity score, but a high escalation score; and (4) Put-Down, which has low scores on both dimensions.

Fights

As I noted above, the term "Fight" is borrowed from Rapoport (1960), who used it to draw an analogy between the spiraling escalation of an arms race and a school-yard fight. A Fight is characterized by symmetrical escalating hostility, described by spiraling coercive actions and reactions of the type described by North, Brody, and Holsti (1964) in their pioneering study of the pre-World War I crisis.[7] The spiraling conflict may be driven either by a mutual desire for retaliation, or by mutual and reinforcing reactions to the threat that each sees in the other side's defensive moves (see Pruitt and Rubin, 1986: 90–91).

An example of a Fight pattern can be seen in the time series of the mix of cooperative and conflictive actions for India and Pakistan in the First Kashmir War, which is illustrated in Figure 4.1. When Pathan tribesmen from Pakistan invaded Kashmir to support their Muslim brethren in the fall of 1947, India sent troops to support the Hindu Maharaja of Kashmir, and the crisis rapidly escalated. Figure 4.1 plots a smoothed time series of the hostility scores, which represents the mix of weighted cooperative and conflictive actions within each seven-day interval.[8]

A variant of this type, which lies on the borderline between a Fight and a Standoff, ends with the exponential escalation characteristic of a Fight, but it begins with a long period of relatively low hostility, which dampens its overall escalation score. The crisis preceding the First Balkan War of 1912, with Serbia, Greece, and Bulgaria pitted against Turkey, which appears in Figure 4.2, is a good example of this subtype. During the spring of 1912, the three Balkan states entered into alliances directed against the Ottoman Empire, but it was not until autumn that the Balkan states began the mobilization that led rapidly to war. Two other cases that fit this borderline category are the crises preceding the Second Central American war and the Second Balkan war.

74

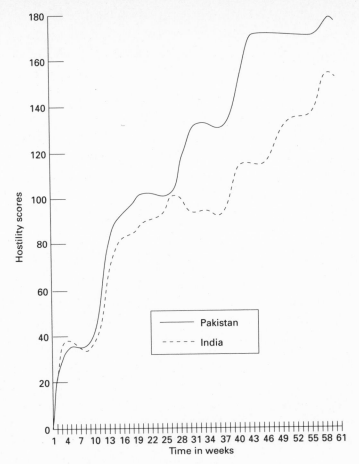

Figure 4.1   Fight: First Kashmir Crisis, 1947

Standoff

A standoff exhibits the high reciprocity of a Fight, but the escalation is controlled; neither party is willing to allow the risk of war to exceed a certain level. In this sense, the crisis is effectively "managed." The parties demonstrate their firmness through mutual threats or military displays, but the escalation either levels off, with the crisis ending in a stalemate, or the crisis deescalates as the parties move toward a settlement. In a Standoff, neither party is willing to submit outright, yet neither is willing to increase the level of conflict beyond a certain point. An example of a Standoff appears in Figure 4.3, which exhibits the time series for the "Cod War," a low level crisis between

75

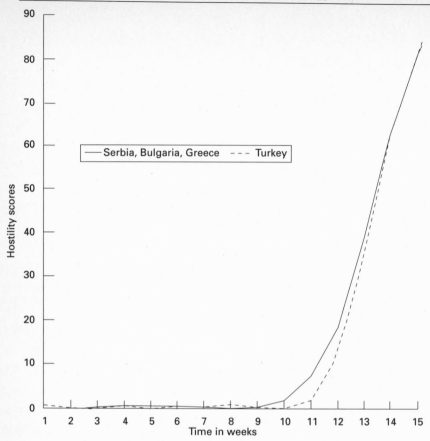

Figure 4.2   Fight/Standoff Variant: First Balkan War Crisis, 1912

Britain and Iceland over fishing rights in 1975–76. The dispute began when Iceland unilaterally extended its territorial limits for fishing rights. When the British refused to accept the new limits, Icelandic forces harassed British fishermen, including cutting the fishing lines of British trawlers. The British responded with a naval show-of-force, which was reciprocated by Iceland, but the crisis did not escalate beyond a number of minor military incidents.

It is interesting to compare this case with another Standoff, the Trieste crisis of 1954. The smoldering dispute over Trieste between Italy and Yugoslavia flared up in 1954, before it was successfully mediated by Italy's NATO allies. As the time series in Figure 4.4 illustrates, the crisis began with a strong upward spike of conflictive behavior, but it was quickly dampened by the peaceful intervention of the United States, Britain, and France.

76

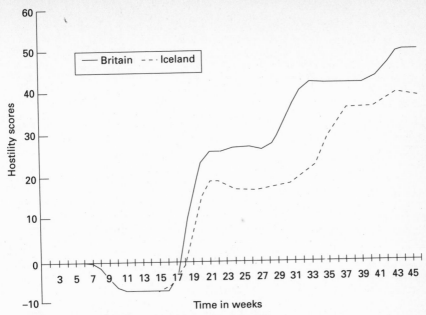

Figure 4.3   Standoff: Cod War Crisis, 1975–1976

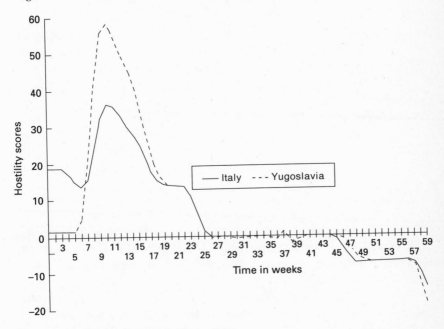

Figure 4.4   Standoff: Trieste Crisis, 1954

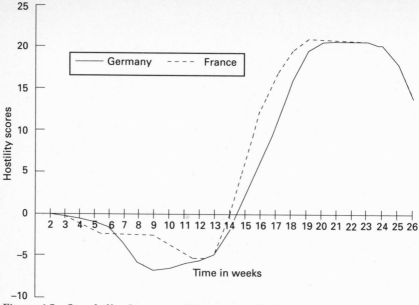

Figure 4.5   Standoff – Cross-over Variant: Agadir Crisis, 1911

The Agadir crisis of 1911, which was a dispute between Germany and France over imperial influence within Morocco, offers another interesting Standoff variant. Notice, in Figure 4.5, how the cooperative and conflictive initiatives move from one party to the other as the crisis evolves. These patterns suggest changes in the relationship between the disputants and in the influence strategies they are employing. Several of the crises in the sample exhibit this "cross-over" pattern. In the case of the Agadir crisis, the changes are related to changes in government, and, consequently, governmental policy in France, as well as the diplomatic intervention of Britain on the French side.

Resistance

The Resistance category contains asymmetrical crises with high escalation, but low reciprocity. These typically are disputes in which one antagonist pursues an escalating coercive strategy, while the other stands firm. The model is similar to Pruitt and Rubin's (1986:89–90) "aggressor–defender" model of escalation. In a typical case, the "aggressor" initiates the contentious tactics and moves to increasingly more coercive influence tactics, until its goals are achieved, or the crisis escalates to war. The defender reacts by responding in kind to the coercive influence tactics of the aggressor.

Thus, one party's behavior is much like that seen in a Fight: an abrupt and continuing pattern of increasingly conflictive actions. Its adversary responds in kind, usually after some initial attempts at more accommodative responses. A typical Resistance pattern is illustrated in Figure 4.6, by the time series for the British–French crisis at Fashoda in 1898–99. The Fashoda crisis was a colonial dispute over territory in the Sudan, in which French expeditionary forces in Fashoda found themselves militarily over-matched by a competing British force, which arrived on the scene shortly after General Marchand's troops raised the Tricolor.

An interesting variant occurs in those instances in which the defender, perhaps recognizing the inevitability of war, escalates the level of matching coercive action to close the gap in the degree of coercion, so that the pattern more closely resembles a Fight as the crisis escalates to a high level. An example of this pattern appears in the time series for the Pre-World War I crisis appearing in Figure 4.7. The early phase of the crisis, following the assassination of the Austrian Archduke, Francis Ferdinand, consisted primarily of interactions between Austria and Serbia. During this phase, Austria employs coercive influence attempts, while Serbia responds with placating moves, so that the early phase of the crisis resembles a Put-Down, in which one party bullies the other. Once the other major powers become involved, however, the pattern changes to more closely resemble the "conflict spiral" model of a fight, with escalating matching coercive behavior on both sides. It is this later phase of the crisis that North, Brody, and Holsti (1964) considered in their pioneering study of the conflict spiral. Similar patterns can be observed in the time series of the Berlin Blockade and Cyprus crises.

Another variant of Resistance occurs when there is a "cross-over" as in the subtypes for the Standoff category. A Resistance pattern with a cross-over is illustrated by the time series from the Bosnian crisis of 1908, a territorial dispute that pitted Austria–Hungary against Russia and Serbia. The cross-over in the degree of coercive action, which can be seen in Figure 4.8, is linked to Germany's political intervention on the side of Austria. The Bosnian crisis has been viewed by many as a dress rehearsal for the crisis preceding World War I, albeit with some of the players revising their performances between the dress rehersal and opening night. It is interesting to compare the behavior patterns in Figures 4.7 and 4.8 with the comparison between those two crises in mind.

79

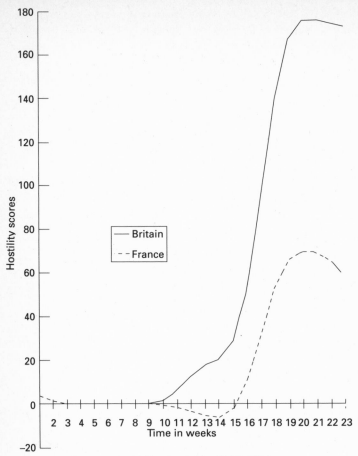

Figure 4.6   Resistance: Fashoda Crisis, 1898–1899

Put-Down

A Put-Down exhibits both low escalation and low reciprocity. One antagonist employs escalating coercive tactics, but the other responds only at a moderate level of conflict intensity, perhaps with one or two short pulses of more conflictive action. Put-Downs typically are disputes between parties that are unevenly matched in capabilities and motivation, so that the more belligerent party simply increases the level of coercion until the other party submits. A typical Put-Down appears in the time series of the Anschluss Crisis between Germany and Austria in 1938 (Fig. 4.9), when Hitler bullied the Austrian government into accepting unification with Germany.

An interesting cross-over variant of a Put-Down occurs in the depic-

80

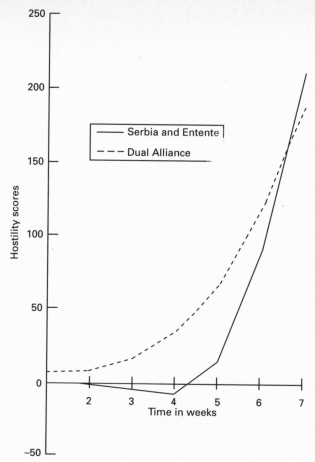

Figure 4.7   Resistance/Fight Variant: Pre-World War I Crisis, 1914

tion of the Manchurian crisis of 1931 (Figure 4.10) which preceded the war between Japan and China. The Chinese began by attempting diplomacy through the League of Nations, but, with the Japanese continuing to demand more and more concessions, the Chinese decided to take a firm stand. When they did the Japanese intensified their military hostilities. The Chinese initiated further attempts at an accommodative settlement, but the Japanese were not interested in a compromise.

The categorization of the forty crises by behavioral types appears in Table 4.1, which suggests a number of intriguing relationships.

The numbers to the left of each case appearing in Table 4.1 indicate the ranking of that case on the combined escalation indicator, with the Pre-World War I crisis ranking the highest and the Polish–Lithuanian

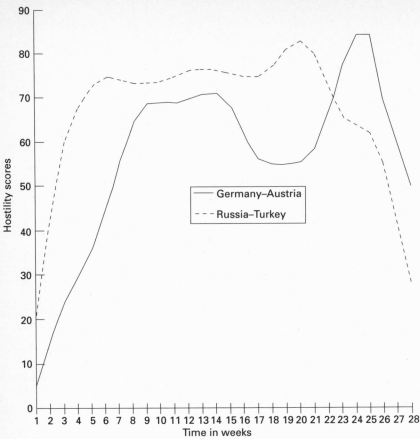

Figure 4.8   Resistance – Cross-over Variant: Bosnian Crisis, 1908

crisis ranking the lowest. Notice that of the twenty-one cases with high escalation scores, ten of the eleven highest scores are in the Resistance category; whereas of the nineteen cases with low escalation scores, eleven of the twelve lowest scores fall into the Standoff category. Thus, when the escalation scores are divided along the median between high and low scores, the highest scores are associated with low reciprocity and the lowest scores are associated with high reciprocity.

The association between low escalation and high reciprocity is not unexpected. Crises that do not escalate to high levels offer better prospects for negotiation and other reciprocated cooperative moves. The high reciprocity scores reflect these moves. By the same token, it is not surprising that all but one of the crises ending in a com-

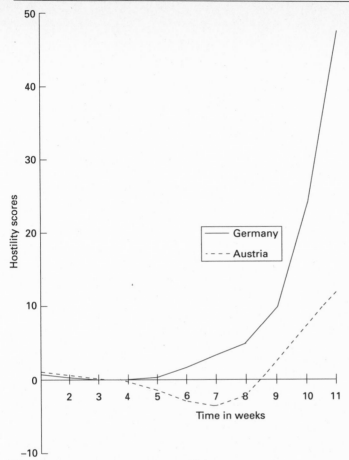

Figure 4.9   Put-Down: The Anschluss, 1938

promise fall into the high reciprocity, low escalation, Standoff category.

That the crises with the highest escalation scores fall into the low reciprocity Resistance category, as opposed to the high reciprocity Fight category is more puzzling. The indicator of the degree of reciprocity works both ways; that is, it reflects reciprocated contentious activity as well as reciprocated accommodative activity. Interestingly, the low reciprocity scores for the crisis falling into the Resistance category are consistent with the outcomes of those crises, that is, they tend to end either in a war, or in submission by one side to the demands of the other. These patterns suggest that one party has taken the initiative and is bullying the other into submission, as would be expected in an "aggressor–defender" (Pruitt and Rubin, 1986:89–92)

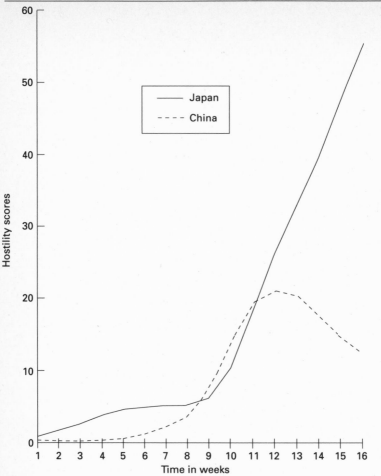

Figure 4.10 Put-Down – Cross-over Variant: The Manchurian Crisis, 1931

model of crisis escalation. The low reciprocity score reflects the intersection of an escalating coercive bargaining strategy on the part of the
more aggressive party and an accommodative, or mixed, strategy on
the part of the other party. The Fashoda crisis, which appears in Figure
4.6, illustrates the expected pattern. But this does not tell us why we
should find higher levels of escalation in crises that approximate the
"aggressor–defender" model of escalation than in those that approximate the "conflict spiral" of a Fight.

Behavioral types and crisis outcomes

Behavioral types and war

Overall, the associations between the behavioral types and crisis outcomes are consistent with what would be expected from the psychological perspective described at the beginning of the chapter. Table 4.1 indicates that thirteen of the seventeen crises ending in war have high escalation scores, with six of the eight high escalation, high reciprocity, Fights ending in war. Only four of the nineteen cases in the two low escalation categories end in war, and only one war occurs among the twelve cases falling into the Standoff category, with its combination of low escalation and high reciprocity. These associations are consistent with what we would expect to find, and they add to our confidence in the break-points for high and low scores on the two dimensions. The strong association between higher escalation scores and the outbreak of war, however, does not encourage confidence in bargaining strategies that prescribe escalating coercive tactics to achieve one's objectives short of war.

An intriguing finding concerns the difference in predictability between the high reciprocity and low reciprocity behavioral types. Within the two high reciprocity categories, wars occur in 75 percent of the fights, when the escalation score is high, and only in only 8 percent of Standoffs, when the escalation score is low. In these cases, the behavioral difference appears to be related to the high reciprocity scores reflecting negotiation efforts in the Standoff category, and high reciprocity in military activities in the Fight category. On the other hand, there is little difference between the high and low escalation categories within the two low reciprocity types. Those crises end in war 54 percent of the time when they fall into the high escalation Resistance category and 43 percent of the time when they are in the low escalation Put-Down category.

The outcomes of crises in the two high reciprocity categories are predictable regardless of whether the two sides become "locked-in" to a pattern of escalating reciprocal conflictive actions, or a pattern of reciprocal cooperative actions. It appears that there is a certain degree of momentum that helps to propel these crises to their most likely outcomes. If that is the case, it would support those critics of the prescriptions of conflict strategists, who emphasize the dangers of coercive bargaining and the benefits of extending cooperative initiatives.

The unpredictability of the cases in the low reciprocity categories

Table 4.1. *Behavioral types and outcomes*

FIGHT	Outcome	RESISTANCE	Outcome
7. 1st Kashmir	War	1. Pre WWI	War
12. Rhineland	Diplomatic Victory	2. Suez	War
15. Beagle Channel	Compromise	3. Cyprus	Stalemate
16. 2nd Balkan	War	4. Berlin Blockade	Diplomatic Victory
17. 1st Balkan	War	5. Italo–Ethiopian	War
19. Central American	War	6. Spanish–American	War
20. 2nd Kashmir	War	8. Munich	Diplomatic Victory
21. Schleswig–Holstein	War	9. Cuban Missile	Diplomatic Victory
		10. Bosnian	Diplomatic Victory
		11. Fashoda	Diplomatic Victory
		13. Danzig	War
		14. Rann of Kutch	War
		18. Crimean	War

STANDOFF	Outcome	PUT-DOWN	Outcome
27. Teschen	Compromise	22. Pastry	Diplomatic Victory
29. Cod War	Compromise	23. British–Russian	Diplomatic Victory
30. Sino–Indian	Compromise	24. Chaco War	War
31. Italo–French	Stalemate	25. Russo–Turkish	War
32. Sino–Vietnamese	War	26. Manchurian	War
33. British–Portuguese	Diplomatic Victory	28. Anschluss	Diplomatic Victory
34. Agadir	Compromise	29. Bizerte	Diplomatic Victory
35. Trieste	Compromise		
36. 1st Moroccan	Diplomatic Victory		
37. Honduran Border	Compromise		
38. Chaco Dispute	Compromise		
40. Polish–Lithuanian	Compromise		

presents a more puzzling picture. The connection between the low reciprocity scores and the outcomes – war or submission by one side – suggests that these are predominantly crises in which one side has taken a strong initiative and is attempting to bully the other into submission, a pattern consistent with the aggressor–defender model mentioned above. But why these crises should escalate to a higher level than Fights, which are consistent with a conflict spiral model of escalation, and why the outcomes of the low reciprocity crisis are less predictable, are more puzzling. Classical realism would predict the opposite, that is, as the disparity in war-fighting capabilities becomes more obvious to the participants, the level of escalation and the likelihood of war should decline (see Blainey, 1973). The weaker party should make the prudent decision to submit, rather than risk the added costs of war, with defeat in the offing anyway.

The answer to this apparent anomaly may lie in nonbehavioral variables, such as the effects of the crisis structure. The relationships among the crisis structure, crisis behavior, and crisis outcomes, will be explored in the next chapter. A possible hint of what is happening is suggested by the variables in the patterns of behavior among crises falling into the high escalation, low reciprocity, Resistance category. Consider the differences in the patterns exhibited by the three crises appearing in Figures 4.6–4.8. The time series for the Fashoda crisis, which is depicted in Figure 4.6, is a classic example of the aggressor–defender model. But, compare that pattern to the time series for the Pre-War I crisis appearing in Figure 4.7. At the outset of the crisis, Austria–Hungary resorted immediately to coercive tactics, while Serbia employed an accommodative strategy. After the Austrians rejected the Serbian response to their ultimatum, other major powers became directly engaged and the crisis escalated dramatically. It appears that the relatively low reciprocity score for this crisis reflects the uncertain, and unbalanced, beginning of the crisis; whereas the high escalation score reflects the second half of the crisis, which resembles a Fight.

The time series for the Bosnian crisis of 1908, which is depicted in Figure 4.8, contains a "cross-over," which reflects the change in the bargaining of the two sides following the intervention of Germany on the side of Austria. With Germany on its side, the Austrian behavior became more contentious, while that of Russia became more accommodative. "Cross-overs" occur in several of the crises in the Resistance category. Some of them appear to reflect changes in the structure of the crisis, as in the Bosnian and Pre-World War I cases, others suggest experimentation with different bargaining strategies.

The time series in the last two cases are influenced by changes in the composition of the parties on the two sides, which affect the pattern of escalation. Unlike the Fashoda crisis, which is very consistent with an aggressor–defender model of crisis escalation, the time series for the 1914 and Bosnian crises describe disjointed patterns of escalation that appear to reflect shifts in influence strategies associated with changes in the crisis structure. Among the other cases in the Resistance category, the time series for the Italo–Ethiopian and Manchurian crises, both of which ended in war, are very consistent with the aggressor-defender pattern exhibited by the Fashoda crisis, which was resolved peacefully. The time series of the Italo–Ethiopian and Manchurian crises suggest a pattern of interaction in which the weaker party begins by attempting accommodation, but switches to matching the coercion of the "aggressor" when it recognizes that the stronger party cannot be persuaded to accept a compromise settlement. But other crises in the Resistance category, such as the Bosnian, Munich, Berlin, and Cyprus crises, suggest less consistency on the part of either party, with each employing different tactics at different stages of the escalating crisis. The time series alone cannot tell us why some of these cases ended in war and others did not, but they do provide a useful map of the evolution of the bargaining of the two sides over the course of the crises. An intriguing question is the extent to which these shifts and inconsistencies in behavior patterns reflect changes in the structure of the crisis, or shifts in bargaining strategies that are the result of reevaluations based on feedback from preceding influence attempts.

Variations in peaceful outcomes

Whereas whether a crisis will end in a peaceful settlement or war is associated with the degree of escalation, variations among nonwar outcomes are related to the degree of reciprocity. Three quarters (nine of twelve) of the cases in which one side achieved a diplomatic victory over the other occurred in crises with low reciprocity scores, whereas *all* nine of the instances of compromise settlements occur in crises with high reciprocity scores. These are not surprising distinctions. One would expect compromises to be preceded by reciprocal cooperative efforts, and a diplomatic victory by one side is likely to be achieved through the coercive efforts of the successful party. Nor is it surprising that eight of the nine compromises occur in Standoffs with both high reciprocity and low escalation. However, when this distribution of cases is compared to that in the high reciprocity, high escalation Fight category, even with the relatively small sample, the differences are striking. Among the crises falling into the two high reciprocity categories, 89 percent of those with low escalation scores ended in compromises, whereas 75 percent of the crises with high escalation scores ended in war. The differences between these two symmetrical categories suggest that it becomes more difficult to maintain a rational and prudent bargaining strategy as a crisis escalates to higher levels. In this respect, the outcomes challenge the wisdom of approaching crisis bargaining as a competition in risk-taking, in which success is dependent on credibly demonstrating a greater willingness to accept the risk of war. The patterns in the Fight category suggest the consequences of symmetrical escalation between the two sides who are each determined to demonstrate their superior resolve. The patterns in the Standoff category suggest the potential benefits of eliciting cooperation through a series of reciprocated cooperative moves. In other words, the patterns observed in the high reciprocity crises raise questions about the wisdom of the prescriptions of conflict strategists.

As I noted above, there is less of a distinction among the outcomes of crises with high or low escalation scores in the low reciprocity Resistance and Put-Down categories. There are no successful compromises in either category, and wars are only slightly less likely to occur in low reciprocity crises when the escalation scores are low, than when they are high.

Summary and conclusion

Based on two salient dimensions of dispute behavior – reciprocity and escalation – we constructed a typology of four behavioral types: Fight, Standoff, Resistance, and Put-Down. The similarities observed in patterns of escalation within the behavioral types, and qualitative descriptions of the evolution of the crises, encourage confidence in the descriptive validity of the typological distinctions. That impression is reinforced by the observation of expected relationships between the behavioral types and outcomes among the forty crises in the sample. Higher escalation scores are associated with war outcomes; all but one of the compromise settlements occur in low escalation, high reciprocity Standoffs; and one-sided diplomatic outcomes are most likely when reciprocity is low. The two high reciprocity categories have both the highest percentage of crises ending in wars, in the high escalation Fight category, and the highest percentage of peaceful outcomes, in the low escalation Standoff category.

These findings are consistent with what I have labeled the

psychological view of the consequences of crisis escalation. The likely outcomes of Fights and Standoffs emphasize the dangers of the two sides becoming locked-in to a conflict spiral of escalating coercion, on the one hand, and the possibilities of employing reciprocating accommodative moves to reach a compromise settlement, on the other. If crisis escalation represents a learning process based on feedback from coercive moves, based on what we have observed to this point, it appears to be a dangerous curriculum, in which the means can overwhelm the ends. On the other hand, of the nine cases that ended in compromise, all but one fell into the high reciprocity, low escalation, Standoff category. Those cases suggest that, when statesmen are able to dampen the escalation of crises, it is possible to set in motion a process of reciprocated accommodative moves leading to a compromise solution.

The distribution of cases within the low reciprocity Resistance and Put-Down categories is more puzzling. Higher escalation scores are associated with a greater likelihood of war in the high reciprocity categories, but that relationship does not hold for the low reciprocity Resistance and Put-Down categories. The distribution of war and nonwar outcomes appears almost unrelated to the escalation scores for these categories. These rather puzzling findings suggest that we need to take a closer look at the relationship between behavioral patterns and structural variables, and, ultimately, the bargaining tactics and strategies employed by the participants. We will begin with the relationship between the crisis structure and crisis behavior in Chapter 5 and then turn to bargaining tactics and strategies in Chapters 6 through 8.

5 STRUCTURE, BEHAVIOR, AND OUTCOMES

The findings in Chapters 3 and 4 have yielded some clues regarding the descriptive and prescriptive validity of the realist perspective on crisis behavior. The structural variables considered most salient by realists – perceived interests and comparative capabilities – are excellent predictors of war or nonwar crisis outcomes when these variables take on particularly high or low values. On the other hand, when there is a high degree of reciprocity in the interactions of the two sides, we find positive associations between high escalation and war, and between low escalation and compromise outcomes. These findings underscore the potential risks and missed opportunities associated with following the prescriptions of conflict strategists. They suggest that, while the structural variables considered most salient by classical realists are likely to be key determinants of crisis behavior, other factors may intervene to confound policy-making based solely on a rational calculation of interests and capabilities. If that is the case, it raises the issue of the relative potency of these two competing forces – a rational calculation of interests and capabilities versus the psychopolitical effects – of an escalating crisis, as well as their relationship to each other. Are the behavior patterns that we have observed dependent on variations in the crisis structure? And, if it is possible to obtain better predictions of the outcomes of crises based on variations in each of these variables, what can we learn from the combined effects of variations in the crisis structure and crisis behavior? These questions will be explored in this chapter, beginning with an examination of the relationship between the crisis structure and patterns of behavior.

Structure and behavior

Structure and reciprocity. The findings in Chapter 4 indicate that the relationship between crisis escalation and war is more predictable when there is a high degree of reciprocity in the interactions of the participants. A plausible structural link to reciprocity lies in the perceived relative capabilities of the participants. From a power politics perspective, we would expect to find higher reciprocity scores when the two sides each had the same expectations regarding the costs and risks of war to their side, and lower reciprocity scores when their expectations differed. That is, if both sides expected to prevail in war, if both sides believed that their war-fighting capabilities were roughly even, or if both sides expected their side to lose, a simple power politics perspective would lead to the prediction that the degree of reciprocity in the interactions of the two sides would be high, because each side would exhibit the same degree of resolve in seeking to obtain or defend its interests.

There are no cases in the sample in which both parties expect to lose in a war, and only one case in which both expect to win easily; therefore a test of the relationship between capability perceptions and reciprocity is essentially a comparison between those cases in which the parties see themselves as evenly matched and those cases in which they perceive an imbalance in capabilities. The power politics prediction that those cases in which the two parties saw themselves as evenly matched in war-fighting capabilities would result in higher reciprocity scores is not supported by the data. In fact, there is no significant bivariate relationship between the comparative capability perceptions of the two sides and higher or lower reciprocity scores. Knowledge of whether or not the two sides have matching views of their war-fighting capabilities yields correct predictions in only twenty-two of the forty cases, or just slightly better than a random selection.

The results are not surprising, given the findings in Chapter 3, which suggests that a power politics expectation of a significant bivariate relationship between perceived capability and behavior is over simplistic, even within the realist tradition. A broader realist perspective would view the conflict behavior of states as the result of the combined influence of perceived comparative capabilities *and* the seriousness of the interests at stake. If, for example, the two sides see themselves as evenly balanced in war-fighting capabilities, so that a war is likely to be long and costly for both sides, their respective choices of influence strategies – and their willingness to accept the risk of war – may differ considerably if one side has vital interests at stake and the other does not. Conversely, an imbalance in capability perceptions might be off-set by a compensating imbalance in interests to produce a high level of reciprocity.

Structure and escalation. If the relationship between the crisis structure and reciprocity requires consideration of the effects of both capability perceptions and the interests at stake, it also is reasonable to expect that the effect of the crisis structure on the escalation of the crisis would combine the influences of both structural variables. Working from a realist perspective, we would expect crises to be prone to exhibit higher levels of escalation when each of the parties holds more optimistic views regarding its war-fighting capabilities, and there are more important interests at stake. By the same token, we would expect lower levels of escalation when neither party was optimistic about the consequences of going to war and neither had any security interests at stake.

Combining the structural measures

The reader may recall that, in Chapter 3, each of the structural measures was ranked on a three-point scale according to the degree of optimism in that side's view of its war-fighting capabilities, and its view of the importance of the interests at stake. With the highest score assigned to the highest rank, the perceived comparative war-fighting capability scores are: (3) win easily; (2) evenly matched; and (1) lose easily. The scored ranks for the interests at stake are: (3) vital security interests; (2) lesser security interests; and (1) interests not directly related to national security.

The method employed to combine the capability and interest variables in Chapter 3 was designed to examine the proposition that the war-proneness of crises was related to the seriousness of the interests at stake and the combined optimism of the two sides with regard to the outcome of a war. The unit of analysis was the crisis. In this chapter we are interested in examining the behavioral patterns that we would expect to find associated with particular *pairings of disputants*, based on the match-up of their structural scores. That is, we are interested in the patterns of escalation and reciprocity that we would expect to observe based on the intersection of each side's perception of its comparative military capabilities and the interests at stake. The unit of analysis is not the crisis *per se*, but the crisis dyad – the structural relationship between the two sides.

Predicting behavioral types from structural scores. The relationships between the structural match-ups and patterns of escalation and reciprocity that would be expected from a realist perspective are straightforward extensions of the realist emphasis on the centrality of considerations of security interests and comparative capabilities. The hypotheses are that: (1) crises are more likely to exhibit a high degree of escalation when both parties are more optimistic regarding the consequences of a potential war, and both parties have higher security interests at stake; (2) crises are more likely to exhibit high reciprocity when the combined capability scores and interests for the two parties are evenly matched.

Based on these two hypotheses, we can predict the behavioral type we would expect to find associated with each pairing for each variable, assuming that the two sides each followed the prescriptions of realism. For example, if both sides have vital interests at stake, the pairing of rank scores on interests would be 3, 3, which we would expect to be associated with the high escalation and high reciprocity of a Fight. We would make the same prediction if the capability scores indicated that both sides expected to win easily in the case of war (3, 3). On the other hand, if one side expected to win easily, and the other saw the two sides as evenly matched (3, 2), we will expect high escalation, but low reciprocity, that is, a crisis that would be closer to the "aggressor–defender" model of escalation associated with low reciprocity Resistance and Put-Down types. There are six possible combinations for each of the variables, so that, when all the pairings of interest and capability rankings, for each side, are taken into account, there are forty-five possible permutations. We can reduce the number to a more manageable size, however, by combining the rank scores on the two variables, and then summing them to obtain a single *motivation* score for each side. When the motivation scores for each side are paired against each other, there are nineteen possible combinations. For each combination, we can predict the behavioral type – Fight, Standoff, Resistance, or Put-Down – with which it would be associated, based on the two realist hypotheses stated above.

An example of the procedure can be seen by looking at the British–Russian crisis of 1877–78. As Russia began to advance closer to Constantinople during the course of the Russo-Turkish War, the British became concerned about a potential threat to their strategic interests in the Eastern Mediterranean, particularly, any changes that might threaten their maritime connections with India. A crisis ensued when Russia ignored British demands to halt the advance of their troops toward Constantinople. The Disraeli government believed that it enjoyed a significant military advantage over Russia, which would give Britain a perceived capability score of 3, and that it had nonvital security interests at stake, which would yield an interest score of 2. The combined motivation score for Britain, therefore, would be 5. The Russians were concerned with their strategic position in the Balkans, but they already were strained militarily by the war with Turkey and the Russian military command recognized that they would be no match for the superior naval power of Great Britain. Consequently, their motivation score would be 3: nonvital security interests at stake, for an interest score of 2, and the expectation that they would be easily defeated in a war against Britain, for a capability score of 1. When this (5, 3) pairing is considered in light of the two hypotheses above, the predicted behavioral type is a low escalation, low reciprocity, Put-Down. A low level of escalation would be predicted because of Russia's pessimism regarding its war-fighting capabilities, and a low level of reciprocity would be predicted because of the imbalance in the motivation scores of the two sides. That, in fact, is what happened. The British initially sent the Russians a verbal warning, but, when that went unheeded, British naval forces set sail for Constantinople, in a show-of-force that bears a remarkable resemblance to their strategy in the Falklands crisis a century later. When the British fleet anchored in Besika Bay, the Russians decided to yield to the British demands.

The predictions become more ambiguous when the motivation scores are at the mid-range. When a party has a motivation score of 4, it can mean either that: it expects an easy victory in the event of war, but has no security interests at stake; it sees itself as evenly matched militarily with nonvital security interests at stake; or it believes that it would be easily defeated in a war, but it has vital security interests at stake. It could be argued that all of these are cases in which the party would be sufficiently motivated to put up considerable resistance in the face of an aggressive opponent, so that we would expect crises with 6, 4, and 5, 4, pairings of motivation scores to reach higher levels of escalation. By the same token, it could be argued that 4, 3 and 4, 2 match-ups would not escalate to higher levels because of the caution of the side with a motivation score of 3 or 2.

It is harder to make a prediction based on a realist perspective when *each* party has a motivation score of 4. From a classical realist perspective, prudence might suggest to each party that the expectations of costs and risks associated with war are not worth fighting even a winning war; a long and costly war should not be undertaken when anything less than vital interests are at stake; and it would be senseless to fight a war in which defeat is virtually certain, even with vital interests at stake. On the other hand, a pure power politics approach might suggest bargaining more aggressively when the balance in capabilities is in one's favor, regardless of the stakes. Furthermore, conflict strategists would see a crisis in which there is an

95

even balance in motivation to be one in which the outcome will favor the side demonstrating greater resolve.

Tensions between the need to exercise prudence versus the admonition to demonstrate power and resolve lie at the heart of the realist prescription itself. It is not surprising that they introduce an element of ambiguity into any attempt to test the extent to which statesmen follow the realist prescription in real world crises; however, if that ambiguity exists in the minds of statesmen as well, it should surface in an examination of predicted associations between the crisis structure and the behavioral types. With that in mind, the analysis begins with a model based on prudential assumptions, which would predict that crises in which the match-up in motivation is 4, 4 would fall into the high reciprocity, low escalation, Standoff category, but we also will consider a model based on the admonition to demonstrate resolve, which would predict that these cases would fall into the high reciprocity, high escalation, Fight category. A list of the possible combinations for interest, capabilities, and motivation (interests and capabilities combined) for the two sides to the dispute appears in Appendix 2 (p. 000). The motivation score for each side, in each crisis, can be found in column 6 of Table 3.1.

Associations between structure and behavior

A comparison of the predicted and observed associations between the paired motivation scores, and the four behavioral types that were described in Chapter 4, appears in Table 5.1.

The combined structural scores accurately predict the behavioral type in only sixteen out of forty cases. These associations yield a standardized *lambda-y* score of 0.19, which indicates that knowing the combined score on the two structural variables yields about a 19 percent improvement over a random selection. As expected, one source of the weak predictions is associated with the ambiguous motivation pairing of 4–4. There are nine of these cases, and only two of them exhibit the behavioral patterns to be classified as Standoffs. The association, however, gets even weaker if we predict an association between 4–4 scores and Fights, as only one of these cases actually falls into the Fight category. If the 4–4 cases are removed altogether from the test, the association for the pairings of motivation scores and behavioral types is somewhat stronger, with a *lambda-y* test of association yielding a score of 0.28. Nevertheless, the overall impression is that of only a weak relationship between the crisis structure and behavioral types.

96

Table 5.1. *Predicted versus observed behavioral types*

Predicted	Observed type				
Predicted	Fight	Resistance	Stand-Off	Put-Down	Total
Fight	3(0.60)	2(0.40)	0(0.00)	0(0.00)	5(1.00)
Resistance	3(0.25)	5(0.42)	1(0.08)	3(0.25)	12(1.00)
Stand-Off	1(0.08)	5(0.42)	5(0.42)	1(0.08)	3(1.00)
Put-Down	1(0.09)	1(0.09)	6(0.55)	3(0.27)	11(1.00)
Total	8(0.20)	12(0.30)	13(0.32)	7(0.18)	40(1.00)

Note: Prediction for motivation combination of 4, 4 = Standoff.
Figures represent frequency counts with percentages in parentheses.

The problematic character of the predictions occurs primarily in the relationship between the crisis structure and the degree of reciprocity. The combined motivation scores accurately predict whether reciprocity will be high or low in just twenty-three of the forty cases, which is only slightly better than a random choice. On the other hand, the degree of escalation is accurately predicted in twenty-eight of the forty cases in Table 5.1. If the border-line 4–4 cases are removed from the table, the accuracy in predicting the degree of escalation based on comparative motivation scores improves to twenty-five of the remaining thirty-one cases, or 81 percent.

The observed association between the match-ups in motivation and crisis escalation is consistent with realist expectations regarding crisis behavior. From a realist perspective, we would expect each side to adopt a more aggressive bargaining strategy when it is more optimistic regarding the consequences of war, and when it has more important security interests at stake. If both parties bargain more aggressively, the crisis should escalate more rapidly and to a higher level.

Structure, behavior, and outcomes

War versus nonwar outcomes

When these results are added to what we found in Chapters 3 and 4, they suggest the following relationships among the crisis structure, escalation, and war or nonwar outcomes. (1) Crises in which both sides are relatively optimistic regarding their war-fighting capabilities, and in which both sides have security interests at stake, are more likely to exhibit high levels of escalation. (2) Crises with high levels of escalation are more likely to end in war. (3) Crises with high

97

combined scores for perceived war-fighting capability and interests at stake are more likely to end in war.

These findings, however, do not indicate whether it is the crisis structure, or the escalation of the crisis, or both, that exerts the strongest influence on decisions to go to war in those crises with high combined structural scores and high escalation. The answer to that question is important to the consideration of the validity of realism as *prescriptive* theory. The prescriptions of conflict strategists are based on the assumption that national leaders decide to go to war, or to seek a peaceful settlement, based on a cool-headed calculation of interests and capabilities; whereas, researchers adopting a psychological perspective view the outbreak of war as a consequence of cognitive and emotional pathologies associated with crisis escalation.

A better sense of the relationships among the three variables can be obtained by partitioning the data on escalation and war into two tables: one containing only those cases in which the combined structural score was high, and one containing only those cases in which the combined structural score was low.[1]

The first thing that strikes one about Tables 5.2 and 5.3 is that, with the borderline 4,4 match-ups removed from the tables, *all* of the wars occurred when the combined structural score was high. On the other hand, the escalation score also was high in eleven of the fourteen wars. In fact, when the structural and escalation scores are in agreement regarding the predicted outcome, they are accurate in twenty-three of twenty-five cases, that is, 92 percent of the time. The two measures disagree in their predictions in only six cases, and, of these, the outcome is consistent with the structural prediction in five instances. The outcomes in these cases suggest that, of the two predictor variables, the crisis structure is a more potent influence on whether or not crises end in war; however, it would be premature to draw even tentative conclusions based on so few cases.

Another way of approaching the question is by taking a closer look at the borderline cases, that is, those nine cases with structural scores of 4, 4. Interestingly, the components of the combined interest and capability scores for the two sides are identical in all nine cases. In each instance, both sides have nonvital security interests at stake and they each perceive themselves to be relatively evenly matched militarily. Six of the nine crises escalated to high levels, but only two of those six crises ended in war. Thus, the variation in outcomes among these cases of evenly matched adversaries is inconsistent with what would be predicted from the degree of escalation. Once again, we are looking at a very small number of cases, but, if the variation in outcomes tells us

Table 5.2. *High structural scores with escalation and war*

Structure = High	Crisis outcome		
Escalation	War	Nonwar	Total
High	11(0.85)	2(0.15)	13(1.00)
Low	3(0.75)	1(0.25)	4(1.00)
Total	14(0.82)	3(0.18)	17(1.00)

Note: Numbers represent frequency counts with percentages in parentheses.

Table 5.3. *Low structural scores with escalation and war*

Structure = Low	Crisis outcomes		
Escalation score	War	Nonwar	Total
High	0	2	2
Low	0	12	12
Total	0	14	14

anything, it is that the degree of escalation alone is not a good predictor of whether or not a crisis will end in war.

In sum, among the crises in the sample, there is a strong association between the crisis structure and crisis escalation and, when those two variables are in agreement, they are excellent predictors of whether or not crises will end in war. When the cases with borderline structural scores are removed from the sample, the crises in the sample with high structural scores escalated to a high level in thirteen of seventeen cases, and eleven of those thirteen crises (85 percent) ended in war. On the other hand, the degree of escalation alone is not a good predictor of crisis outcomes. In the four cases in which the crisis structure and crisis escalation make contradictory predictions, the crisis outcomes are more consistent with what would be predicted from the crisis structure. Moreover, in those borderline cases in which the combined structural scores do not offer a clear prediction, the outcomes are not consistent with what would be expected from the escalation score.

Taken together, these findings suggest that calculations of interests and capabilities are salient variables in influencing the escalation of crises, and that they may well be exerting a strong influence over decisions to go to war. Recent studies by other scholars have supported both of these propositions. Brecher and James (1986) have found a positive association between the presence of security interests at stake and higher levels of hostility in crises; Snyder and Diesing (1977) have found some evidence to indicate that the crisis structure is a strong determinant of crisis behavior, and they argue that the structure is a potent factor in determining crisis outcomes; Buena de Mesquita (1981) has found military capabilities and interests to be associated with decisions to go to war. All of these findings are consistent with a classical realist perspective.

Variations among peaceful outcomes

War was avoided in twenty-three of the forty crises in the sample. Twelve of those twenty-three crises ended in a diplomatic victory for one side; nine of them ended in compromises; two ended in inconclusive stalemates. As we saw in Chapter 4, all nine of the compromises occurred in crises with a high degree of reciprocity in the interactions of the two sides, whereas nine of the twelve cases in which one side achieved a diplomatic victory over the other occurred in crises with low reciprocity. When the degree of reciprocity was high, we found strong associations between high escalation and war, and between low escalation and compromises, but when the degree of reciprocity was low, there was no discernible association between the degree of escalation and war or nonwar outcomes.

The positive associations between high reciprocity scores and compromises, and between low reciprocity scores and diplomatic victories, hold true regardless of variations in the crisis structure. Variations in reciprocity, as well as variations among nonwar outcomes, appear to be independent of the crisis structure. That is not what would be expected from a realist perspective, which would predict that compromises would be more likely to occur when the motivation scores for the two sides are equal, and that one side would be likely to yield to the other when they are not equal. The data, however, suggest that we should look elsewhere for an explanation of why some crises, and not others, are characterized by the combination of low escalation and high reciprocity that we find associated with compromise outcomes. One hypothetical explanation, which is consistent with classical realism (Morgenthau, 1960:ch. 31), would be that these crises are more effectively managed because of the active participation of experienced major powers, either as participants, or as third party mediators. Morgenthau's argument is that experienced major powers are better able to conduct a prudent policy without being carried away by ideological or emotional restrictions; consequently, they are more likely to achieve settlements that avoid unwanted wars.

Major power diplomacy. One of the intriguing findings in Chapter 3 was that, of the thirteen crises in the sample in which major powers were pitted against each other, only three (23 percent) ended in war, as opposed to fourteen of the remaining twenty-seven cases (52 percent). Some empirical support for the validity of the proposition that major powers are more effective managers of crisis diplomacy also was found in an earlier study (Gochman and Leng, 1983), undertaken with a smaller sample of crises. That study also suggested that major powers performed an effective mediating role by intervening in crises between minor powers. It is worth taking a closer look at that possibility among the crises in the sample at hand.

The distinction between major and minor powers is based on the Correlates of War criteria (Small and Singer, 1982) described in chapter 3.[2] Major powers are identified as intervening in disputes between other states, when they engage in diplomatic efforts to achieve a negotiated settlement outside of the public efforts of intergovernmental organizations. It is not required that representatives of the intervening major powers be officially designated as mediators, provided that they become actively involved in efforts to bring the dispute to a negotiated settlement.

The associations between the classification of adversaries as major or minor powers, and the outcomes of the crises in the sample appear in Table 5.4. Each cell of the table presents the frequency of the outcome for that category of adversaries, with the frequency of major power intervention appearing in parentheses alongside it. Row 1 of column 1, for example, tells us that major powers intervened diplomatically in an attempt to achieve a settlement in none of the eight minor power crises that ended in war.

The associations appearing in Table 5.4 support the classical realist view that the major powers can be expected to behave in a responsible manner in controlling the escalation of crises to war. Only a quarter of the crises with major powers on both sides ended in war, as opposed to roughly half of those cases which had minor power adversaries, or which pitted major powers against minor powers. One good reason for the exercise of greater restraint can be seen in the outcomes of the three major power crises in the sample that did end in war: World War II, World War I, and the Crimean War rank first, second, and eighth among all international wars in severity (battle-connected deaths) for the period between 1816 and 1980 (Small and Singer, 1982:102–3).

When major powers intervened in disputes involving other powers,

Table 5.4. *Adversary types, outcomes, and major power intervention*

Participants	War	Compromise	Diplomatic Victory	Stalemate	Total
Minor–Minor	8(0)	6(3)	0(0)	1(1)	14(4)
Major–Major	3(0)	1(1)	7(2)	1(0)	12(3)
Major–Minor	6(1)	2(0)	5(1)	0(0)	13(2)
Total	17(1)	9(4)	12(3)	2(0)	40(8)

Note: Numbers in parentheses indicate frequency of cases of major power intervention.

war was avoided in seven of eight instances. The interventions in three minor power crises – the Teschen, Polish–Lithuanian, and Trieste disputes – all resulted in compromises. The three major power interventions in crises involving other major powers, however, were not mediatory; the interventions served to tip the balance in favor of one side. These were the interventions by Germany on the side of Austria in the Bosnian crisis, and by Britain on the side of France in the First Moroccan and Agadir crises. The other instances of major power intervention is that of Great Britain and France in the Munich crisis of 1938–39, when they persuaded, or coerced, the government of Czechoslovakia to yield to German demands.

The overall record for major powers is consistent with what would be predicted by classical realism. When major powers were involved in crises, either as participants on both sides, or as intervening third parties, the crises escalated to war in only four of eighteen cases, or 22 percent of the time. When major powers were not involved, the crises escalated to war in thirteen of twenty-two cases, or 59 percent of the time. These findings, however, do not help us explain the relationship between high reciprocity and compromise outcomes. There is no observable relationship between the involvement of major powers on both sides in crises, or as intervening third parties, and high reciprocity scores.

Compromises. Most of the compromise outcomes in the sample, in fact, occur in crises between minor powers. There are six instances of minor power crises ending in compromise, and all six include mediating efforts, either by major powers, or by intergovernmental organizations. The three instances of major power mediation were mentioned above. The other three cases – the Chaco Dispute, and the Honduran Border, and Beagle Channel crises – were all Latin American territorial disputes in which the OAS assisted the parties in obtaining compromises. Thus, all six of these cases involved active efforts at mediation; all six exhibited high levels of reciprocity; and all six ended in compromises.[3] Based on the evidence that we have seen so far, we can only speculate on the relationship among these variables. A plausible hypothesis would be that we are observing the effects of mediation efforts that have led to reciprocal diplomatic exchanges associated with the move to compromise settlements.

One-sided outcomes. It is not surprising to find that, among the crises with peaceful outcomes, those with high reciprocity tend to end in compromises and those crises with low reciprocity tend to have one-sided outcomes. Those findings are consistent with the notion that reciprocal exchange is the key to cooperative settlements. What remains puzzling is the lack of any observable relationship between the level of escalation and war or nonwar outcomes among the crises with low reciprocity scores. From a classical realist perspective, the most plausible explanation would be that the determinant variables lie not in the behavior patterns of the participants, but in the crisis structure. A realist explanation would be that the crises with one-sided outcomes tend to be cases in which there is a distinct imbalance in perceived war-fighting capabilities, with the outcome – war or submission by the weaker side – determined by the interests at stake for the weaker side. Specifically: (1) if there is a distinct imbalance in perceived war-fighting capabilities, and the weaker party does not have vital interests at stake, the weaker side will yield to the demands of the stronger side; (2) if the stronger side perceives that it can win easily in the event of war, and the weaker party has vital interests at stake, the crisis will end in war.

A close look at the nine cases that ended with one side achieving a diplomatic victory over the other, includes some crises that fit these propositions rather neatly. Among the nine crises ending in one-sided peaceful outcomes, there are four cases that are consistent with the first proposition: the "Pastry War" between France and Mexico in 1838, the British–Russian crisis of 1878, the Fashoda crisis of 1899, and the Bosnian crisis of 1908. These cases offer examples of prudent power politics in action: both sides had nonvital security interests at stake, but the stronger party expected to win easily in the event of war, and the weaker party expected to be defeated. All, interestingly, are crises occurring in the period prior to World War I, when the classic balance of power system is presumed to have worked most effectively.

There also are three cases among the ten low reciprocity crises ending in war that fit the second proposition, that is, they are cases in which a weaker party with vital interests at stake refused to yield to the demands of a stronger adversary: the Russo-Turkish War crisis of 1876–77, the Italo-Ethiopian crisis of 1934–35, and the Manchurian crisis of 1932.

103

In sum, although there are several crises that fit the classical realist hypothesis, those crises account for less than half of the nineteen cases with low reciprocity scores that ended either in war or one-sided peaceful outcomes. Since the structural conditions do not provide a sufficient explanation for the linkage between behavior patterns and outcomes, it makes sense to take a closer look at the behavior of the participants. Here too, there is a realist proposition to consider.

Initiators, escalation, and war

The association between low reciprocity and either war or one-sided peaceful outcomes is so strong that all but one of the cases in the low reciprocity Resistance and Put-Down categories end either in war or submission by one side to the demands of the other. In Chapter 4, the unbalanced patterns of escalation appearing in these two categories were compared to Pruitt and Rubin's (1986:89–90) "aggressor–defender" model of crisis escalation. In this model, the "aggressor" takes the initiative and attempts to coerce the other side into yielding and the "defender" simply reacts – forcefully in the case of the Resistance category, less forcefully in the case of a Put-Down.

The aggressor–defender model implies that one of the parties is controlling the escalation of the crisis, and, ultimately, its outcome, by exhibiting greater resolve through more aggressive behavior. Some evidence suggesting the plausibility of this hypothesis was found by Maoz (1983) in a study of 164 militarized disputes[4] occurring between 1816 and 1976. Maoz found that the party first to threaten the use of force was likely to be the party to exhibit the highest level of hostility during the dispute, and the party most likely to prevail. Maoz's study was limited by the availability of data for only a small subset of the actions of the disputants, so he was unable to track the pattern of escalation over the course of the crisis, but his findings are suggestive and provocative.

Maoz (1983:199–200) hypothesized that the initiator's high rate of success, which had been observed in a previous study by Buena de Mesquita (1981), was a function of its greater resolve, which it demonstrated through more aggressive behavior. Borrowing from Dollard's (1939) frustration-aggression hypothesis, Maoz (1983:199) speculated that the more aggressive side's actions were prompted by its dissatisfaction with the status quo. The empirical linkage between the frustration-aggression hypothesis and the behavior observed by Maoz is problematic, because Maoz identified dissatisfaction with the status quo with the side that was the first to threaten, display, or use military

104

force. While these two characteristics may be found together in many instances, it is not difficult to think of examples in which the first party to threaten force is the party defending the status quo, such as Austria in 1914, or the United States in the Cuban Missile crisis. Nevertheless, aside from the frustration-aggression hypothesis, one could argue that the state that is the first to raise the level of escalation, and the risk of war, by issuing a threat of force, is likely to be the state demonstrating the greatest resolve, whether it is challenging the status quo, or defending it. For example, in the Cuban Missile crisis of 1962, the challenge to the status quo came from the Soviet Union, but the United States issued the first threat of force, and, in its defense of the strategic status quo in the Western hemisphere, the United States adopted the more aggressive strategy.

Maoz's measurement of resolve based on the use of coercive actions, on the other hand, is of interest, because it offers a view of resolve that is consistent with that of the conflict strategists (Schelling, 1960, 1966; Kahn, 1965). Maoz's definition of resolve ties the concept to an offensive, risk-taking, strategy, as opposed to associating it with firmness in the face of attempts at coercion. In that respect, it has an aggressive character that would associate it with coercive bargaining.

Besides raising troubling questions regarding the positive relationship between aggressive behavior and success, Maoz's findings suggest a possible explanation for the distribution of outcomes among the low reciprocity cases in our sample, which are dominated by crises that end either in war, or a diplomatic victory by one side over the other. Perhaps these are predominantly cases in which the greater resolve of one party controls the escalation of the crisis and forces the other party into choosing between war or submission. If that is the case, we should find a high percentage of cases in our sample in which the same party initiates the crisis, exhibits a higher overall level of escalation, and, ultimately, prevails, either through a diplomatic triumph or a military victory.

Testing the initiation-aggression hypothesis. There are two potential operational indicators of the crisis initiator. If we view the initiator as the first party to challenge the status quo, then the best indicator is the *precipitant act,* an action taken by one party that disturbs the status quo to the extent that it is challenged by the other party (see Snyder and Diesing, 1977:11). On the other hand, if we view the initiator of the crisis as the first party to escalate the dispute to the point at which war is threatened, then the best indicator is the *first threat of force.* Conceptually, the two are distinct. The precipitant act initiates the dispute by challenging the status quo; the first threat of force escalates the dispute

105

to the level of a militarized dispute (see Chapter 2) by introducing the threat of force. The same actor can carry out both acts. The precipitant action itself may contain the threat or use of force, or a protest from the other side may trigger a threat of force from the party challenging the status quo. In fact, in our sample of forty crises, the same party initiates the precipitant action and issues the first threat of force in roughly half (nineteen) of the cases.

The escalation measure,[5] which combines the rate and magnitude of escalation in the behavior of the participants on each side, can be used to determine which party acts more aggressively over the course of the crisis. This will give us a more comprehensive measure than the sampling of threats and uses of force employed in Maoz's study. Appendix 3 (p. 000) presents a table which identifies, for each crisis in the sample: (1) the side taking the precipitant action; and (2) the side issuing the first threat of force; (3) the standardized escalation score for each side; (4) the outcome of the crisis; and, in those cases in which the crises escalated to war (5) the relative severity; and (6) outcome of a war.

It turns out that the first threat of force is more strongly associated with the other measures of interest – escalation and crisis outcomes – than with the precipitant act, although both exhibit positive associations. For the sake of brevity, I will adopt Maoz's (1983) approach, and use the threat of force as the initiating action in the remainder of this discussion. To spare the reader from the task of trudging through a series of two-by-two tables, the associations among the variables simply will be summarized.

Diplomatic victories. If we exclude the four cases in the sample in which the first threat or use of force by each party occurs simultaneously, as in a border clash between patrols from the two sides, the side responsible for the first threat or use of force is also the side exhibiting a higher level of escalation in twenty-four of thirty-six cases. Among the crises in the sample ending in one-sided peaceful outcomes, the same side initiates the threat or use of force and exhibits the higher overall level of escalation in ten of twelve cases. In eight of those ten cases, the more aggressive side is also the diplomatic victor.

The positive association between aggressive behavior and success is consistent with the view of crisis bargaining power as a function of perceived comparative resolve (Snyder and Diesing, 1977:190), in which resolve is demonstrated through a state's willingness to risk war to achieve its objectives. In this respect, these cases offer support for the prescriptions of conflict strategists. So far, however, we have considered only those cases in the sample in which a clear winner emerged without the crisis escalating to war. The risk associated with adopting a more aggressive influence strategy is not that of suffering a diplomatic defeat, but of slamming the door on opportunities for compromise and plunging into a costly war.

Crises ending in war. Small and Singer (1982:196–97) find that in sixty-two interstate wars occurring between 1816 and 1980, the state initiating military hostilities emerged victorious in forty-two cases, that is, roughly two-thirds of the time. When that proportion is considered along with the 80 percent success rate favoring the more aggressive side in low reciprocity interstate crises that end peacefully, there would appear to be a good argument for adopting an aggressive bargaining strategy of the sort prescribed by conflict strategists. With this in mind, it is worth taking a closer look at the crises in our sample that ended in war.

A consideration of the prescriptive validity of adopting a belligerent bargaining strategy that may lead to war suggests that we should apply a measure of the consequences of war that will tell us more than which party emerged as the military victor. After all, it is hard to imagine that the participants on *either* side would have allowed the 1914 crisis to escalate to war if they had foreseen the costs of World War I. A bargaining strategy that leads to a severe war, with enormous costs for both sides, can hardly be considered a diplomatic success. To the extent to which a decision to go to war can be considered rational, most realists would agree with Blainey (1973:ch. 3) that it requires confidence that the war can be won at a reasonable cost. What constitutes a reasonable cost is dependent on the interests at stake. In the classical realist terms of Clausewitz (1966[1832]:ch.1.11): "the political object, as the original motive of the War, will be the standard for determining both the aim of the military force and the amount of effort to be made."

Small and Singer (1982:69–71) have followed Richardson's (1960) example in adopting a measure of a war's *severity* based on the number of persons killed, although Small and Singer limit their accounting to the number of combat-connected fatalities among military personnel.[6] To place the fatalities within the perspective of the relative costs to particular states, we will measure severity according to the number of combat-connected military fatalities on a per capita basis. Obviously, fatalities measured in the tens of thousands have different implications for a state the size of Israel, than for a state the size of China. The Small and Singer data do not present an obvious cut-off point for moderate or severe wars; however, a reasonable break-point for the cases in our sample occurs between the upper third and lower two-thirds of the

107

Table 5.5. *Crisis initiator, escalation, and war outcomes*

| Crisis initiators | War outcome | | | | | | |
| | Moderate wars | | | Severe wars | | | |
	Victory	Defeat	Stalemate	Victory	Defeat	Stalemate	Total
Higher escalation	4	2	1	2	1	0	10
Lower escalation	0	2	0	0	2	1	5
Even escalation	0	0	0	0	1	0	1
Total	4	4	1	2	4	1	16
Other cases	4	4	2	4	2	0	16

ranking of combat-connected fatalities for the entire population of international wars. The highest number of fatalities per 1,000 persons in the population for the victor in any of the "moderate" wars in our sample would be 5 for Nicaragua in the Second Central American War, which is ranked thirty-ninth in fatalities per capita for all international wars. The lowest number of fatalities per 1,000 persons for the victorious side among the "severe" cases would be 12.4 for Greece, Romania, Serbia, and Turkey in the Second Balkan War, which is ranked twentieth in fatalities per capita among the 118 international wars. As the reader will see from the table in Appendix 3 (p. 000), the break-point between moderate and severe wars is quite consistent with the views of those wars held by most diplomatic historians.

There are five war outcomes of interest: (1) victory in a moderate war; (2) defeat in a moderate war; (3) victory in a severe war; (4) defeat in a severe war; and a (5) compromise peace settlement, or stalemate. Even from a pure power politics perspective, only the first of the five possibilities can be considered a successful outcome to a militarized crisis. Table 5.5 presents the associations between the initiation of the threat or use of force, the higher mean escalation scores, and the outcomes of those crises that end in war.

If the frequencies in Table 5.5 are viewed from a purely competitive perspective, the states that initiate crises and exhibit a higher overall level of belligerence over the course of the crisis are those that are most likely to prevail in war. Their record of victories, defeats, and ties, if 6–3–1, as compared to a record of 0–4–1 for those states initiating the crisis, but not exhibiting a higher overall escalation score, and 8–6–2 for all other states engaged in wars.[7] If we judge success according to what is accomplished with regard to what realists would call the "national interest," the only wars that could be considered successes are those in which victory was achieved at a reasonable cost, that is, victories in moderate wars.[8] If severe wars are treated as losses, the "won–lost" record for the more aggressive sides is 4–6. It is not an impressive performance record when we remember that these are the states that took the lead in the escalation of the dispute to war.

It is worth taking a closer look at the four crises in which the states initiating the crisis achieved military victories in less severe wars, that is, those who were relatively successful. The four cases are: the Schleswig-Holstein War crisis of 1864, the Spanish–American War of 1897–98, the Manchurian War crisis of 1931, and the Italo-Ethiopian crisis of 1934–35. In three of the four cases, the party precipitating the dispute – Prussia in the Schleswig-Holstein crisis, Japan in the Manchurian crisis, and Italy in the Italo-Ethiopian crisis – believed that it could prevail easily in the event of war and planned on going to war at the beginning of the crisis. In other words, these were cases in which the bargaining strategy simply was to seize the objective by force. The fourth case, the crisis leading to the Spanish–American War, is notorious for the presumed effect of domestic pressures on the United States government to go to war with Spain over the issue of Spanish colonial practices in Cuba. All four cases appear to be instances in which a power challenging the status quo took advantage of an opportunity to employ military force against a weaker adversary.[9] Only in the Spanish–American case was diplomacy pursued seriously by the revisionist power, and, in that instance, domestic pressures helped propel the American government to war.

These four cases are of particular interest because they appear to reflect a power politics model at work, and working successfully. Each is consistent with what Morgenthau (1960:58) describes as a policy of "military imperialism." Morgenthau, however, goes on to warn of its danger: "war is a gamble, it may be won or lost." One could add that it also could be "won" at costs that far exceed the value of the original objectives. Only four of the wars fought by the parties initiating and leading in the escalation of a crisis resulted in military victories in conflicts classified as "moderate" wars. Moderate, of course, is a subjective term, particularly when the estimate of human fatalities is limited to those suffered on the battlefield. Japan suffered 10,000 military fatalities in its victory in the Manchurian War, while China suffered 50,000 military dead, but civilian fatalities in China are estimated in the hundreds of thousands. The other thirteen cases were all wars that either reached levels of severity that would place them in the

109

upper third for all international wars occurring between 1820 and 1980, or ended in defeats or stalemates for the initiator.

Summary and conclusion

Summary

The investigation in this chapter started from the seemingly contradictory findings of Chapters 3 and 4. In Chapter 3 we found an association between the crisis structure and war outcomes that was consistent with classical realist predictions. The examination of crisis behavior and crisis outcomes in Chapter 4, on the other hand, yielded associations that were more consistent with the psychological perspective. To obtain a more complete picture of the relationships among these variables, we began by examining possible associations between the two predictor variables: the crisis structure, as indicated by the combined perceived comparative war-fighting capabilities and interests at stake for each side, and the behavioral type, as indicated by patterns of escalation and reciprocity in the actions and interactions of the two sides. We found a positive association between the crisis structure and crisis escalation, with the degree of escalation accurately predicted in twenty-eight of the forty crises in the sample, and in twenty-five of thirty-one cases when structural scores on the border between those cases predicting high or low escalation were removed from the sample. The findings to this point suggested that states are likely to behave in a more contentious manner as the security stakes increase and they become more optimistic regarding their chances in a war, and that crises are more likely to escalate to higher levels when the stakes and optimism regarding the consequences of war are relatively high for both sides. Classical realism, with its strong emphasis on the predominance of considerations of relative power and security interests, appears to do well as a descriptive theory of crisis behavior at a macroscopic level.

Classical realists also argue that the best way to manage escalating crises is through the skillful diplomacy of experienced major powers. We found, in fact, that when major powers were involved in the crises in the sample, either as participants on each side, or as mediating third parties, the crises escalated to war only 22 percent of the time, as opposed to 59 percent of the time when major powers were involved on just one side, or not at all.

Among the more intriguing findings in Chapter 4 were the associations between patterns of reciprocity, escalation, and different types of outcomes. It comes as no surprise to find that high reciprocity, high escalation Fights are likely to end in war, or that high reciprocity, low escalation Standoffs are more likely to end in compromises. In this chapter, we found some indication of a positive association between efforts at mediation and Standoffs ending in compromises, but we will have to take a closer look at the bargaining of the participants to get a more complete picture of what is happening in these cases.

One also would expect to find, as we did in Chapter 4, that low reciprocity Resistance and Put-Down behavioral types are more likely to end in either one-sided peaceful outcomes, or in war. A plausible explanation of this phenomenon is that these are crises with a distinct imbalance in the capabilities of the disputants, so that the degree of escalation is controlled by the stronger party, with the party that perceives itself as weaker ultimately yielding, or, if it has vital interests at stake, resisting until the dispute escalates to war. The behavior patterns in such cases would fit the "aggressor–defender" model of escalation that we associated with our Resistance and Put-Downs. Although we did find a number of crises that exhibited the structural characteristics that one would associate with these patterns, those cases accounted for less than half of the crises with low reciprocity scores that ended in war or one-sided outcomes.

Another type of explanation for the observed association between low reciprocity and either one-sided outcomes, or war, focuses on the behavioral characteristics of an aggressor–defender model, without tying it to the structural attributes of the two sides. This approach posits that one side is able to control the escalation of the crisis and force the other side into a choice between war or submission, by exhibiting greater resolve through more aggressive behavior. The pattern is of particular interest to us, because of its consistency with the prescriptions of conflict strategists. Within our own sample, we found that, in ten of twelve cases of peaceful one-sided outcomes, the same side was the first to threaten or use force and to exhibit a higher overall level of conflictive behavior. In eight of those ten cases, the more aggressive side also emerged with a diplomatic victory.

The greatest danger in adopting an aggressive approach to crisis bargaining is that of missing opportunities for a compromise settlement and becoming embroiled in a costly war. Half of the crises in the sample with low reciprocity scores ended in war. Although the record of victories and defeats in war is slightly better for those parties initiating the crisis and exhibiting a higher overall level of escalation over the course of the crisis, it is not impressive if one considers the costs of severe wars. The initiators of crises were able to achieve

111

military victories without facing the costs of a severe war in just four of sixteen cases; those parties that both initiated the crisis and exhibited a higher level of escalation did only slightly better, with a record of four successes in ten wars. Overall, those states that have been identified as the crisis initiator, and that have exhibited a higher level of escalation over the course of the crisis, achieved successful outcomes in eight of sixteen crises; in other words, they were successful half of the time.

Conclusions

Although we have treated realist and psychological views of crisis behavior as competing perspectives, the descriptive findings in support of one or the other view are not necessarily contradictory. A plausible interpretation of what we have found up to this point is that crises are more likely to escalate to higher levels when there are higher interests at stake for the two sides, and when each side is relatively optimistic regarding its war-fighting capabilities; that the same considerations exert a significant influence on decisions to go to war, except that those decisions may also be influenced by the pathological effects of the escalatory process. Such an interpretation implies that the realists are correct in pointing to the centrality of considerations of interests and power in crisis decision-making, but that, as crises escalate to higher levels, rational decision-making may be increasingly contaminated by the cognitive and emotional effects of escalating conflict. If we accept this interpretation of what we have found so far, the critical unanswered question concerns the relative potency of rational calculations of power and interests, versus confounding psychological variables, in influencing crisis behavior. The answer to that question ultimately is essential to an evaluation of the prescriptive validity of realism, particularly as it has been extended to serve as a guide to crisis bargaining by conflict strategists.

Over the next three chapters, we will take a more microscopic look at crisis behavior, by focusing on the influence tactics and strategies of the two sides. As we do so, we will devote more of our attention to the prescriptions of conflict strategists. We will begin, in Chapter 6, with a consideration of the relative effectiveness of different varieties of cooperative and conflictive influence tactics.

6 INFLUENCE TACTICS

When they find themselves faced with escalating crises, statesmen must ask what influence techniques will most effectively contribute to the protection of their interests without plunging their states into costly wars. The theoretical discussion in Chapter 1 introduced two competing perspectives on crisis bargaining: the realist and psychological perspectives. Working within the realist tradition, conflict strategists have devoted their attention to techniques of manipulative bargaining designed to demonstrate superior resolve in escalating conflicts. From this perspective, coercive inducements are presumed to be the predominant, and most effective, influence techniques. Consequently, a good deal of the theorizing of conflict strategists is devoted to the credible use of threats and punishments. Crisis bargaining becomes, in Kahn's words (1965:16), "a competition in risk-taking," in which the risk is the outbreak of war.

The main restraint on a potentially reckless pursuit of a strategy of escalating coercive influence tactics lies in the classical realist admonition to demonstrate prudence (Morgenthau, 1960:10). Realists recognize that prudent diplomacy frequently requires some degree of accommodation (see Morgenthau, 1960:ch. 31). For classical realists, the issue must be resolved through a careful calculation of capabilities and interests. Prudential considerations require national leaders to recognize the limits of their power, and to seek an accommodative settlement if the costs and risks of war outweigh the objectives being pursued. On the other hand, conflict strategists note that the credibility of coercive threats is tied to demonstrated commitments to carry them out (see Schelling, 1960). A militarized crisis represents the supreme test of a state's power and resolve. In such a situation, the line between the exercise of prudence and what may be perceived as a failure of nerve is not easily drawn.

In earlier chapters, we noted that a number of studies by behavioral scientists have suggested that conflict bargaining, whether between persons or states, has exhibited a tit-for-tat pattern, which suggests

113

that the adversaries are motivated by considerations other than a cool-headed calculation of their interests in terms of power. Several possible explanations for the observed prevalence of reciprocated exchange were suggested in Chapter 1. In addition to psychopolitical pressures, which statesmen may identify with their role as guardians of national security and prestige, there may be strong domestic political pressures on statesmen to respond with toughness in the face of overt threats from other states.

The tendency on the part of individuals, or states, to respond to influence attempts in a reciprocating manner, that is, to respond in kind to both cooperative and coercive influence attempts, has been observed in a variety of contexts, ranging from interpersonal bargaining experiments (Esser and Komorita, 1975), to computer tournaments (Axelrod, 1984), to empirical research on bargaining strategies employed in interstate crises (Leng and Wheeler, 1979). These studies raise an important issue regarding the efficacy of the prescriptions of conflict strategists. If states are most likely to respond to influence attempts in a reciprocating, or tit-for-tat, manner, then relying on escalating coercion to obtain compliance with one's demands is a prescription for war. On the other hand, realists would argue that a reliance on accommodative moves, under the assumption that the other side will respond in a reciprocating manner, runs the risk of signaling weakness and encouraging coercive tactics by the other side.

A middle ground between essentially coercive or accommodative influence techniques might be through a reliance on carrot-and-stick inducements that demonstrate firmness, while also exhibiting a willingness to move to a mutually accommodative settlement. Some indication of the efficacy of carrot-and-stick inducements was found in a study of US–Soviet crises in the post-World War II era (Leng, 1984).

This chapter explores the varieties of inducements that accompany influence attempts, and then considers their association with the immediate responses of the target state. Most of our attention, however, will focus on a comparison of the effectiveness of the competing approaches to crisis bargaining associated with the conflict strategists and those who emphasize the reciprocal nature of interstate interaction. In the course of the discussion that follows, I will refer to the two approaches as the *realist* and *reciprocating* models of crisis behavior. Which of these two models best describes how states bargain in crises? Which of them offers the best prescription for sucess?

114

Obtaining operational indicators

Influence attempt–response model

The analysis begins with the design of a simple model of influence attempt–response sequences. The model that we will employ is based on a theoretical model of internation influence suggested by Singer (1963) and elaborated in operational form by Leng (1980). The model assumes that the bargaining process consists of sequences of influence attempts – requests or demands which may, or may not, be accompanied by inducements – and responses. Each sequence consists of three moves: (1) state A attempts to influence the behavior of state B through a demand accompanied by positive and/or negative induce-ments; (2) state B responds to the influence attempt; (3) state A observes state B's response, and, according to A's understanding of the proper approach to crisis bargaining, A uses that information in selec-ting the inducement(s) to accompany its next demand.

The *influence attempt* represents the action component of the action–response model. It is composed of a *request* demanding some action by the target (or a request that the target not act), which may or may not, be accompanied by an *inducement* indicating the actor's intentions should the target respond, or fail to respond, as the actor requested. Requests are categorized according to the *cost of compliance*, that is, the costs to the target should it comply with the actor's request. *Induce-ments* are categorized according to *type* (positive, negative, and carrot-and-stick), the *degree* of coerciveness, and the *specificity* of the actor's commitment to carry them out. The target's *response* to an influence attempt is categorized according to the degree of accommodation or defiance in its response.

Based on this model, there are four variables determining the target's immediate response to an influence attempt: (1) the cost of complying with the request; (2) the type of inducement accompanying the request; (3) the degree of inducement; and (4) the credibility of the actor's intention to carry out the inducement.

The reciprocating model makes no prediction regarding the effects of the first of these variables, but the realist model predicts a negative association between the cost of compliance and accommodative responses. The two models, however, present directly competing pre-dictions with regard to the second variable, the type of inducement employed by the actor. Realists argue that coercive tactics, which raise the level of cost and risk to the target, are more effective in achieving accommodative responses; positive inducements, they argue, are

115

likely to be interpreted as signs of weakness and evoke the positive response. The reciprocating model, on the other hand, posits that states are most likely to respond to inducements in kind: positive inducements yield positive responses; coercive inducements encourage defiant responses. Both the realists and their critics agree that increasing the degree of inducement, or the specificity of the commitment to carry it out, should increase the likelihood of the predicted response associated with a particular inducement type. These predicted associations will be discussed in more detail in the analysis section, but first it is necessary to describe how operational indicators of the variables of interest have been obtained from the BCOW data.

Perception and Behavior. In the course of the methodological discussion in Chapter 2, I argued that the most reliable indicators of the foreign policy perceptions of states appear in their actions, as opposed to after-the-fact explanations of those actions by the participants or others. This is not to say that the perceptions of policy-makers are always accurate. Rather it is to argue that the best way to test two competing perspectives of crisis behavior, both of which are based on the assumption that certain types of influence attempts are likely to yield certain types of responses, is through a direct observation of the actual behavior of states in crises. For either perspective to be supported, however, we must find some consistency in the patterns of responses associated with particular types of influence attempts. If there are no consistent patterns, then the "behavior begets behavior" assumption that underlies this approach becomes problematic.

Constructing the indicators

The BCOW coding scheme contains several properties that are useful in analyzing influence attempts and responses. Perhaps the most important of these is the coding of the content of those verbal actions – requests and statements indicating intended future actions – that are the source of data on the cost of compliance to the target and on the type, degree, and specificity of inducements accompanying requests. The indicators for each of those variables are described in the following sections.

Cost of compliance. For each influence attempt, the BCOW data are searched for a description of *what* action is requested or demanded of the target. Requests are categorized into six types, based on the cost of compliance to the target of the demand. They are:

1 *Reduce hostility.* The actor requests that the target behave in a more accommodative manner, but no particular action is requested.

2   *Negotiate, or mediate.* The actor proposes negotiations, or some form of third party mediation, arbitration, adjudication, investigation, observation, or peace-keeping.
3   *Reduce military action.* The actor requests that the target reduce or cease military action directed against the actor, including actual hostilities, a blockade, alert, mobilization, or show-of-force.
4   *Economic.* The actor demands an economic good from the target, such as, payments of reparations, an end to nationalization of property, better trade conditions, etc.
5   *Political.* The actor issues demands that significantly affect the political or strategic position of the target. This could range from asking for political independence for a colony, to declaring war on a third party.
6   *Vital interests.* These are demands that would sacrifice the territorial integrity and/or political independence of the target state.

When the actor requests that the target respond verbally, that is, that the target *promise* to do something – the request is categorized as if it were for the physical action itself, with one exception: when the actor requests that the target make a conditional promise to yield vital interests, that is classified in the "political" category rather than in the "vital interests" category.[1]

The next three independent variables are attributes of the inducements accompanying the actor's demands. Inducements are assumed to be associated with particular demands if they are directed at the same target, and occur on the same day, or on the following day, provided no new requests are made on the following day.

Type of inducement. There are four basic types of inducements:

1   *Negative.* Threats and punishments.
2   *Positive.* Promises and rewards.
3   *Carrot-and-Stick.* A combination of positive and negative inducements.
4   *No inducement.* No inducement accompanies the request.

Within the BCOW data set, these distinctions are based on (1) the descriptions of the intended actions accompanying requests, along with (2) the description of the tempo and direction of those stated intentions, that is, whether the actor intends to start, increase, decrease, stop, or refrain from the specified action. For example, if the actor indicates that it intends to *refrain from* mobilizing its forces, that intended action would be classified as a promise; if it intended to *increase* the action by moving from partial to full mobilization, it would be described as a threat.

117

Degree of inducement: The second inducement attribute of interest is the degree of inducement, which, given our interest in the prescriptions of conflict strategies, is categorized according to the *degree of coercion*. The four categories of degree of inducement, in ascending coercion, are:

1 *Positive inducement*. Positive concessions, such as a reductions, or promises of reductions, in the use of force.
2 *Negative: no threat or use of force*. Economic or political threats and/or punishments short of the threat or use of force.
3 *Threat of force*. Physical actions, such as show-of-force, alerts, and mobilizations, as well as verbal threats to use force.
4 *Use of force*. Military hostilities, blockades, occupations, and seizures of territory.

Specificity of inducement. An attribute of inducements of particular interests to conflict strategists is their credibility. A number of factors can enter into the credibility of the actor's inducements, but that which has been stressed most particularly by conflict strategists (Schelling, 1960) is *commitment*: the extent to which the actor demonstrates its willingness to carry out the threatened or promised inducement or inducements. Two other frequently mentioned factors are the actor's reputation for resolve and the target's perception of the interests at stake for the actor, but their salience is more debatable.[2]

The indicator of the actor's commitment to fulfill its threats and promises is based on the *specificity* of the actor's communication: (1) of the conditions under which it will, or will not, carry out the threatened or promised action and (2) the specificity of the threatened or promised action. In the first case, a distinction is made between those instances in which the action to be taken is dependent on some specified action, or failure to act, on the part of the target, and when it is dependent on less specific conditions, such as references to "grave conditions," or possible third party action. Regarding the second, the specificity of the intended action, a three-fold classification distinguishes among: (a) ultimatums, and highly specified promises, in which the action to be taken and a deadline for the requested target action are specified; (b) simple threats or promises, in which only the threatened or promised action is specified; and (c) warnings or unspecified promises, in which there is no explicit action threatened, but only an ambiguous statement with no commitment to any explicit action. The descriptive distinctions for these indicators can be found in the BCOW data set in the descriptions of *how* statements of intended actions are communicated to the target (see Chapter 2).

118

Among the potential nonbehavioral influences on the credibility of the actor's inducements, probably the two most prominently mentioned factors are the target's perceptions of the actor's reputation for resolve and of the actor's capability. It can be argued that a reputation for unshakable resolve can enhance the credibility of the actor's stated commitment to carry out its threats and promises (see Schelling, 1960).[3] Short of a detailed content analysis of intragovernmental communications, however, it is difficult to disentangle the target's overall perception of the actor's resolve from the effects on the target's perception of the actor's resolve that are the result of the influence attempts employed by the actor during the course of the dispute.

A similar problem occurs with regard to the effects of perceptions of comparative capabilities on the credibility of inducements. It can be argued that the credibility of an actor's threats or promises is affected by the target's perception of the actor's capability to carry out its inducements without suffering high costs to itself. But, the target's perception of comparative capabilities may affect its choice of response more directly as well, that is, through its prediction of the consequences of the actor's action or inaction. In the case of a threat of force, for example, comparative capability considerations can enter into the target's choice of response in two ways; (1) through its prediction of the likelihood that the actor will go through with its threat, and (2) through its perception of the comparative war-fighting capabilities of the two sides should the actor carry out the threat.[4] To avoid using the same variable to predict two different effects,[5] we will consider the effects of the target's perception of comparative capability on its choice of responses below, in a separate section on the role of crisis structure; nevertheless, its dual role should be borne in mind as we do so. By the same token, the potential confounding effects of the target's perception of the actor's resolve and capabilities on the credibility of the actor's signaled commitment to carry out its threats and/or promises should be borne in mind when we consider the bivariate association between the specificity of the actor's inducements and the target's responses.

This section completes the description of the four predictor variables in the examination of influence attempts and responses: (1) the cost to the target of complying with the actor's demand; and (2) the type; (3) degree; and (4) specificity, of inducements accompanying the demand. The operational indicators for the dependent variable – the target's response – can be described more simply.

Responses. Following an influence attempt, the target's response is defined operationally as consisting of any actions that the target

119

directs to the actor – or to a third party if the actor requested that the target take action directed at that third party – within the seven days following the influence attempt, or until the actor issues another demand, whichever comes first. Thus, the response represents the target's overall reaction, which may take a few days to unfold, as opposed to its most immediate response. Responses are categorized into one of four basic types.

1 *Positive*. The target responds in an accommodative manner, un-accompanied by any negative action, either by complying with the actor's request, or by offering an alternative concession.[6]
2 *Mixed*. The target's response combines positive and negative actions.
3 *Ignore*. The target's response consists of no action beyond evalua-tive statements (praise, protests, etc.).
4 *Defy*. The target responds with negative actions (threats and/or punishments), directed at the actor or another participant on the actor's side in the dispute.

In addition to these four basic distinctions, and in keeping with the conflict strategists' emphasis on the threat or use of force, *defy* and *mixed* responses are divided into those in which the threat or use of force is included in the response and those in which it is not, to yield six categories.

Identifying influence attempt and response types

In earlier studies of influence attempts and responses (Leng, 1980, 1984) the identification of the categories mentioned above was done by human coders. Because of the complexity of these judgments, the effort was not only time-consuming, but prone to error. The computer software for the current study was devised to identify and extract all of the categorizations and subcategorizations mentioned below. The program makes adjustments for any combination of actor and target (including requests for actions directed at third parties), for whether the request and/or response are for physical or verbal actions, and for all the complications ensuing from the effect of various combinations of request and/or response action tempos – to start, increase, decrease, stop, or refrain from undertaking the action – on the request, inducement, and response action categories. This approach has yielded a level of efficiency and reliability in generating the influence attempt and response categories from the BCOW data that were not possible in earlier studies.

Analysis

Bivariate associations

The comparison of the realist and reciprocating models of crisis bargaining begins with cross-tabular analyses of the association between each of the influence attempt attributes of interest with the responses predicted by the competing models. Following the bivariate analyses, a log-linear approach is taken to construct the most parsimonious multivariate influence attempt-response model.

Cost of compliance. From a realist perspective, the higher the costs, in terms of target interests that must be sacrificed in order to comply with the actor's demands, the greater the likelihood of a defiant response by the target, and the lower the likelihood of a positive response. Table 6.1 shows the frequencies and percentages across the rows for the six basic response types associated with five demand types for 677 influence attempts occurring within the sample of 40 crises.

Table 6.1 provides some intriguing descriptive findings. One is the very low number of demands that states give up their vital interests – territorial integrity or political independence. A plausible explanation is that if these are indeed "interests worth dying for" (Walzer, 1977), then statesmen are rather careful not to make explicit demands that they be sacrificed, even if that is the ultimate goal.

The most frequent response, across categories, is "ignore," although it would be less predominant if the "mixed" and "defy" categories had not been subdivided according to whether or not these responses included the threat or use of force. Positive (comply or placate) responses are most often associated with requests for negotiation or a reduction in hostility. On the other side of the coin, demands that the target reduce its military activities produce the highest frequency of negative responses, particularly responses coupled with the threat or use of force, a result that is consistent with a finding from Brecher and James's (1986) crisis study.

Overall, the cross-category differences in Table 6.1 are large enough to yield a chi square score of 46.61, with 25 degrees of freedom, which is significant at the $p = .01$ level. These associations, however, may be more a function of the *inducements* accompanying the demands, than of the nature of the demands themselves. Requests for negotiation, for example, virtually always are accompanied by promises to reciprocate, and demands for reductions in military activities frequently are backed up by military action. If that is the case, we should find evidence of it in the analysis of the relationship between inducement types and responses.

Table 6.1. *Cost of compliance: demand types and responses*

Demand	Response Types						
	Positive	Mixed	Ignore	Defy	Mixed-F[a]	Defy-F[a]	Total
Vital interests	0 (0.00)	4 (0.36)	4 (0.36)	0 (0.00)	2 (0.18)	1 (0.09)	11 (1.00)
Reduce military	26 (0.11)	29 (0.12)	65 (0.28)	21 (0.09)	49 (0.21)	43 (0.19)	233 (1.00)
Economic political	18 (0.14)	14 (0.11)	55 (0.43)	9 (0.07)	19 (0.15)	12 (0.09)	127 (1.00)
Negotiate mediate	46 (0.21)	29 (0.13)	74 (0.33)	23 (0.10)	25 (0.11)	26 (0.12)	223 (1.00)
Not specified	12 (0.14)	12 (0.14)	37 (0.45)	8 (0.10)	5 (0.06)	9 (0.10)	83 (1.00)
Total	102 (0.15)	88 (0.13)	235 (0.35)	61 (0.09)	100 (0.15)	91 (0.13)	677 (1.00)

[a] Mixed-F and Defy-F are mixed and defy responses that include the threat or use of military force.
Figures represent frequency counts with percentages across rows in parentheses.

Inducement types. The predicted associations between the type of inducement employed by the actor and the target's response offer a direct contrast between the two models. The realist model predicts that considerations of power lead target states to respond most positively to negative, or coercive, influence attempts in which the actor demonstrates its resolve and willingness to accept the risks of conflict escalation to achieve its objective. Positive inducements, on the other hand, are presumed to communicate weakness on the part of the actor, thereby encouraging negative responses.[7]

The reciprocating model predicts that the target is most likely to respond in kind, whether it be to the challenge presented by a negative inducement, to an offer to cooperate signaled by a positive inducement, or to the mixed response encouraged by a carrot-and-stick inducement. As I noted above, advocates of the reciprocating approach stress the influence of norms of equity and reciprocity among states, and the arousal of aggressive reactance to threats to freedom.

The observed associations between inducement types and responses for the sample of forty crises can be seen in table 6.2

An inspection of the percentage scores in Table 6.2 indicates striking support for the reciprocating model over the realist model. Negative inducements yield predominantly negative responses; most positive responses follow positive inducements. The highest percentage (30 percent) of positive responses follow positive inducements. The target

Table 6.2. *Inducement types and responses*

Inducement type	Response Types						
	Positive	Mixed	Ignore	Defy	Mixed-F[a]	Defy-F[a]	Total
None	20 (0.10)	19 (0.09)	104 (0.50)	26 (0.13)	15 (0.07)	24 (0.12)	208 (1.00)
Positive	41 (0.25)	22 (0.14)	57 (0.35)	11 (0.07)	25 (0.15)	7 (0.04)	163 (1.00)
Carrot-and-stick	20 (0.17)	24 (0.20)	14 (0.12)	6 (0.05)	33 (0.27)	24 (0.20)	121 (1.00)
Negative	21 (0.11)	23 (0.12)	60 (0.32)	18 (0.10)	27 (0.15)	36 (0.20)	185 (1.00)
Total	102 (0.15)	88 (0.13)	235 (0.35)	61 (0.09)	100 (0.15)	91 (0.13)	677 (1.00)

[a] Mixed-F and Defy-F are mixed and defy responses that include the threat or use of military force.
Figures represent frequency counts with percentages across rows in parentheses.

responses to influence attempts without accompanying inducements and to carrot-and-stick inducements also are consistent with the reciprocating model. Influence attempts with no accompanying inducements are those most likely to be ignored (50 percent), and carrot-and-stick inducements are those most likely (47 percent) to produce mixed, or mixed-force, responses. Moreover, in a distinction not shown in Table 6.2, carrot-and-stick inducements that are accompanied by the threat or use of force are most likely to result in mixed responses that include the threat or use of force, whereas carrot-and-stick inducements that do not include any threat or use of force are more likely to be associated with positive responses. In sum, the bivariate analysis of the association between inducement and response types consistently supports the reciprocating over the realist model. The differences across categories, in fact, are quite impressive, yielding a chi-square statistic significant at the $p = 0.001$ level.

An interesting descriptive finding in Table 6.2 appears in the relatively even distribution of types of inducements across the four basic categories: none (31 percent), negative (27 percent), positive (24 percent), and carrot-and-stick (18 percent). The even distribution, particularly between positive and negative inducements, contradicts the view that crisis bargaining is predominantly coercive, at least in so far as the frequency of particular types of inducements is concerned.

Degree of coercion. The second inducement attribute of interest is the degree of coercion. The predictions of the two models with regard to the degree of coercion are comparable to those for inducement types. According to the realist model, the greater the degree of coercive inducement, particularly a demonstration of resolve and risk

123

Table 6.3. *Degree of coercion and response types*

Degree of coercion	Response Types						
	Positive	Mixed	Ignore	Defy	Mixed-F[a]	Defy-F[a]	Total
No inducement	20 (0.10)	19 (0.09)	104 (0.50)	26 (0.07)	15 (0.13)	24 (0.12)	208 (1.00)
Positive	39 (0.25)	22 (0.14)	54 (0.34)	11 (0.07)	25 (0.16)	7 (0.04)	158 (1.00)
Threat	23 (0.22)	17 (0.17)	30 (0.29)	9 (0.09)	14 (0.14)	10 (0.10)	103 (1.00)
Threat of force	17 (0.10)	25 (0.15)	47 (0.29)	14 (0.09)	31 (0.19)	30 (0.18)	164 (1.00)
Use force	3 (0.07)	5 (0.11)	0 (0.00)	1 (0.02)	15 (0.34)	20 (0.46)	44 (1.00)
Total	102 (0.15)	88 (0.13)	235 (0.35)	61 (0.09)	100 (0.15)	91 (0.13)	677 (1.00)

[a] Mixed-F and Defy-F are mixed and defy responses including either the threat or use of force.
Figures in parentheses are percentages.

acceptance through the threat or use of military force, the greater the likelihood of an accommodative response, on the other hand, any reduction in the degree of coercion would be perceived as a sign of weakness and encourage a negative response. Once again, the reciprocating model predicts target responses in kind, that is, the more severe the threat, the more defiant the response, the more accommodating the positive inducement, the more accommodating the response.

Table 6.3 presents the association of influence attempts, categorized according to the degree of coercion, with types of responses. The frequencies and percentages appearing in Table 6.3 are once again consistent with the reciprocating model, while running counter to the predictions of the realist model. The highest percentage (25 percent) of positive (comply or placate) responses occurs when the actor offers a positive concession. In fact, as inducements become more coercive in the remaining categories, there is a *consistent decline* in the percentage of positive responses and a *consistent upward* trend in defy responses and in mixed and defy responses containing the threat or use of force. The proportion of coercive response types associated with the degree of coercion employed in the inducements are: positive inducements = 27 percent, nonmilitary threats = 33 percent, threats of force = 46 percent, and the use of force = 82 percent. Thus, the responses to the degree of inducement are again remarkably consistent with the predictions of the reciprocating model, as well as statistically significant. The differences across categories in Table 6.3 yield a chi-square score of 132 which, with 20 degrees of freedom, is significant at the $p = 0.001$ level. Given what we observed with regard to inducement *types* and responses, these results are not surprising. That is, we should expect that whatever pattern is observed in the association between inducement types and responses would become more pronounced as the degree of positive or negative inducement is increased.

Specificity of inducements. The indicator of the actor's commitment to carry out its threats and promises is based on the specificity of the actor's communication of the conditions under which it will act, and of the action that it intends to take if those conditions materialize.

Table 6.4 divides each of the three types of inducements (positive, negative, and carrot-and-stick) into three subcategories based on degree of specificity. *Ultimatums and unconditional promises* are inducements that are: (1) conditional upon action or inaction by the target; and (b) that specify the action to be taken in the case of noncompliance, in the case of threats, or compliance in the case of promises, along with the deadline for compliance. Thus the conditions for acting, the deadline for compliance, and the action to be taken in the event of compliance, or noncompliance, are all specified. In the case of simple *threats or promises*, the conditions for acting and the action to be taken by the actor are specified, but the target is not presented with a deadline. *Warnings and unspecified promises* are the vaguest of inducements; there may be ambiguity regarding the conditions for acting, as well as the action to be taken. The distinctions among these three subcategories are based on the assumption that the more specific the actor is in communicating what it intends to do, when it intends to do it, and under what conditions it will or will not do it, the greater the credibility of its commitment to carrying out the promised or threatened action.

Realism posits that, as the actor's commitment to carry out its inducements increases, so should the likelihood of an accommodative response from the target. The reciprocating model predicts that increases in the actor's commitment to carry out its inducements would increase the target's likelihood to respond in kind in both instances.

The relationships between inducement specificity and responses depicted in Table 6.4 once again are more consistent with the reciprocating model of crisis bargaining, although the associations are not as impressive as those found with type and degree of inducement. Ultimatums are most frequently associated with defy responses, which is what would be predicted by the reciprocating model. Threats are more likely than warnings to be associated with mixed or defy responses that include the threat of force. The associations, however, are less

Table 6.4. *Inducement specificity and responses*

Specificity	Response Types						
	Positive	Mixed	Ignore	Defy	Mixed-F[a]	Defy-F[a]	Total
Warning	2 (0.15)	2 (0.15)	3 (0.23)	4 (0.31)	2 (0.15)	0 (0.00)	13 (1.00)
Threat	16 (0.12)	12 (0.09)	50 (0.37)	9 (0.07)	22 (0.16)	25 (0.19)	134 (1.00)
Ultimatum	0 (0.00)	3 (0.20)	5 (0.33)	0 (0.07)	1 (0.07)	5(0.33)	15 (1.00)
Unspecified promise	0 (0.00)	0 (0.00)	3 (0.75)	0 (0.00)	1 (0.25)	0 (0.00)	4 (1.00)
Promise	23 (0.26)	8 (0.09)	35 (0.40)	8 (0.09)	9 (0.10)	5 (0.06)	88 (1.00)
Unconditional promise	9 (0.25)	4 (0.11)	11 (0.31)	2 (0.06)	8 (0.22)	2 (0.06)	36 (1.00)
C&S ultimatum	0 (0.00)	1 (0.33)	0 (0.00)	0 (0.00)	0 (0.00)	2 (0.67)	3 (1.00)
C&S Threat	12 (0.19)	9 (0.15)	9 (0.15)	5 (0.08)	18 (0.29)	9 (0.15)	62 (1.00)
C&S Warning	1 (0.25)	0 (0.00)	0 (0.00)	0 (0.00)	2 (0.50)	1 (0.25)	4 (1.00)

[a] Defy-F and Mixed-F are defy and mixed responses accompanied by the threat or use of military force. C&S = Carrot-and-stick
Numbers represent frequencyy counts with percentages in parentheses.

impressive than those for either the type or degree of inducement. In fact, none of the three tables representing the three levels of specificity within a particular type of inducement produces associations that are statistically significant.

Some tentative conclusions: The findings in Tables 6.1–6.4 overwhelmingly support the predictions of the reciprocating model over those of the realist model. These results, however, are based solely on a model that assumes that behavior begets behavior, and no examination of the validity of the realist model would be complete without including distinctions based on the structure of the crisis. In Chapter 3 and 5 we found evidence indicating positive associations between the crisis structure and crisis outcomes, and between the crisis structure and the degree of crisis escalation. Could it be that the reciprocating response pattern that we have found is a consequence of *both* parties following the prescriptions of realism in crises between evenly matched adversaries? This is an intriguing question in light of an earlier study of influence attempts (Leng, 1980:149), which found a slightly higher rate of defiant responses occurring in crises where the disputants were roughly evenly matched in military capabilities.

Crisis structure and influence attempts

The critical structural components, from a realist vantage point, are two: the interests at stake and the comparative war-fighting

126

capabilities of the two sides. The intersection of the interests and capabilities of the two sides defines the crisis structure and, according to the realist model, the risk acceptance of the two sides. The operational indicators of the two structural variables were described in detail in Chapter 3, so I will restate only their principal components in the discussion that follows.

Interests. The interests at stake range from vital interests (territorial integrity or political independence), to other security interests, to political or economic issues not involving national security. The realist expectation would be that states would respond more belligerently to all influence attempts when the stakes, defined in terms of security interests, were higher.

In fact, an examination of subtables of associations of inducements and responses, subdivided according to the category of interests at stake for the target, does not indicate any significant differences across the three interest categories. Based on the interests at stake, the target responses offer no support for the realist model. On the other hand, there is an interesting pattern in the relationship between the interests at stake for the target and the *actor's choice of type of inducement*. As the *target's* stakes increase, there is a consistent upward trend in the percentage of total inducements that are coercive (17 percent, 25 percent, 35 percent) and a consistent downward trend in positive inducements (25 percent, 21 percent, 13 percent). These percentages suggest an intriguing possibility, that is, although policy-makers in crises do not respond to influence attempts in accordance with the prescriptions of realism, they may assume that their adversaries do. That would lead to a particularly dangerous mix of the two models: policy-makers would be behaving according to the reciprocating model in responding in a tit-for-tat manner to threats and promises, but, in assuming that their adversaries are rational and prudent, they would rely upon escalating coercive inducements in their own influence attempts. The combination is a recipe for escalating conflict.

In Chapter 3 we found that, even if the two sides were unevenly matched in capabilities, if the weaker party had vital interests at stake, the crisis was likely to escalate to war. We now may have found a clue as to why that is the case.

Perceived comparative capabilities. Each of the categories of response types remains relatively constant across the three capability categories, indicating no significant relationship between the target's perceived comparative war-fighting capability and its responses to influence attempts.[8] The slightly higher rate of defiant responses associated with crises in which the adversaries were evenly matched in military capa-

127

bility, which was observed in an earlier study (Leng, 1980), does not hold up in the larger sample employed in this study; the percentages across capability categories are virtually even.[9] Nor is there evidence to suggest that capability considerations affect the credibility of inducements.

These results are not entirely surprising given findings from other studies. In a review of a wide range of empirical studies focusing on deterrence, and responses to threats, in militarized disputes and crises, Levy (1988:507) concludes that the overall balance of military capabilities between two states has little influence on the effectiveness of military threats in general.[10] Nor is it difficult to think of historical examples that fit the aggregate findings. The classic example is Thucydides account of the Melian decision to resist an Athenian ultimatum despite an overwhelming military disadvantage. The first major quantitative study of the events and perceptions of leaders in a modern crisis, the Stanford study of the origins of World War I, concluded that for German and Austrian leaders perceptions of the hostility of the Entente powers overshadowed their perception of military inferiority in deciding to go to war (Zinnes, North, and Koch, 1961; North, Holsti, and Brody, 1964). Interestingly, most of the studies cited by Levy (1988) indicate that interests, or interests combined with capabilities, are the key determining variables.

Combined capabilities and interests. With that point in mind, a more adequate test of the realist model might be to combine the two structural variables for each side, as we did in Chapter 5, into a single *motivation* score. The motivation scores for each side, in each crisis, appear in column 6 of Table 3.1

This time, although the patterns are not dramatic, there is some indication of modest support for the realist model. Accommodating responses occur most frequently (18 percent of all responses) when the motivation score is low (2) and more consistently downward to a low of 9 percent when the target's motivation is high (5 or 6). Defy or mixed responses, which include the threat or use of force, occur more frequently when the motivation is 4 (17 percent) or 5 or 6 (14 percent) than when it is 2 (9 percent) or 3 (10 percent). These patterns are consistent with the realist model; however, the patterns of mixed and defy responses without accompanying threats of force are not. The former occurs most often (18 percent) when the motivation level is 2, the latter occurs most often when it is 5 or 6 (15 percent).

When the findings are examined at the micro-level, that is, with regard to the link between inducement categories and responses across different levels of target motivation, the distribution of response types across inducement categories remains consistent with the findings obtained in our analysis of categories of inducements alone, and those findings supported the reciprocating model. Bearing in mind that the reciprocating model's predictions are indifferent to the crisis structure, what we appear to be seeing is a weak effect of structural variables on responses in the direction predicted by the realist model, but only in those instances for which the reciprocating model makes no prediction. However when the predictions of the two models are contradictory, we find strong support for the reciprocating model over the realist model, regardless of variations in the crisis structure.

A multivariate model

To this point, the analysis has focused on the bivariate relationships between each of six independent variables with the target's response. The observed bivariate associations of each of the independent variables may be summarized as follows. There appears to be: (1) strong associations, consistent with the predictions of the reciprocating model, between types of inducements and responses; (2) a fairly strong association, consistent with the reciprocating model, between the specificity of inducements and response types; (3) a weak association, consistent with the realist model, between response types and cost of compliance, interests, and combined capabilities and interests (motivation).

This gives us a sense of the relative salience of the individual predictor variables, but it does not tell us anything about possible interaction effects among those variables. Given the assumptions with which we began the analysis, we would expect some interaction effects among three of the independent variables: type, degree, and specificity of inducements. The assumptions of both the realist and reciprocating models indicate that the predicted patterns of responses following particular types of inducements should become more pronounced as the degree and/or specificity of those types are increased. There also is the related question of which of the eight putative predictor variables are necessary components of a predictive model of influence attempt–response sequences, and which could be excluded. Given the constraints of categorical data, a log-linear approach represents the most efficient means of attempting to answer these questions.

Log-linear analysis is based on fitting a hierarchical model to a multivariate table containing the cell frequencies for each of the categories of each of the variables. The procedure is analogous to that of analysis of variance, except that one is working with cell frequencies or probabilities rather than with individual scores. Logarithms of the

129

expected cell frequencies are written as additive functions of the main effects and interactions of the variables of interest. The presence or absence of these effects provides insight into the relationships, if any, among the variables of interest.[11]

Determining the model. A log-linear model containing all the variables of interest, with all potential effects and interactions, is termed a "saturated" model. For example, a saturated model consisting of three variables: x, y, and z, would have the following effects: x, y, z, xy, xz, yz, and xyz. A saturated model, containing all possible effects, would fit the data perfectly. Thus, one way of searching for the most parsimonious model is by beginning with a saturated model and deleting terms in a stepwise manner to determine what levels of interaction, and which variables, are necessary to obtain a model providing a good fit to the data. The goodness-of-fit of the model can be estimated with a Pearson chi-square or likelihood ratio chi-square.[12]

The size of the sample (677 observations) does not permit simply beginning with all eight of the variables, including all possible effects, in a saturated model, so some partitioning was necessary in beginning the analysis. The first step was to screen out unnecessary interaction effects through tests of partial and marginal associations among factors. These operations test the hypothesis that the partial and marginal associations between factors in a specified effect is zero. The test of marginal and partial associations enabled us to reduce the number of necessary variables to four: type (t), degree (d), and specificity (s) of inducements, and response (r). The chi-square scores for this test, for these four variables and their possible effects, appear in Table 6.5. Note that the variables that have been dropped from the model (cost of compliance, interests, capabilities, and motivation) are those that also yielded the weakest bivariate associations with target responses.

The result of this initial pass through the data also indicated that only one-third order interaction effect (type, degree, and specificity, or *tds*) is a necessary component of the model. Given the hierarchical nature of the model, this also includes the terms: t, d, s, td, ts, and ds. Two other second-order interactions (tr) and dr) also yielded significant chi-square scores ($p < 0.05$). The second-order effect, sr, was not significant.

These results suggest a model consisting of all possible interactions of: (1) type, degree, and specificity (*tds*) with each other; (2) type with response (tr); and (3) degree with response (dr). A second screening, using a step-wise deletion process, was conducted, beginning with the four variables identified in the test of marginal and partial associations,

Table 6.5. *Log-linear partial and marginal associations: four variabales*

| Variable | \| Partial association \| \| \| | \| \| \| \| | \| \| | Marginal association | | |
	DF	Chi-sq.	Probab-ility	Iter-ations	DF	Chi-sq.	Probab-ility	Iter-ations
type	3	20.21	0.0002					
degree	4	104.77	0.0000					
specificity	3	344.97	0.0000					
response	3	46.27	0.0000					
td	12	616.37	0.0000	16	12	1044.95	0.0000	2
ts	9	51.15	0.0000	13	9	473.90	0.0000	2
tr	9	27.69	0.0011	12	9	75.86	0.0000	2
ds	12	110.37	0.0000	20	12	498.21	0.0000	2
dr	12	27.31	0.0070	13	12	76.57	0.0000	2
sr	9	5.40	0.7979	20	9	12.82	0.1707	2
tds	36	72.04	0.0003	16	36	78.73	0.0001	16
tdr	36	10.61	1.0000	20	36	18.83	0.9918	20
tsr	27	4.51	1.0000	10	27	26.41	0.4959	13
dsr	36	18.05	0.9945	10	36	38.16	0.3715	14

DF = Degrees of Freedom
t = type; *d* = degree; *s* = specificity of inducement; *r* = response type

but with only one third order interaction effect (*tds*). This approach yielded the same results as the test of marginal and partial associations, that is, a model consisting of *tds*, *tr*, and *dr*. A test of the overall fit of this model to the observed frequencies in the data, yielded a likelihood ratio chi-square of 65.43 and 216 degrees of freedom, and a probability of 1.00, which is a very good fit.

The model tells us that there are significant associations in the data among all three of the remaining independent variables – type, degree, and specificity of inducements – and, most interesting, given the purpose of this investigation, not only are the most significant associations with response obtained from simple second order interactions with degree of inducement and type of inducement, but this model provides an excellent overall fit to the data. An intuitive interpretation of these results suggests that, although there are significant interaction effects *among* the three inducement attributes, the variation in responses may be explained by the direct effects of variations in type of inducements employed and the degree of coercion.

Estimating parameters. Log-linear analysis allows us to go one step further to estimate the nature and strength of the relationships between the variables through an analysis of the effect parameters. This provides a useful check against some of the specific relationships observed in the cross-tabular analysis discussed earlier. Estimates of

131

Table 6.6. *Log-linear parameter estimates: inducement type and response*

Response	Inducement type			
	None	Positive	Carrot & Stick	Negative
Positive	−0.103	0.248	0.102	−0.246
Mixed	−0.233	−0.074	0.381	−0.085
Ignore	0.293	0.149	−0.549	0.107
Defy	0.033	−0.323	0.066	0.244

the log-linear parameters for the two effects of interest – *tr* and *dr* – appear in Tables 6.6 and 6.7. The scores confirm the bivariate findings, while adding some insights into the strength of those associations.

Table 6.6 presents the parameter estimates for *tr*, that is the relationship between inducement type and response. Note the high level of reciprocity exhibited in the relationships between positive, negative, and carrot-and-stick inducements with positive, negative, and mixed responses respectively, and the negative associations between positive inducements and defy responses, and between negative inducements and positive responses. The pattern is consistent with the bivariate findings favoring the reciprocating model over the realist model. One intriguing relationship that did not stand out in the contingency table analysis, however, is the strong negative relationship (−0.55) between carrot-and-stick inducements and ignore responses. This indicates that carrot-and-stick inducements are more likely to elicit some response, usually mixed, than either threats or promises alone.

Table 6.7 presents the parameter estimates for the interaction effects between degree of inducement and response. The scores in Table 6.7 also are consistent with the findings favoring the reciprocating model in the cross-tubular analyses. The most striking of these are the parameter estimates for the positive relationship between the use of force and defy responses (0.52) and, not surprisingly, the negative relationship between the use of force and ignore responses (–0.71). The one exception to the pattern suggested by the reciprocating model is the lack of a positive relationship between threats of force and defy responses. This is intriguing in light of the strong association between negative inducements and defy responses noted above. It may be that threats of force accompanying carrot-and-stick inducements are associated with mixed responses, but it could also be that target states employing a "firm-but-flexible" reciprocating bargaining strategy might respond in a mixed manner to threats of force, for example, with a counter-threat accompanied by an offer to negotiate.

132

Table 6.7. *Log-linear parameter estimates: degree of inducement and response*

	Degree of Inducement				
Response	None	Reduce force	No threat of force	Threat of force	Use of force
Positive	−0.227	0.145	0.324	−0.196	−0.047
Mixed	−0.239	0.057	−0.107	0.050	0.239
Ignore	0.390	0.084	0.089	0.149	−0.713
Defy	0.076	−0.286	−0.307	−0.003	0.521

Summary of log linear findings. The log-linear analysis has allowed us to uncover the structure of a model that indicates that the key to predicting target responses to influence attempts in our sample of forty crises lies in the type and degree of inducements employed. These two variables interact with each other and with the specificity of inducements. It also is important to note what is *not* necessary to obtain an adequate fit of the model: the cost of compliance, the target's perception of its relative capability, of its interests, and of its interests and capability combined, are not significant predictors of how the target will respond to individual influence attempts. The strongest association lies in the bargaining techniques employed by the would-be influencer. In addition to uncovering the structure of a remarkably parsimonious model, the analyses confirm the consistent superiority of the reciprocating model of influence over the realist model. In this respect the relationships appearing in the parameter estimates in Tables 6.6 and 6.7 are consistent with the findings in the cross-tabular analyses of bivariate relationships.

Summary and conclusion

Summary

The analyses in this chapter have focused on a comparison of two competing perspectives on influence techniques in militarized crises, which I have labeled the realist and reciprocating models. We have found only modest support for the realist model, and then only when its predictions did not contradict those of the reciprocating model. We found a weak positive association between the target's motivation, that is, a combination of its perception of its comparative war-fighting capabilities and the interests at stake, and defiant responses. While this finding is consistent with the realist model, it is in no way inconsistent with a reciprocating model.

On the other hand, in every instance where the two models made contradictory predictions, and most particularly with regard to target responses based on the type of inducement or the degree of inducement, the findings *consistently* have supported the reciprocating model over the realist model. Moreover, the results of the log-linear analysis have added confirmation to the impression, gained from the bivariate analyses, that these two variables accounted for the greatest degree of variation among the types of responses chosen by the target state. In fact, although eight variables were used in the study, a model based solely on the three attributes of inducements (type, degree, and specificity) and response types provides an excellent fit to the data from the sample of forty militarized crises. This model tells us: (1) that the states in the sample were overwhelmingly likely to respond in kind to inducements from would-be influencers; (2) that as inducements became more coercive, there was a consistent pattern toward more coercive responses; and (3) that this pattern was not significantly affected by the relative capabilities of the disputants and/or the interests at stake for the target.

In the process of conducting the tests of the competing models, a number of intriguing *descriptive* findings also emerged. (1) Contrary to the common view that crisis bargaining is primarily coercive, we found that the types of inducements employed by states in the sample are relatively evenly distributed across accommodative, coercive, and carrot-and-stick inducements. (2) The threat or use of force is rarely ignored, but it is used less often than one might expect in militarized crises. Influence attempts employ the threat of force about 24 percent of the time; the use of force appears in only 6 percent of the influence attempts. (3) As we noted in a different context in an earlier study (Gochman and Leng, 1983), actions speak louder than words; there are very few instances of attempts being ignored when they are accompanied by either rewards or punishments. (4) And, we found that carrot-and-stick inducements are more likely to elicit *some* response than either threats or promises alone.

Conclusions

The realist and reciprocating models of crisis bargaining each prescribe an approach to crisis bargaining that is based on predictions regarding how states are likely to respond to different influence attempts. The findings in this chapter clearly and consistently support the predictions of the reciprocating model over those of the realist model.

It is important, however, to recognize the limitations of the approach that we have taken in this chapter. One limitation lies in an analysis of individual influence attempt–response sequences that neglects the overall patterns that may obtain when one has the opportunity to observe influence strategies employed over the course of a crisis. For example, have we been observing instances of accommodative responses to positive inducements that have come only at the end of a series of escalating coercive inducements by the other party? By taking individual influence attempt–response sequences out of the context of an overall influence strategy, we cannot answer that question. We need to examine the influence *strategies* employed by states over the course of the crisis.

A corresponding limitation lies in our observation of the target's response. Do policy-makers tend to respond in kind initially in order to maintain their prestige and reputation for resolve, in the case of threats, or their reputation for fairness, in the case of promises, and then move to a more prudent response at a later date? The answer to that question also requires an examination of the target's overall response strategy as well. We will turn to an examination of influence strategies and, to a lesser extent, response strategies, in the next chapter.

7 INFLUENCE STRATEGIES

What constitutes the most effective influence strategy in a militarized crisis? The classical realist prescription is to "demonstrate power" through coercive inducements, albeit within the bounds of a prudential assessment of comparative military capabilities. That prescription is extended to the techniques of crisis bargaining by conflict strategists, who emphasize coercive techniques designed to credibly demonstrate resolve. Realism's critics, on the other hand, have pointed to the dangers associated with undertaking a strategy of escalating coercion, as well as to the possibilities of deescalating the crisis through a series of reciprocated accommodative moves.

Two books published in the early 1960s were particularly influential in setting the course of the debate over these two perspectives. The first was Schelling's *Strategy of Conflict* (1960), a game theoretic discussion that treated interstate conflicts as games of strategy, in which the object was to win. The second was Osgood's *An Alternative to War or Surrender* (1962), a proposal for a graduated reduction in US–Soviet tensions (GRIT), which focused on the tendency of disputants to respond to accommodative initiatives in a reciprocating manner.[1] These studies are representative of the ensuing debate between strategic and psychological approaches to understanding interstate conflict, and between realist and reciprocating bargaining prescriptions. Much of the discussion of the conflict strategists' approach to crisis bargaining in the preceding chapters has been drawn from Schelling. In this chapter, we will begin with a closer look at research that has proceeded in a direction closer to that suggested by Osgood, and then proceed to compare the effectiveness of influence strategies based on the different assumptions underlying the two perspectives.

Eliciting cooperation

Osgood (1962) proposed that one side initiate a reduction in tensions through a series of pre-announced unilateral accommodative steps. The program of unilateral accommodative initiatives would be continued for some time regardless of the initial responses from the other side, but its progress would be accelerated or decelerated in frequency and magnitude depending on the degree of reciprocation by the other party. The central assumption behind GRIT is that the deescalation of conflict begins with the removal of those psychological factors that propel escalation – insecurity, distrust, threats to prestige – through accommodative initiatives.

An influence strategy that might achieve a balance between the conflict strategists' emphasis on the need to credibly demonstrate resolve, on the one hand, and avoidance of the dysfunctional psychological consequences of aggressive behavior that are emphasized by social psychologists like Osgood, on the other hand, was suggested in a series of interpersonal bargaining experiments conducted by Esser and Komorita (1975). Esser and Komorita found that the most effective influence strategy was one that combined firmness in the face of threats, or other bullying tactics, with a willingness to move to reciprocal accommodation. What Esser and Komorita called a "firm-but-fair" strategy, combined tit-for-tat responses to either positive or negative inducements with occasional unilateral concessions to encourage positive responses from the other party.

Esser and Komorita's (1975) investigation grew out of experiments with Prisoner's Dilemma games. There will be several references to experiments with Prisoner's Dilemma games in the course of the discussion in this chapter and the next, so a brief description of the game may be useful.

Prisoner's Dilemma is one of a series of two-by-two games in which each player chooses between two strategies: cooperate or defect. In drawing an analogy to an interstate crisis, "cooperate" can be viewed as the selection of an accommodative influence attempt, and "defect" can be interpreted as the use of coercion. The game appears as a simple two-by-two outcome matrix, with the outcome of each game determined by the intersection of the strategy choices of the two players. In an experiment like that of Esser and Komorita, the moves of the two players are made simultaneously, with each player aware of the "pay-offs" to each side that are associated with each outcome. Based on the pay-offs that they will receive, each player can estimate its own and the other side's preferences among the four possible outcomes. The game can be played for any number of repetitions, with each player having the option of changing its strategy after viewing the outcome following each play of the game.

The matrix for a Prisoner's Dilemma game is displayed in Table 7.1.

Table 7.1. *Prisoner's Dilemma game*

		Column strategies	
		Cooperate	Defect
Row strategies	Cooperate	Compromise (3,3)	Column victory (1,4)
	Defect	Row victory (4,1)	War (2,2)

The numbers within the cells in Table 7.1 represent the ranked outcome preferences for each of the players: 4 represents the player's best outcome; 3 is its next best outcome; 2 is its second worst outcome, and 1 represents the player's worst outcome. Within each cell, the outcome utility for row appears on the left, and the outcome utility for column appears on the right. In the Prisoner's Dilemma game depicted in Table 7.1, we can view the outcomes represented in each cell as analogous to crisis outcomes, with both sides preferring victory over compromise, compromise over war, and war over submission. Working clockwise from the upper left hand cell (row 1, column 1), the outcomes would appear as: r1c1 = compromise settlement, r1c2 = row submits to column, r2c1 = column submits to row, and r2c2 = war. Since neither side knows which strategy the other will choose, the dominant strategy choice, for either player, in Prisoner's Dilemma, is Defect (D). By choosing strategy D, a player either receives its best outcome (4), or its second worst outcome (2), while strategy C yields the player either its second best outcome (3), or its worst outcome (1).

The "dilemma" in Prisoner's Dilemma results from the fact that, if both players defect (D), they each end up with their second worst outcomes (2,2); whereas had they each chosen to cooperate (C), they would both have attained their second best outcomes (3,3). Prisoner's Dilemma illustrates the tension between individual rationality and collective rationality, or between short-term and long-term rationality (see Rapoport, 1974:ch. 1). In this respect, Prisoner's Dilemma captures the tension between the prescriptions of the conflict strategists, which are based on the assumptions of self-interested rationality, and the dysfunctional escalatory consequences suggested by the psychological perspective.

In experiments like those of Esser and Komorita, Prisoner's Dilemma is played over many iterations, with the pay-offs from each play of the game accumulating, and with each player aware of the outcomes of previous plays of the game. Beyond choosing the strategy for a particular play of the game, the players conceive of longer term strategies based on the pattern of outcomes of previous plays. Working from this perspective, it is possible to conceive of strategies that are more likely to elicit mutual compromise, so that both players can attain their second best, rather than their second worst, outcomes.

Perhaps the most widely discussed Prisoner's Dilemma experiment was a computer tournament organized by Axelrod (1984), in which the contestants were asked to design what they considered the most effective iterative strategy. Each of the strategies submitted was paired against each of the other submissions for many iterations of a Prisoner's Dilemma game. The winning strategy, was submitted by Anatol Rapoport, a noted game theorist. Rapoport's Tit-for-Tat (TFT) strategy began with an initial cooperation move, and then followed a strict strategy of responding in kind to the other player's previous move for the remainder of the repetitions of the game. If the other side defected, the Tit-for-Tat player would defect on the next move, if the other side cooperated, Tit-for-Tat would chose cooperation on its next move, and so on.

Computer games, of course, are far removed from interstate crisis bargaining; moreover, the rules of simultaneous play that were employed in the tournament do not fit the pattern of alternating moves that characterize real world bargaining. Nevertheless, the potential effectiveness of TFT has suggestive implications for interstate crisis bargaining, where reciprocity assumes such a prominent role, both as a norm for relations among states (see Gouldner, 1960), and as an observed component of interstate conflict behavior. It is of immediate interest to us, because of the high level of reciprocity that we observed between individual influence attempts and responses in Chapter 6. Moreover, the effectiveness of an overall influence strategy based on reciprocating inducements was suggested in the results of an earlier study by Leng and Wheeler (1979), of the influence strategies of states engaged in twenty crises occurring between 1900 and 1975. The Leng and Wheeler findings indicated that a Reciprocating influence strategy, based on the Esser and Komorita (1975) model, was the most effective overall influence strategy among the types considered in the sample. Similar results have been reported by Huth (1988) in a subsequent study of extended deterrence.

Coercive bargaining

The findings from these studies challenge the conflict strategists' view that the most effective influence strategy in a militarized crisis, where national security is threatened directly, is one that demonstrates a willingness to accept a high risk of war in order to achieve national objectives. According to this perspective, a strong demonstration of resolve, coupled with escalating coercive inducements designed to raise the costs and risks of noncompliance, is the best way to lower the opponent's aspirations and to further the interests of your own state. Much of the writing of conflict strategists (Schelling, 1966; Kahn, 1965) deals with the manipulation of risk through a policy of controlled escalation in coercive inducements, or what Leng and Wheeler (1979) have labeled a "Bullying" influence strategy.

Some empirical support for the effectiveness of an escalating coercive approach has been found in interpersonal bargaining experiments (Bartos, 1970; Yukl, 1974), and we found, in Chapter 5, that the side employing the first threat of force and exhibiting more aggressive behavior over the course of the crisis was more likely to prevail in those crises that ended in one-sided peaceful outcomes. On the other hand, experiments by Worchal and Brehm (1971) support the reactance hypothesis described in Chapter 1, which posits that individuals or groups whose freedom is threatened are likely to respond in an aggressive manner to defend their freedom. The examination, in Chapter 6, of the responses of states to coercive influence attempts suggested that the behavior of states in militarized crises is more consistent with the reactance hypothesis, than with realist views.

It is possible that what we observed in Chapter 6 were only the *immediate* responses of prestige conscious policy-makers, who were anxious to save face before a domestic audience. Following the initial gesture, they may then have yielded before what they perceived as superior capability and resolve. In fact, there may be a pattern of several coercive influence attempts meeting defiant responses until the weaker, or less determined, party finally yields. While such patterns would indicate that there is some validity to the reactance hypothesis, they would not negate the ultimate effectiveness of a Bullying influence strategy.

The analyses in this chapter return to the comparison of the relative effectiveness of Bullying and Reciprocating influence strategies, along with two other types initially reported by Leng and Wheeler (1979), but with a considerably larger sample of crises and more rigorous

140

INFLUENCE STRATEGIES

measurement techniques. We will consider also the relationship between policy-makers' perceptions of the crisis structure and their choices of influence strategies. The first steps in this undertaking are to describe the four basic types of influence strategies and the means of determining which is the predominant type employed by each side in a given crisis.

Influence strategies

Bullying

A Bullying influence strategy is based on escalating coercive inducements. Any response short of compliance with the actor's demands is met with a more severe threat or punishment. This pattern continues with each successive influence attempt–response sequence until the target has been induced to comply with the actor's demands. A modest departure from the purely coercive bargaining may occur when the actor follows a series of escalating coercive inducements with a carrot-and-stick inducement containing a modest "face-saving" concession for the other side.

Bullying strategies are based on the conflict strategists' view of crisis bargaining as akin to a competition in risk-taking, where the risk is the outbreak of war. By escalating the level of coercion, the actor demonstrates its resolve: its willingness to accept high costs and risk to achieve its objectives and its confidence in its ability to prevail in war. Crisis bargaining power, as Snyder and Diesing (1977:190) define it, is viewed as a function of "perceived comparative resolve"; the party communicating greater resolve should prevail, all other things being equal. The objections to this view have been noted above: the encouragement of an escalatory process that can run out of control, the absence of accommodative inducements to encourage compromise, and the neglect of psychological variables influencing conflict behavior, particularly psychological reactance to threats.

Reciprocating

A Reciprocating influence strategy consists of responding in kind to the actions of the other side, along with occasional unilateral cooperative influence attempts. The cooperative moves are terminated immediately if the other side does not respond in kind. The reciprocating party, however, does not *initiate* any coercive influence attempts.

A Reciprocating strategy differs from a strict TFT strategy in the

141

timing of cooperative initiatives. TFT requires that the player issue a cooperative initiative on the first move of the game. But, the "first moves" in an interstate crisis are, almost by definition, conflictive: the precipitant action and the challenge to that action from the other side. Thus, as in a GRIT strategy, the cooperative moves in a Reciprocating strategy come after the crisis has begun, and they serve the purpose of signaling a willingness to cooperate in an environment that already has become quite contentious. The approach conforms with TFT rather than GRIT, however, in that the cooperative moves are quickly terminated if the other side does not respond in a positive manner.

The objective of a Reciprocating strategy is to demonstrate firmness in the face of coercive inducements, along with a willingness to respond in kind to accommodative moves. Advocates of a reciprocating approach base their prescriptions on its consistency with the reciprocity norm in international politics, the observed tendency of states to behave in a reciprocal manner in the course of conflicts, and the strategy's nonthreatening and forgiving qualities.

Appeasing

An Appeasing influence strategy is the opposite of the Bullying strategy. Anything short of compliance by the target results in more positive inducements. The key assumption behind an Appeasing influence strategy is that the opponent has finite demands that can be satisfied at an acceptable cost to the appeaser.

Appeasement has been infamous ever since the Munich crisis of 1938–39, but it is not an entirely illogical strategy. It would appear to be an appropriate approach for a state dealing with weaker opponents, who would not be likely to interpret concessions as signs of weakness, or when dealing with stronger opponents who have limited objectives. In any event, how often states actually employ Appeasing strategies in crises, and the relative effectiveness or ineffectiveness of Appeasing strategies are open questions that are worth a closer look.

Trial-and-Error

Each of the first three influence strategies assumes that the actor holds definite assumptions about what is most likely to motivate the target to comply with the actor's demands, and that the actor has developed an influence strategy based on those assumptions. A Trial-

and-Error influence strategy makes no such assumptions. The actor simply adjusts its choice of inducements based on the target's response to the preceding influence attempt. Inducements that produce positive responses are repeated; inducements that produce negative responses are changed. The decision-makers proceed inductively, by trying one approach after another until they find an influence attempt that produces the desired response.

The experimental research that has been done on trial-and-error has been directed to its efficiency as an approach to learning. Most of the work done by social psychologists (Braver and Rohrer, 1978; Stephan, 1975) suggests that it is less effective than vicarious learning, particularly when the learner is being conditioned to move to less competitive behavior. As an influence strategy in interstate conflicts, it would appear to suffer from inefficiency and inconsistency. On the other hand, there are good reasons to expect to find evidence of Trial-and-Error strategies by nations trying to bargain in an uncertain environment. In fact, what appears as a conscious Trial-and-Error strategy may well be the result of disagreement within the decision-making body, particularly between hard-line and soft-line factions, with one faction or the other gaining ascendency as the crisis evolves.

Stonewalling

A fifth influence strategy consists of essentially ignoring all inducements from the other party, without initiating any influence attempts. The "Stonewalling" party attempts to assume the position of an immovable object, without attempting any coercive or accommodative inducements of its own.

This category has been added to the typology of influence attempts after observing a few cases in which this appeared to most accurately describe the behavior of one of the disputants. The policy appears to occur when the Stonewalling government has decided that the other party is unalterably bent on hostilities to achieve demands that are clearly too excessive to be yielded, yet the Stonewalling side has no feasible means of influencing the behavior of the other party. National leaders who are faced with nothing but unacceptable choices may do nothing rather than choose the lesser of two evils. They may stall in the hope that the situation will improve, perhaps through the intervention of a third party, or they may be immobilized by indecision. Others may deem the demands of the opposite side unworthy of attempts at bargaining, and simply prepare for war.

143

Outcomes

The comparative effectiveness of each of the five types of influence strategies will be judged according to the outcomes of the crises in our sample. There are five possibilities: (1) a diplomatic victory short of war; (2) a compromise settlement; (3) a stalemate; (4) an unwanted war; and (5) a diplomatic defeat. The comparative merits of a diplomatic defeat, a stalemate, or an unwanted war, of course, can vary from one situation to another, or in the minds of one set of decision-makers or another. Consequently, the distinction that will be of most interest to us will be that between a diplomatic victory or compromise on the one hand, and stalemate, war, or defeat on the other. Nevertheless, the five category distinction will be useful in allowing us to observe which outcomes are most often associated with which influence strategies.[2]

Indicator construction

Influence strategies

Determination of the overall influence strategy for a given side in a crisis is complicated by several factors. Actors can change their strategies over the course of the dispute; the decision-making body itself may not be entirely clear regarding the strategy it is employing; the observable behavior of the actor may coincide with more than one strategy with enough frequency to make it difficult to tell which is the intended strategy. In the face of these potential ambiguities, we will examine four different indicators of the *predominant* influence strategy employed by a given side: (1) the behavior patterns represented by the time series of cooperative and conflictive actions; (2) the predominant influence strategy appearing in the sequence of influence attempts by that side; (3) the predominant influence strategy appearing in the sequence of responses to influence attempts from the other side; and, in (4) those cases in which the three operational indicators do not provide sufficient information for a decision, an intuitive reading of narrative accounts of the crisis behavior of the participants. The operational rules for employing the first three indicators are somewhat complex, so only a brief description of each will be presented here. Detailed accounts of the decision rules for identifying strategies appear in Appendices 4–6 (pp. 229–32).

Behavior patterns. The time series described in Chapter 4 exhibit the pattern of cooperative and conflictive actions by each side over the

144

course of the crisis. It is possible to interpret the pattern for each side as consistent with one or another of the five influence strategies:

(1) *Bullying*. The actions of the Bullying side describe a secular trend of increasing escalation, with no deescalatory or accommodative shifts in the pattern. The level of hostility for the Bullying side remains equal to, or higher than, that of the other side over the course of the crisis.

(2) *Reciprocating*. The Reciprocating side matches the coercive and accommodative moves of the other side, with a level of escalation equal to, or slightly lower than, that of the other side. There may be one or more unilateral spikes in cooperative activity, which are quickly extinguished if they are not matched by the other side.

(3) *Trial-and-Error*. A Trial-and-Error strategy is notable for a low degree of reciprocity in matching the actions of the other side, with frequent switches in direction from escalation to deescalation, and vice versa.

(4) *Appeasing*. An Appeasing strategy exhibits a pattern of increasing accommodative moves, which rise with increases in the intensity of the conflictive behavior of the other party.

(5) *Stonewalling*. A Stonewalling strategy can be identified by a very low level of activity for long periods; those actions that do occur will be primarily conflictive and will lag behind those of the other party.

The determination of which influence strategy best describes the time series for each side, is based on a visual inspection of smoothed frequency distributions similar to those presented in Figures 4.1–4.10 in Chapter 4. The decision rules for making those choices are listed in Appendix 4 (p. 229).

Influence attempt strategy. Crisis bargaining is viewed as a series of influence attempt–response sequences. Each disputant's influence strategy contains a set of decision rules prescribing appropriate adjustments in the inducements it chooses, based on feedback from the target's responses to preceding inducements. Each time a disputant chooses an inducement to accompany an influence attempt, the choice can be classified as consistent with the decision rules for one or more of the first four influence strategies described above.[3] The decision rules are presented in Appendix 5 (p. 230).

The decision rules for the appropriate adjustment in the choice of inducement following an inducement–response sequence may well be the same for more than one influence strategy. If, for example, an actor employs a negative inducement and the target issues a defiant response, then, if the actor were employing *either* a Bullying or Reciprocating influence strategy, the appropriate inducement to accompany the next influence attempt by the actor would be a more

145

coercive negative inducement. To add to the ambiguity, decision-makers do not always consistently follow the same influence attempt strategy throughout the course of the crisis. Consequently, the influence attempt strategy identified represents the *predominant* influence strategy employed, as opposed to a clear and consistent strategy throughout the course of the dispute. To qualify as the predominant influence attempt strategy, one of the five strategy types must meet two criteria: (1) more inducement choices must be consistent with its decision rules than those for any other strategy, and (2) these inducement choices must represent the majority of inducement choices over the course of the dispute. If no single influence strategy meets both criteria, then the predominant influence strategy cannot be chosen by this method.

Besides the potential ambiguities that I have noted above, this method, which was the only method used in our earlier study of influence strategies (Leng and Wheeler, 1979), is limited by its focus being solely on influence attempts. Its most notable omission is its neglect of the actor's *responses* to influence attempts by the other party. How a state responds to influence attempts by the other party represents the other half – the defensive half – of its influence strategy.

Response strategy. The actor's predominant response strategy is identified by comparing the target's response (comply, placate, ignore, defy, or mixed) to the inducements employed by the other party. For example, if the other side employs a positive inducement, and the actor responds by placating the would-be influencer, the response would fit a Reciprocating strategy; if the actor responds with defiance, it would fit a Bullying strategy; if the actor ignores the demand, it would fit a Stonewalling strategy, and so on.[4] The decision rules for identifying response strategies appear in Appendix 6 (p. 232).

Taken together, the three indicators provide a more complete perspective than the predominant influence attempt strategy alone. The inspection of the time series allows us to observe the trend of conflictive and cooperative behavior produced by *all* of the actions that each side directs to the other. This allows us to consider what Schelling (1960:ch. 3) called "tacit bargaining" – signaling intentions and attempting to persuade the other party through physical actions as a component of each side's overall influence strategy. Adding consideration of the response strategy, along with identification of the influence attempt strategy, provides a more complete picture of the attempts at signaling and persuasion associated with explicit influence attempts.

A complicating feature of this approach is that states do not always exhibit consistent patterns of behavior across the three indicators. In the Munich crisis, for example, Hitler employed a predominantly Bullying approach in the influence attempts communicated to Czechoslovakia, but his responses to positive initiatives from the other side were more consistent with an Appeasing influence strategy. It is not hard to see the logic behind Hitler's bargaining. The tough demands on Czechoslovakia were backed up by a willingness to use force against the Czechs, coupled with a readiness to respond positively to appeasing moves by other major powers in order to encourage them to pressure Czechoslovakia to yield to his demands, or, at least, to provide Britain and France with a rationale for staying out of a war if the Czechs did not yield to Germany's demands. It turns out that the third indicator – Germany's overall behavior – is consistent with the Bullying strategy identified in Hitler's influence attempts. In this instance, and in other cases like it, if two of the three operational indicators agree, I have selected the influence strategy for which there is the greatest amount of agreement.

There are nineteen cases among the eighty in the sample, however, in which the operational indicators are evenly split, either among three strategies, or between two strategies in cases in which one of the indicators provided insufficient information for a choice. In those cases, I have relied on more qualitative accounts to reach a final judgment.

Qualitative judgments. The commentaries of diplomatic historians and participants provide a useful means of either confirming the decisions reached by the operational techniques, or making a choice in the nineteen more ambiguous cases. Historians, of course, do not use the categories that are employed in this study, so I have used my own best judgment in transforming their descriptions into one of the five types of influence strategies.

A single predominant influence strategy. Before leaving this section, a rationale should be offered for the decision to combine the influence attempts and responses exchanged by several pairs of actors on opposite sides of a particular dispute to determine the predominant influence strategy for each side. In the Munich crisis, for example, Germany's bargaining with Czechoslovakia is consistent with a Bullying strategy, but its exchanges with Britain and France more closely fit a Reciprocating strategy. I have designated the *predominant* German influence attempt strategy as Bullying, because that is what the combined record most closely resembles; nevertheless, it masks the difference in Germany's approaches to the different states. The argument for combining the influence strategies, by all parties on one side that

147

are directed at all parties on the other side, into a single predominant influence strategy, is based on the assumption discussed in Chapter 2. That is, it is assumed that the outcome of the crisis, including the outcome for any particular pair of participants, is influenced by the interactions of all the parties who are directly involved in the crisis. In other words, since it is the combined effect of the actions by all parties on one side that determines their fate, it makes sense to include the actions of all those parties in any analysis of the effects of influence strategies, rather than to treat the interactions of each pair of participants as if they were involved in separate disputes. How Britain and France responded to the influence strategy of Germany was influenced by the strategy Germany employed in its attempts to influence Czechoslovakia, and vice versa.

The influence strategies identified by each of the four indicators, along with the predominant influence strategy for the crisis, appear in Appendix 7 (p. 233).

Analysis

The examination of influence strategies focuses on three relationships of interest. We will begin by examining the possibility of a direct, bivariate association between particular types of influence strategies, particularly Bullying and Reciprocating strategies, and crisis outcomes. The second relationship of interest is that between the crisis structure and influence strategies. From a realist perspective, which overall influence strategy is employed should be a function of the actor's perceived comparative capabilities and the gravity of the interests at stake.

Ultimately, however, we are interested in the relationship among all three variables. There may be an interaction effect between the crisis structure and the influence strategy, which exerts the most potent influence on the crisis outcome. Snyder and Diesing (1977), for example, describe crisis bargaining as a process of signaling and persuasion in which the influence strategy is intended to assume a dual role. On the one hand, the inducements employed are designed to persuade the target that it would be in its interest to act in the manner desired by the actor; on the other hand, the actor's demands and inducements, as well as its responses to the inducements of the other side, are intended to communicate the actor's view of the seriousness of the issues at stake and its understanding of its capabilities. Thus, the actor is attempting to communicate its perception of the crisis structure to the target and to reconnoiter the target's perception of the crisis structure by observing the target's responses to the actor's influence attempts. Viewed from this perspective, each side's perception of the balance in capabilities and interests is likely to be influenced by the other side's influence strategy. Which influence strategy is chosen, in turn, is influenced by the crisis structure. We do not have enough crises in our sample to undertake a multivariate test of these potential interactive effects, but we may be able to gain some additional insights from the data at hand.

The predominant influence strategy, motivation score, and outcome classification, for each side in the forty crisis sample, appear in Table 7.2. The motivation scores are the same as those presented in Chapter 5. They represent an indicator combining that side's perception of its interests at stake and comparative war-fighting capabilities, on a scale ranging from two to six, with six representing vital interests at stake and a perception that a military victory can be achieved at a moderate cost.

Influence strategies and outcomes

The bivariate associations between influence strategies and outcomes, with the three cases[5] in which war was planned at the outset excluded, are presented in Table 7.3.

The initial findings are strikingly consistent with what was found in our comparison of the reciprocating and realist approaches to influence attempts in Chapter 6. The Bullying and Reciprocating strategies are virtual mirror images of each other. Escalating coercive Bullying strategies lead to war or submission in 69 percent of the cases, and to a victory or compromise in 27 percent of the cases; whereas Reciprocating influence strategies lead to a victory or compromise in 64 percent of the cases, and to war or submission in 28 percent of the cases. When Bullying strategies are successful, they do tend to result in diplomatic victories (23 percent), rather than compromises (4 percent), but Reciprocating strategies also achieve diplomatic victories in 20 percent of the cases in which they are employed, along with compromises 44 percent of the time. These results are generally consistent with those obtained in an earlier study (Leng and Wheeler, 1979:676) of influence strategies.

Trial and Error influence strategies do slightly better than Bullying strategies in achieving compromise outcomes (32 percent), but they lead to war or submission in 58 percent of the cases in which they are employed. There are too few cases of either Appeasing or Stonewalling strategies to draw any conclusions, although the associations are

149

Table 7.2. *Motivation score, influence strategy and crisis outcome*

Crisis	Actor(s)	Motivation[a]	Strategy	Outcome
Pastry	France	4	Bully	Victory
	Mexico	3	Trial & Error	Submit
Crimean	Russia	5	Trial & Error	War
	Britain *et al.*	5	Bully	War
Schleswig-	Germany, Austria	5	Bully	War[b]
Holstein	Denmark	4	Stone-Wall	War
Russo-	Russia	5	Bully	War
Turkish	Turkey	4	Stone-Wall	War
British-	Britain	5	Bully	Victory
Russian	Russia	3	Appease	Submit
British-	Britain	5	Bully	Victory
Portuguese	Portugal	3	Trial & Error	Submit
Spanish-	US	4	Bully	War
American	Spain	4	Reciprocate	War
Fashoda	Britain	5	Reciprocate	Victory
	France	3	Trial & Error	Submit
1st Moroccan	France	3	Reciprocate	Victory
	Germany	3	Trial & Error	Submit
Central American	Nicaragua	5	Bully	War
	Honduras	5	Bully	War
Bosnian	Austria, Germany	5	Reciprocate	Victory
	Serbia, Russia, Turkey	4	Reciprocate	Submit
Agadir	France, Britain	4	Reciprocate	Compromise
	Germany	3	Reciprocate	Compromise
1st Balkan	Serbia, Bulgaria, Greece	5	Bully	War[b]
	Turkey	4	Bully	War
2nd Balkan	Bulgaria	5	Stone-Wall	War
	Serbia, Greece, Romania	5	Bully	War
Pre-WWI	Germany, Austria	4	Bully	War
	Serbia, Russia, Britain, France	4	Reciprocate	War
Teschen	Poland	3	Trial & Error	Compromise
	Czechoslovakia	5	Reciprocate	Compromise
Chaco Dispute	Bolivia	4	Trial & Error	Compromise
	Paraguay	4	Reciprocate	Compromise
Chaco War	Bolivia	4	Bully	War
	Paraguay	4	Trial & Error	War
Manchurian	Japan	5	Bully	War
	China	4	Trial & Error	War
Italo-	Italy	5	Bully	War[b]
Ethiopian	Ethiopia	4	Trial & Error	War
Rhineland	France, Britain, Belgium	4	Reciprocate	Submit
	Germany	3	Reciprocate	Victory
Anschluss	Austria	4	Appease	Submit
	Germany	5	Bully	Victory
Munich	Czechoslovakia, Britain, France	5	Trial & Error	Submit
	Germany	4	Bully	Victory
Polish–	Poland	5	Reciprocate	Compromise
Lithuanian	Lithuania	3	Trial & Error	Compromise
Danzig	Germany	5	Bully	War
(Pre-WW2)	Britain, Poland	5	Reciprocate	War
French–	Italy	2	Trial & Error	Stalemate
Italian	France	4	Reciprocate	Stalemate

Table 7.2 (*cont.*)

Crisis	Actor(s)	Motivation[a]	Strategy	Outcome
1st Kashmir	India	5	Bully	War
	Pakistan	5	Bully	War
Berlin Blockade	US, Britain, France	4	Reciprocate	Victory
	USSR	4	Bully	Submit
Trieste	Italy	3	Reciprocate	Compromise
	Yugoslavia	3	Trial & Error	Compromise
Suez	Egypt	4	Trial & Error	War
	Britain, France, Israel	5	Bully	War
Honduran Border	Honduras	3	Reciprocate	Compromise
	Nicaragua	3	Trial & Error	Compromise
Sino-	India	4	Trial & Error	Compromise
Indian	China	4	Reciprocate	Compromise
Bizerte	France	4	Reciprocate	Submit
	Tunisia	3	Trial & Error	Victory
Cuban Missile	US	4	Bully	Victory
	USSR, Cuba	4	Trial & Error	Submit
Cyprus	Greece	4	Bully	Stalemate
	Turkey	4	Reciprocate	Stalemate
Rann of Kutch	India	4	Bully	War
	Pakistan	5	Reciprocate	War
2nd Kashmir	India	4	Bully	War
	Pakistan	5	Bully	War
Cod War	Iceland	3	Bully	Compromise
	Britain	5	Reciprocate	Compromise
Beagle Channel	Argentina	4	Reciprocate	Compromise
	Chile	4	Reciprocate	Compromise
Sino-	China	5	Bully	War
Vietnam	Vietnam	4	Trial & Error	War

[a] Motivation: Actor's combined interests and perceived comparative capability scores.
[b] Cases where war was the actor's intended outcome from the onset of the crisis.

Table 7.3. *Influence strategies and outcomes*

Strategy	Outcomes					
	Victory	Compro.	Stale.	War	Defeat	Total
Bullying	6(0.23)	1(0.04)	1(0.04)	17(0.65)	1(0.04)	26
Reciprocating	5(0.20)	11(0.44)	2(0.08)	4(0.16)	3(0.12)	25
Trial & Error	1(0.05)	6(0.32)	1(0.05)	5(0.26)	6(0.32)	19
Appeasing	0(0.00)	0(0.00)	0(0.00)	0(0.00)	2(1.00	2
Stonewalling	0(0.00)	0(0.00)	0(0.00)	2(1.00)	0(0.00)	2
Total	12(0.16)	18(0.24)	4(0.05)	28(0.38)	12(0.16)	74

Note: Numbers represent frequency counts with percentages in parentheses.

consistent with what one would expect in both cases. If these last two categories are dropped from the table – to remove the cells with zero entries – a chi square test is statistically significant at the $p = 0.001$ level.

Table 7.4 offers another perspective on the relationship between influence strategies and outcomes, by presenting the association

Table 7.4. *Influence strategy pairings and outcomes*

Strategy pairing	Diplomatic victory	Diplomatic defeat	Compromise	Stalemate	War	Total
			Crisis outcome			
Bully–Bully	0	0	0	0	4	4
Bully–Reciprocate	0	1	1	1	4	7
Bully–Trial-and-Error	4	0	0	0	6	10
Bully–Appease	2	0	0	0	0	2
Bully–S.W.	0	0	0	0	3	3
Reciprocate–Reciprocate	2	0	2	0	0	4
Reciprocate–Trial-and-Error	2	1	6	1	0	10
Total	10	2	9	2	17	40

Note: The diplomatic victory and defeat columns list the outcome for the first of the two strategies listed. For example, column two of row two indicates one diplomatic defeat for the side employing a Bullying strategy in the Bullying–Reciprocating pairing.

between the influence strategy and pairings and crisis outcomes. The associations in Table 7.4 indicate that, with the exception of those crises in which the other side employs an Appeasing strategy, Bullying strategies most often lead to war, regardless of the strategy employed by the other party. On the other hand, the only incidences of Reciprocating or Trial-and-Error strategies ending in war occur when they are paired against Bullying strategies.

In sum, the associations in Tables 7.3 and 7.4 suggest that Reciprocating influence strategies are likely to be more effective overall than Bullying strategies. Those findings are not surprising given the strong tendency of states to respond to individual influence attempts in a tit-for-tat manner, which was observed in Chapter 6. But, they do raise some interesting questions regarding the positive associations between the crisis structure and crisis outcomes, which were found in Chapters 3 and 5. The first of these questions is: what effect, if any, do the parties' perceptions of the crisis structure have on the choice of influence strategies?

Influence strategy choices and the crisis structure

As we noted in Chapter 3, the structural components of a crisis that are most important from a realist perspective are two: the security interests at stake, and the actor's perceived comparative war-fighting capabilities. In Chapter 3 we generated a three level ranking on each of

Table 7.5. *Crisis structure perceived by actors and influence strategy choices*

Motivation score	Influence strategy					
	Bullying	Reciprocating	Trial & Error	Appeasing	Stonewalling	Total
5	18(0.64)	7(0.25)	2(0.07)	0(0.00)	1(0.04)	28(1.00)
4	11(0.32)	12(0.35)	8(0.24)	1(0.03)	2(0.06)	34(1.00)
3	1(0.06)	6(0.35)	9(0.53)	1(0.06)	0(0.00)	17(1.00)
2	0(0.00)	0(0.00)	1(1.00)	0(0.00)	0(0.00)	2(1.00)
Total	30(0.38)	25(0.31)	20(0.25)	2(0.02)	3(0.04)	80(1.00)

Note: Numbers represent frequency counts with percentages in parentheses.

these variables for each side in a dispute. In Chapter 5, we added these two scores together to obtain a *motivation* score for each actor.[6] The bivariate associations between motivation scores and influence strategies appear in Table 7.5.[7]

The associations in Table 7.5 are consistent with what classical realism tells us to expect. When the interests at stake and war-fighting optimism are at the highest levels, states choose Bullying influence strategies in 64 percent of the cases; whereas there is only one instance of a Bullying strategy being employed when the combined motivation score falls into the lowest two ranks. In other words, statesmen are more likely to chose coercive escalating Bullying strategies when the security stakes are higher and they are more optimistic regarding the consequences of war.

More generally, Table 7.5 exhibits a trend that runs from the choice of Bullying strategies when the motivation score is at its highest level, to Trial-and-Error strategies when it is at its lowest level, to a fairly even balance among Bullying, Reciprocating, and Trial-and-Error strategies when the motivation level is on the border between high and low. If we consider just these three major influence strategies, and collapse the last two rows of Table 7.5 into one to reduce the zero entries, a chi square test indicates that the differences are statistically significant at the $p = 0.001$ level.

Overall, the associations in Table 7.5 are remarkably consistent with the classical realist admonition to demonstrate power when it is justified by the interests at stake and one's military capabilities, and to exercise prudence when the conditions do not justify taking large risks. Thus, when it comes to the *choice of influence strategies*, the leaders of the states in the sample have behaved in a manner consistent with the precepts of realism. On the other hand, the influence of prudential considerations appears to weaken over the course of the crisis. As we saw in Table 7.3, when states in the sample employed Bullying strategies, in most instances (65 percent) they found themselves in wars.

Motivation, outcomes, and influence strategies

In Chapter 3 we found a positive relationship between optimistic perceptions of comparative war-fighting capabilities and the outbreak of war. Wars occurred most frequently when at least one side believed that they could win easily and the other side believed that they had at least an even chance of winning. When we combined the indicators of capability and interests into a single structural measure, we found that, when one side believed that they could prevail easily in a war, and the other thought that they had at least an even chance, *and* both sides had security interests at stake, the crisis escalated to war in nine of ten cases. We also found that, even if the parties perceived themselves as unevenly matched militarily, the crisis would escalate to war if the weaker party had vital interests at stake. On the other side of the coin, we found that war was avoided in *all* of the crises in which there were no security interests at stake for either party. Those findings suggested that the key structural components identified by classical realists – security interests and perceptions of comparative war-fighting capabilities – are excellent predictors of war or nonwar outcomes at the more extreme ends of the continuum, that is, given the conditions described above. Twenty-three of the forty crises in the sample, however, fall into an intermediate category where the combination of interests and comparative capabilities for the two sides yields moderate scores. Based on the crisis structure alone, it is difficult to predict crisis outcomes in these cases.

The analyses in Chapter 3 were based on the association between the *crisis* structure and outcomes. The question at hand, however, concerns the relationship between the perceived comparative war-fighting capabilities and interests at stake, or motivation score, *for a particular side*, and the outcome that it experiences. Table 7.6 depicts the associations between the motivation scores for parties to the dispute and the outcomes that they obtain.

The first impression that one receives from the frequency counts in Table 7.6 is consistent with the findings in Chapter 3. The states in the sample were most likely to find themselves in unwanted wars[8] when the stakes were high and they were optimistic regarding the outcome of the war. Moreover, when the combination of interests and perceived comparative capability scores were in the lowest two categories, those sides avoided war entirely. The distributions in Table 7.6 present

154

Table 7.6. *Motivation scores and outcomes*

Motivation score	Diplomatic victory	Compromise	Stalemate	War	Diplomatic defeat	Total
		Crisis outcome				
5	6(0.21)	3(0.11)	0(0.00)	19(0.68)	0(0.00)	28(1.00)
4	3(0.09)	7(0.21)	3(0.09)	15(0.44)	6(0.18)	34(1.00)
3	3(0.18)	8(0.47)	0(0.00)	0(0.00)	6(0.35)	17(1.00)
2	0(0.00)	0(0.00)	1(1.00)	0(0.00)	0(0.00)	1(1.00)
Total	12(0.15)	18(0.23)	4(0.05)	34(0.42)	12(0.15)	80(1.00)

Note: Numbers represent frequency counts with percentages in parentheses.

a somewhat cloudier picture once we go beyond the simple distinction between war and nonwar outcomes in extreme cases; nevertheless, the proportions of diplomatic victories, compromises, and defeats are consistent with what would be expected from a realist perspective. The distribution of outcomes across the different motivation levels is statistically significant at the $p = 0.001$ level.[9]

The most telling of these distributions is that for parties with the highest motivation score (5). In all but three of twenty-eight cases (89 percent), these sides either achieved diplomatic victories or went to war. We saw in Table 7.5 that eighteen (64 percent) of these states also chose Bullying influence strategies. In fact, these cases account for 60 percent of all instances in which states chose Bullying strategies. Taken together, these distributions and associations suggest that: (1) states are most likely to choose Bullying strategies when the security stakes are higher and they are more optimistic regarding the outcome of a war, and (2) when they do so, the crisis is more likely to end in either submission by the other party, or a war.

Influence strategies, behavioral patterns, and outcomes

The motivation score for each side is a relative score in the sense that that side's capability score reflects its perception of its war-fighting capabilities relative to those of the other side. Nevertheless, we would expect the best structural predictor of the crisis outcome to be the *intersection* of the degree of motivation of each of the contending sides. Earlier in the investigation, in Chapter 5, we found that crises in which the combined motivation scores of the two sides were high were more likely to escalate to high levels. We also know, from the findings in Chapter 4, that crises with high reciprocity tend to end in war when they escalate to high levels, and tend to end in

155

Table 7.7. *Influence strategy pairings and behavioral types*

Influence Strategies	Behavioral type				
	Fight R=H, E=H	Resistance R=L, E=H	Standoff R=H, E=L	Put-Down R=L, E=L	Total
Bully–Bully	4(4)	0(0)	0(0)	0(0)	4(4)
Bully–Reciprocate	0(0)	6(4)	1(0)	0(0)	7(4)
Bully–Trial & Error	0(0)	5(3)	2(1)	3(2)	10(6)
Bully–Appease	0(0)	0(0)	0(0)	2(0)	0(0)
Bully–Stonewall	2(2)	0(0)	0(0)	1(1)	3(3)
Reciprocate–Reciprocate	2(0)	1(0)	1(0)	0(0)	4(0)
Reciprocate–Trial & Error	0(0)	1(0)	8(0)	1(0)	10(0)
Total	8(6)	13(7)	12(1)	7(3)	40(17)

Note: Cell entries in parentheses indicate war outcomes.
R = Reciprocity, E = Escalation, H = High, L = Low.

compromises when the level of escalation is low, and that crises with low levels of reciprocity tend to end in either one-sided peaceful outcomes, or in war.

There was a puzzling aspect to the findings in Chapter 4 in the generally higher escalation scores observed in cases exhibiting low reciprocity. The reader may remember that the two low reciprocity behavioral categories – the high escalation Resistance category and the low escalation Put-Down category – were presumed to be consistent with an "aggressor–defender" (Pruitt and Rubin, 1986:89–92) model of escalation, in which one party is controlling the escalation of the conflict and the other party is reacting in a defensive manner. If one party was pursuing an escalating coercive strategy, then the outcome of the crisis would depend primarily on the resolve of the other party. This reasoning implies that one party is employing a Bullying strategy, and that the other is likely to be employing either a Reciprocating strategy in the crisis falling into the high escalation Resistance category, or a Trial-and-Error or Appeasing strategy in those crises falling into the low escalation Put-Down category. That expectation would be consistent with the finding in this chapter indicating that when states employ Bullying strategies they are most likely either to achieve a diplomatic victory (23 percent) or to find themselves in an unplanned war (65 percent). If this is the case, it may be that the use of an escalating coercive Bullying strategy by one side is the cause of the higher escalation scores in the low reciprocity crises.

Table 7.7 includes the influence strategy pairings observed in the sample of forty crises, and their associations with the four behavioral types. The frequencies with which the pairings yield the behavioral patterns described by the types appears in each column, with the number of cases that ended in war included in parentheses. The presumption that the low reciprocity Resistance and Put-Down categories were consistent with aggressor-defender models of escalation is supported by the fact that, in sixteen of the twenty cases (80 percent) falling into these categories, one of the two sides was employing a Bullying influence strategy. Moreover, more than half of the cases falling into the high escalation Resistance category are instances in which the "defender" employs a Reciprocating strategy, whereas, the defender does not employ a Reciprocating strategy in any of the cases in the Put-Down category. These associations offer a plausible answer to the puzzling results found in Chapter 4. The high escalation scores found in the low reciprocity Resistance category are associated with cases in which one party is employing an escalating coercive Bullying influence strategy and the other party is responding in a tit-for-tat manner with a Reciprocating strategy. Why three of the cases in the low escalation Put-Down category ended in war cannot be explained by the choice of influence strategies; however, in two of those cases – the Russo-Turkish War of 1877–78, and the Manchurian War of 1932 – the stronger party, which adopted a Bullying strategy, expected to prevail easily in the case of war, and the weaker party had vital interests at stake.

The associations between influence strategies and behavioral types are no less impressive in the high reciprocity Fight and Standoff categories. In six of the eight crises falling into the high escalation Fight category, at least one of the parties is employing a Bullying influence strategy. Those also are the six cases that ended in war. In four of those cases both parties employed Bullying strategies; in the other two cases, one of the parties employed a Stonewalling strategy. Eight of the twelve crises ending in low escalation Standoffs pitted a Reciprocating strategy against a Trial-and-Error strategy. We will take a closer look at this match-up, and at Reciprocating strategies more generally, in the next chapter, but it is not hard to imagine why the intersection of an essentially tit-for-tat strategy and a Trial-and-Error approach should lead to low escalation and a high degree of reciprocity. Overall, the associations between the pairings of influence strategies and the behavioral types are remarkably consistent with what would be expected from the descriptions of the influence strategies.

157

The crisis structure, influence strategies, and behavior types

The observed associations between influence strategies and behavioral types shed light on the earlier findings regarding the relationship between each of these variables and the crisis structure. Consider what we have found to this point.

Structure and influence strategy. Earlier in this chapter, we found positive associations between high motivation scores and the choice of Bullying strategies, and between low motivation scores and Trial-and-Error influence strategies. The choice of Reciprocating strategies, however, appeared unrelated to variations in motivation, although it was the second most likely choice under all conditions.

Structure and behavioral type. In Chapter 5, we found that a positive association between high combined structural scores and high crisis escalation, and between low motivation scores and low escalation, but there was no discernible relationship between the crisis structure and the degree of reciprocity in the interactions of the disputants.

Influence strategy and behavioral type. Finally, we have found that Bullying influence strategies are highly associated with high escalation scores, that: (1) a pairing of two Bullying strategies is associated with high reciprocity, high escalation, Fights; (2) a pairing of Bullying and Reciprocating strategies is associated with high escalation, low reciprocity, Resistance; and (3) that a pairing of Reciprocating and Trial-and-Error strategies is associated with high reciprocity, low escalation, Standoffs.

The size of the sample does not permit a multivariate test of the relationships among these three variables; however, it is possible to draw some reasonable hypotheses from the bivariate findings. To the extent to which the crisis structure affects the choice of influence strategies and consequent behavioral patterns, it appears to be in encouraging more coercive bargaining and greater risk-taking when the security stakes are high and policy-makers are optimistic regarding their war-fighting capabilities. There appears to be a stronger, and more comprehensive, relationship between the choice of influence strategies and behavioral types. The influence strategy is an effective predictor of the degree of reciprocity as well as of the degree of escalation. Moreover, the positive relationship observed between the crisis structure and crisis escalation is impossible to separate from the same positive association between Bullying influence strategies and crisis escalation. Based on these associations, the most plausible relationship among the three variables would be a developmental sequence in which the choice of influence strategy is partially dependent on that side's perception of the crisis structure (motivation), and the behavioral type, in turn, is dependent on the type of influence strategy employed.

Crisis structure, influence strategies, and outcomes

Given the investigation's concern with the validity of realist prescriptions, the question of greatest interest concerns the relative influence of the crisis structure in determining crisis outcomes, as opposed to that of either the influence strategies chosen by the participants, or the behavioral patterns resulting from the intersection of influence strategies. Realists prescribe crisis bargaining based on the assumption that the other party will act in accordance with a rational calculation of its interests and capabilities, that is, based on its perception of the crisis structure. Researchers viewing crisis behavior from a psychological perspective stress the confounding effects of such factors as psychological reactance to coercive influence strategies, the effects of the growing tension and stress associated with crisis escalation, and the tendency of states to respond to influence attempts in a reciprocating manner.

Once again, the size of the sample makes it impossible to conduct a multivariate statistical analysis of all the possible relationships among the three predictor variables and crisis outcomes. Because we have found influence strategies and behavioral types to be closely associated and to yield the same predictions regarding crisis outcomes, we can simplify the comparison of the realist and psychological perspectives by focusing on just one of these two variables. The bivariate tests conducted to this point indicate strong associations between influence strategies and all three of the other variables, whereas only weak associations were found between behavioral types and either the crisis structure or crisis outcomes. Consequently, the comparison will be limited to an examination of the relative potency of the crisis structure and influence strategies as predictors of crisis outcomes.

Based on the findings to this point, we can hypothesize three relationships among these variables. (1) The variation in crisis outcomes is a direct function of variations in the crisis structure. The observed association between influence strategies and crisis outcomes is spurious. It is a result of the dependence of the choice of influence strategy on the crisis structure. (2) The variation in crisis outcome is a direct function of variations in influence strategies. There is a developmental sequence in which the crisis structure encourages the choice of a particular influence strategy, but, once the influence strategy has

Table 7.8. *Influence strategies and outcomes with high motivation scores*[a]

Influence strategy	Crisis outcomes					
	Victory	Compromise	Stalemate	War	Defeat	Total
Bullying	2(0.13)	0	0	14(0.87)	0	16
Reciprocating	1(0.25)	0	0	2(0.50)	1(0.25)	4
Trial & Error	0	0	0	4(0.80)	1(0.20)	5
Appeasing	0	0	0	0	1(1.0)	1
Stonewalling	0	0	0	2(1.0)	0	2
Total	3(0.11)	0	0	22(0.78)	3(0.11)	28

[a] Motivation scores = 5–5, 5–4, or 4–5.
Numbers represent frequency counts with percentages in parentheses.

been chosen, the crisis outcome is not influenced by the crisis structure. (3) The variation in crisis structure is a function of the combined effect of the crisis structure and influence strategy. A particular influence strategy is more likely to be associated with a particular outcome when the combined interests and capabilities of the two parties take on particular values, and vice versa.

To get some sense of which of these three relationships is most plausible, the data have been partitioned into two subtables, one of which presents the associations between influence strategies and crisis outcomes when the combined motivation scores are high, and one which presents the associations between influence strategies and outcomes when the motivation scores are low. Table 7.8 contains those cases in which the combined motivation scores were 5–5, 5–4, or 4–5. These are the motivation scores that have been found to be most highly associated with war outcomes. Table 7.9 contains the remaining cases, with the exception of those three crises in which one of the sides was bent on war from the start.

One of the first things that an observer notices about Tables 7.8 and 7.9 is that the positive association between the motivation scores and choices of influence strategies leaves few cases in which the two are not in agreement regarding the predicted outcome. Consequently, it is difficult to draw comparisons between the two as predictors. Nevertheless, there are some suggestive associations in the two tables.

The most notable difference between Tables 7.8 and 7.9 is that 78 percent of the wars occur among the cases with the higher motivation scores appearing in Table 7.8. That is not surprising, since the division between the two tables is based on the association between motivation scores and war or nonwar outcomes. More revealing is the fact that the percentage of cases ending in war is higher when the motivation score

Table 7.9. *Influence strategies and outcomes with lower motivation scores*[a]

Influence strategy	Crisis outcomes					
	Victory	Compromise	Stalemate	War	Defeat	Total
Bullying	4(0.40)	1(0.10)	1(0.10)	3(0.30)	1(0.10)	10
Reciprocating	4(0.19)	11(0.52)	2(0.10)	2(0.10)	2(0.10)	21
Trial & Error	1(0.07)	6(0.43)	1(0.07)	1(0.07)	5(0.36)	14
Appeasing	0	0	0	0	1(1.00)	1
Stonewalling	0	0	0	0	0	0
Total	9(0.20)	18(0.39)	4(0.09)	6(0.13)	9(0.20)	46

[a] *Motivation scores* = 5–3, 3–5, 4–4, 4–3, 3–4, 3–3, 3–2, 2–3, or 2–2.
Numbers represent frequency counts with percentages in parentheses.

is higher for *all types* of influence strategies. The percentage of cases with Bullying strategies ending in war in Table 7.8 is 87 percent, whereas it is 30 percent in Table 7.9; for Reciprocating strategies, the percentages are 50 percent and 10 percent, and for Trial-and-Error strategies, they are 80 percent and 7 percent. By the same token, the percentage of crises ending in either victory or compromise is higher for all types of influence strategies, and *all* instances of compromises or stalemates occur when the motivation scores are moderate or low, that is, in Table 7.9. These distributions suggest that the crisis structure, as indicated by the intersection of the motivation scores of the two sides, is exerting some influence on war and nonwar outcomes beyond the selection of the influence strategy. Therefore, it appears that we can rule out hypothesis 2, which suggests that the crisis structure exerts no direct influence on the crisis outcome.

On the other hand, Bullying influence strategies are still the most likely influence strategies to end in war in *both* tables, suggesting that the influence strategies employed, as well as the crisis structure, are exerting an influence on the crisis outcomes. In fact, in all of the cases ending in war in Table 7.8, at least one side employed a Bullying influence strategy. Similarly, in all compromise outcomes, at least one party employed a Reciprocating influence strategy. More generally, Table 7.9 suggests considerable variation in the distribution of *nonwar* outcomes among the three major influence strategies. Thus, it would seem that we also can rule out hypothesis 1, which suggests that the crisis outcome is independent of the influence strategy employed.

In sum, based on the distribution among outcomes in Tables 7.8 and 7.9, the most reasonable hypothesis appears to be the third, that is, that while the choice of influence strategy is dependent to some degree on the crisis structure, as indicated by the intersection of the motivation scores of the two sides, the crisis outcome is influenced by both the crisis structure and the influence strategies employed by the dispu- tants. The empirical basis for this judgment is tenuous, given the small number of cases in which one is able to make any distinction between the predictions of the two independent variables, but it does offer a plausible explanation for the seemingly conflicting findings appearing in earlier chapters and in other studies dealing with realist or psycho- logical perspectives on crisis bargaining.

Conclusion

The findings in this chapter indicate that, among the milita- rized crises in the sample, national leaders have tended to follow the realist prescription to think and act in terms of the national interest and their comparative military capabilities in choosing influence strategies. Moreover, they have been likely to choose more belligerent influence strategies, and to allow the crisis to escalate to war, when the stakes have been high and they have been optimistic regarding the outcome of a war. In these respects, classical realism provides an accurate description of how states have been likely to behave in militarized crises. These findings are consistent not only with the views of classical realist thinkers like Morgenthau (1960) or Blainey (1973), but also with the rational choice models of Buena de Mesquita (1981).

On the other hand, the high association between aggressive Bully- ing influence strategies and war suggests the high risks inherent in the policy prescriptions that follow from the realist perspective. Moreover, the high association between Reciprocating influence strategies and compromise solutions is consistent with findings from interpersonal bargaining experiments (Esser and Komorita, 1975), as well as our earlier empirical findings (Leng and Wheeler, 1979), which suggested the advantages of a firm-but-fair influence strategy in eliciting cooper- ation from the other side. Those findings are more consistent with a psychological perspective.

A plausible explanation for these seemingly contradictory results is that, while considerations of interest and power are always an impor- tant ingredient in crisis decision-making, other factors are at work as well, factors that make the realist prescription a dangerous one. Those factors include the dynamics of crisis escalation associated with the interaction of two parties behaving in a manner consistent with the prescriptions of conflict strategists, and psychological reactance to threatening behavior, which make crisis decision-making a less

162

rational process. The strong positive association between Reciprocating influence strategies and compromise outcomes suggests as well that the norm of reciprocity plays a stronger role in crisis behavior than realists recognize. In Chapter 8 we will take a closer look at Reciprocating influence strategies and the attributed and conditions contributing to their success in eliciting cooperation in militarized crises.

8 RECIPROCATING INFLUENCE STRATEGIES

Reciprocity serves as the guiding principle for social exchange in anarchic systems, and, in the international system, with its assumption of the sovereign equality of states, the reciprocity norm lies at the heart of diplomacy and international law.

Empirical evidence of the prevalence of reciprocating, or tit-for-tat behavior has appeared in a number of studies of interstate behavior (see Chapter 6). In the course of this investigation, we have found evidence of a marked degree of reciprocity in responses to both accommodative and coercive influence attempts (Chapter 6). We have found also that states employing Reciprocating influence strategies achieved the greatest degree of success in obtaining successful peaceful outcomes to militarized crises (Chapter 7). In short, an examination of the crises in the sample suggests that states in crises tend to interact in a reciprocal manner, and that when states base their influence strategies on that assumption, they are more likely to be successful.

This chapter takes a closer look at Reciprocating influence strategies and the reasons for their success. The results found in Chapter 7 are consistent with a previous empirical study of interstates crises by Leng and Wheeler (1979), but most of the research on the relative effectiveness of different types of influence strategies has appeared in interpersonal, or computer programming, experiments with Prisoner's Dilemma (PD) games. A variety of strategies for eliciting cooperation have been examined in these experiments, with the Tit-for-Tat (TFT) and GRIT strategies described in Chapter 7 competing for the status of being viewed as most effective overall (see Patchen, 1987). A Reciprocating strategy contains some of the features of both of these strategies, but it is most simply described as a modification of TFT.

A simple TFT strategy begins with a cooperative opening move. Then, on all successive moves, the TFT player responds in kind to whatever strategy was chosen by the other player on the previous play of the game. A Reciprocating strategy follows the basic approach of TFT, but it relaxes the requirement that there be a single unilateral initiative on the opening move, to allow one or two cooperative initiatives to be initiated later in the crisis. As I noted in Chapter 7, cooperation on the opening move is impossible in an interstate crisis, which begins with a precipitant action by one side and a challenge to that action by the other. The use of a cooperative initiative within an already contentious environment is a characteristic that Reciprocating strategies share with GRIT, but, unlike GRIT, Reciprocating strategies return for a tit-for-tat approach immediately following the cooperative initiative.[1] Another important departure from experiments with TFT strategies concerns the openness of communication in the environment in which the strategy is employed. Most TFT experiments employ PD games in which there is no communication between the two sides; our analysis of the use of Reciprocating strategies in real world crises includes open communication between the two sides.[2] As we shall see below, these are not insignificant differences; however, the basic combination of tit-for-tat with a cooperative initiative to signal a willingness to negotiate lies at the heart of both Reciprocating and TFT strategies.

With so much attention and research devoted to TFT strategies and their alleged effectiveness in eliciting cooperation, one way of evaluating the success of Reciprocating strategies is by examining them in light of qualities that are assumed to contribute to the success of TFT strategies.

Attributes of an effective reciprocating strategy

After reviewing the results of his computer tournament, Axelrod (1984) speculated that there were four key ingredients that led to the success of a TFT strategy: (1) It is "nice." The side playing TFT opens with a cooperative move and it is never the first to defect from cooperation. (2) It cannot be exploited. The TFT player immediately responds in kind to any conflictive moves from the other side. (3) It is forgiving. The TFT player also responds in kind to any cooperative move from the other side, regardless of what has preceded it. (4) It is clear and recognizable. The other side easily recognizes that the TFT player is matching its moves.

With the exception of the TFT requirement that the cooperative initiatives come on the first move, Reciprocating strategies contain all of those features that Axelrod presumed to contribute to the success of TFT. Thus a closer look at the use of Reciprocating strategies in real world crises, with Axelrod's four criteria in mind, provides a good starting point for an evaluation of their effectiveness in eliciting cooperation. It also allows us to consider the possibility of a more finely calibrated balance between demonstrating firmness, or resolve, and a willingness to move to a cooperative settlement.

The examination begins with operational definitions of each of the four critical attributes of TFT, and then proceeds to consider variations in their application in Reciprocating strategies, and their contributions to the success of those strategies.

Niceness: cooperative initiatives

The TFT player indicates his or her willingness to cooperate on the first move and is never the first to defect on any succeeding moves. The cooperative first move requirement works in games, because the opening move – even in sequential games – is made simultaneously by both players. But real world disputes do not begin that way. One party initiates the dispute by challenging the status quo with a competitive move. TFT's second criteria – nonexploitability – demands a conflictive response, which is likely to encourage another conflictive move by the other side. If both parties then follow a strict TFT strategy for the remainder of the crisis, they will be "locked-in" a pattern of escalating conflict.

A Reciprocating strategy relaxes the rigid opening move requirement of TFT to allow the party to initiate one or two cooperative moves as the crisis evolves, in order to break the deadlock of escalating conflict. There has been some evidence from experiments with PD games indicating that, in uncertain environments, adding unilateral cooperative moves after the opening move improves the success rate of TFT strategies (Molander, 1985). The relaxation of the opening move requirement, however, raises new questions. First, there is the question of *timing*. When have the states in our sample been most likely to signal their willingness to cooperate? Moreover, how have they done so? Because, in addition to the issue of timing, there are questions regarding the *degree* of accommodation represented by the initiatives, the *conditions* that may be attached to them, and the *types* of cooperative initiatives that have been used most frequently. Beyond all of these descriptive questions, there is the issue of success. What combinations have worked best in eliciting cooperation from the other side?

Timing

When should the Reciprocating party signal a willingness to break out of the escalatory pattern and move to a cooperative settlement? The answer to that question depends on the policy-makers' views regarding potential trade-offs between a desire to communicate clearly a willingness to move to a cooperative settlement, versus the risk of having the move interpreted as a sign of irresolution, or weakness. To put it another way, the issue of timing is related to the balance between firmness and flexibility in a firm-but-flexible influence strategy. We will consider three possibilities, beginning with that placing the greatest emphasis on signaling flexibility.

(1) *An early cooperative initiative.* The closest approximation to the game theoretic model of TFT would be for the state employing a Reciprocating strategy to offer a cooperative initiative at the earliest possible opportunity. This approach offers the advantage of encouraging a response in kind before the crisis escalates to the point at which the increased belligerency, interests at stake, and public pressures make it more difficult to do so. In other words, an early cooperative initiative offers the advantage of initiating movement toward a cooperative settlement before the situation gets out of hand.

(2) *Cooperation only after demonstrating resolve.* Critics of an early cooperative move might argue that it has the disadvantage of sending a signal that suggests a lack of resolve on the part of the party making the initiative. Harford and Solomon (1967) found that in Prisoner's Dilemma, a strategy that consisted of initial noncooperation to demonstrate resolve, followed by one or two unconditional positive inducements, and then a move to tit-for-tat for the remainder of the dispute, was more effective than a standard TFT strategy.[3] The rationale behind this approach is that by demonstrating toughness and resolve, one lowers the aspirations of the other party, thus laying the groundwork for a more receptive response to cooperative initiatives later in the bargaining. The positive concession would be followed immediately by a return to a strict TFT strategy, which would remind the other party of the player's continuing resolve. The timing is consistent with what some students of diplomacy have suggested is the most effective approach to negotiation more generally: start with a high opening position, continue an unyielding stance until the other party is convinced of your resolve, and then offer a significant concession to move quickly to agreement (see Zartman and Berman, 1982:170–71). Critics of the approach would argue that the pathologies associated with crisis escalation might result in the cooperative moves coming too late to be effective.

(3) *Strict Tit-for-Tat.* A third approach would be to adopt a strict tit-for-tat approach from the outset, with cooperative moves only in response to those of the other party. In order words, the party offers no positive *initiatives*, but it does respond in kind to those of the other

167

party. This approach offers the possibility of moving to a cooperative settlement of the crisis without running the risk of appearing irresolute. On the other hand, getting to a cooperative settlement becomes dependent on an initiative from the other side. If the other party does initiate cooperation, then the pattern of action exhibited by the tit-for-tat player would fit our behavioral definition of a Reciprocating strategy. But, if the other party does not take the first cooperative step, the two sides would remain deadlocked in escalating coercive behavior.

Degree of accommodation

Related to the issue of timing, is the degree of commitment to cooperation represented by the initiative. An unequivocal demonstration of a willingness to grant concessions offers the advantage of unambiguously signaling flexibility, but it runs the risk of unintentionally signaling a lack of resolve as well. As in the case of the three examples in timing, I will begin with the most accommodative approach and then move to increasingly conservative options.

(1) *Unilateral concession.* The most straightforward approach is to offer a unilateral concession, unaccompanied by any coercive action. One or two cooperative offers are made, followed by a return to a strict TFT strategy. The approach offers the advantage of an unambiguous signal of a willingness to cooperate. The unilateral concession is consistent with Osgood's (1962) GRIT strategy of calculated deescalation, and there is some evidence from game theory experiments (Lindskold, Betz, and Walters, 1986:99–100) that a contentious atmosphere can be altered when one party acts "deliberately and unambiguously in a manner incompatible with that sort of relation." As in the issue of timing, the risk is that of encouraging a coercive response by an adversary that considers the positive initiative a sign of weakness.

(2) *Carrot-and-Stick.* A more cautious option is to follow a coercive move by the other party by responding in kind, but with an accompanying carrot, such as an offer to negotiate the issue, or to move to a reciprocal reduction in hostile actions. The Reciprocating party offers the prospect of moving to a cooperative solution while continuing to demonstrate its resolve. The "carrot" also can serve as a "face-saver," a concession to the other party for yielding.

(3) *Less than proportionate retaliation.* A third option is to respond to coercive initiatives in kind, but at a lower level of hostility. This approach signals a desire to avoid escalating the level of conflict, although it does not offer an unambiguous signal of willingness to offer any concessions to the other side.

As with the timing issue described above, the three subcategories of degree of accommodation represented by a cooperative initiative are designed to allow a distinction based on the trade-off between the clarity of the signal of a willingness to move to a cooperative solution, versus the danger of appearing weak and irresolute.

Conditionality

The conditions attached to cooperative initiatives are a third consideration. Again, a simple three category distinction, will be employed, with the clearest concession ranked first. In each case we will note whether the concessions are (1) unilateral (2) require reciprocal action by the other side, or (3) ask for *more than* reciprocal action by the other party. Some actions can be taken unilaterally, such as a unilateral withdrawal of troops; others, such as negotiations, require reciprocity. But, even in the case of reciprocal actions, the party may offer to undertake them only if the other side grants an additional concession, such as a withdrawal of troops from disputed territory, or it agrees to a particular formula for a settlement.

Type of action

We also would expect the effect of the signaled intention to seek a cooperative settlement to be dependent on *what* is offered. We will distinguish among four broad categories of types of cooperative moves, or offers based on the categories of *requests* described in Chapter 6: (1) negotiation or other forms of peaceful settlement techniques (mediation, arbitration, adjudication); (2) a reduction in hostile nonmilitary activity; (3) a reduction in military activity; and (4) substantive political or economic concessions.

Cooperative initiatives: Findings. Table 8.1 lists the attributes of the initial cooperative initiatives employed in the twenty-five instances in the sample in which states employed predominantly Reciprocating influence strategies. The numbers appearing in the cells in Table 8.1 represent the categories listed above. Table 8.1 reveals some interesting patterns. With regard to the issue of *timing*, most cooperative initiatives come, not at the outset of the crisis, but only after the party has exhibited its resolve through its responses in kind to attempts at coercion by the other side. There are sixteen instances of the latter and only six instances of the former. Thus, the approach that the states are taking is consistent with the view that cooperative initiatives may be effective in breaking deadlocks *after* they have demonstrated their resolve through competitive moves, as opposed to signaling a willingness to cooperate at the outset. The timing exhibited by these real

169

Table 8.1. *Reciprocating strategies: first cooperative initiatives*

Crises	Actor	Timing	Degree	Condition	Type	Response	Outcome
Spanish–American	Spain	1	1	2	1	Ignore	War
Fashoda	Britain	2	2	2	1	Comply	Victory
1st Moroccan	France	1	1	2	1	Mixed	Victory
Bosnian	Austria, Germany	1	1	2	2	Defy	Victory
Bosnian	Serbia, Romania, Turkey	2	1	2	1	Ignore	Submit
Agadir	France	1	1	2	1	Comply	Compromise
Agadir	Germany	2	1	2	1,2	Comply	Compromise
Pre-WWI	Entente	2	2	2	4	Defy	War
Teschen	Czecho-slovakia	3	2	2	1	Comply	Compromise
Chaco Dispute	Paraguay	2	2	2	1	Comply	Compromise
Rhineland	France, Britain, Belgium	2	1	2	1	Placate	Submit
Rhineland	Germany	2	2	2	2	Defy	Victory
Polish–Lithuanian	Poland	3	2	3	3	Comply	Compromise
Danzig	Britain, Poland	2	1	2	4	Ignore	War
French–Italian	France	3	[a]	[a]	[a]	[a]	Stalemate
Berlin Blockade	US, Britain, France	1	2	2	1	Comply	Victory
Trieste	Italy	2	2	2	1	Ignore	Compromise
Honduran B.	Honduras	2	2	2	1	Comply	Compromise
Sino-Indian	PCR	1	2	2	1	Mixed	Compromise
Bizerte	France	2	2	2	1	Comply	Submit
Cyprus	Turkey	2	1	2	4	Ignore	Stalemate
Rann of Kutch	Pakistan	2	2	2	1,3	Defy	War
Cod War	Britain	2	1	2	1,3	Defy	Compromise
Beagle Channel	Argentina	2	2	2	1	Defy	Compromise
Beagle Channel	Chile	2	2	2	1	Comply	Compromise

Note: [a] France employed strict tit-for-tat responses to Italy's coercive moves, without any cooperative initiatives.

world states is not surprising, given the nature of crises, which begin with at least one party challenging the other through a competitive initiative. This, along with the findings of Harford and Salomon (1967) cited above, offers a clue as to why game theorists have found standard TFT strategies relatively ineffective in hostile environments (Axelrod and Dion, 1988). It also suggests that statesmen who become embroiled in the highly competitive environment of a crisis find it prudent to demonstrate their firmness before indicating a willingness to be flexible.

Carrot-and-stick inducements are slightly (14–10) favored over unilateral cooperative moves in signaling a willingness to cooperate, suggesting, again, that statesmen are concerned with demonstrating their firmness – or avoiding any impression of weakness – even when signaling cooperative initiatives. It is interesting to note that the parties employing carrot-and-stick initiatives have been more successful in eliciting positive responses.

The last two attributes of cooperative initiatives can be discussed together, as they are highly interrelated. All of the cooperative initiatives found in the twenty-three cases require a reciprocal response by the other side, and eighteen of them ask that the other side either join in negotiations or in accepting mediation, in an effort to obtain a peaceful settlement.

All in all, the initial cooperative moves by the states employing Reciprocating strategies have been quite conservative. The modal pattern is for the move to come only after the party has demonstrated its firmness by responding in kind to conflictive moves by the side, and for the cooperative initiative to be an offer to negotiate, which, more often than not, is accompanied by a threat or warning. The pattern is not surprising, given the high degree of mutual hostility and distrust characteristic of militarized crises. Although it is a pattern that may be fairly characterized as prudent realism, it is perfectly consistent with the intent of a "firm-but-flexible" influence strategy.

Firmness: responses in kind to attempts at coercion

Another presumed advantage of TFT strategies is that they cannot be exploited. When a TFT strategy is employed in Prisoner's Dilemma, any defection by the other side is immediately punished by a response in kind on the next play of the game. One of the interesting findings from experiments with PD games is that subjects playing the game tend to be quite consistent in their inclination to immediately reciprocate defection by the other party (see Komorita, Hilty, and Parks, 1991: 496). The findings in Chapter 6 indicated that states in real world crises also tend to respond in kind and degree to coercive influence attempts.

This is not to say that strict TFT is necessarily the best way to respond to coercive influence attempts. Game theorists continue to experiment with a number of variations in the degree of tit-for-tat to determine the optimal response to coercion. Is it better, for example, to overreact, in order to alert the other side to the costs and risks of any further attempts at coercion? Or is it more prudent to underreact to discourage rapid escalation of the dispute? Brams and Kilgour (1988: ch. 6) have conducted experiments with "Chicken" games,[4] which suggest that, in crises in which the outbreak of war is viewed as disastrous for both sides, as in a nuclear crisis, the optimal response may be to overreact to low level attempts at coercion and to underreact

171

Table 8.2. *Reciprocating strategies: responses to coercive influence attempts*

Crisis	Actor	Response to threat of force			Response to no threat of force			Outcome
		Higher	Same	Lower	Higher	Same	Lower	
Spanish American	Spain	0	2	2	0	0	0	War
Fashoda	Britain	0	4	0	1	0	2	Victory
1st Moroccan	France	0	0	0	0	1	3	Victory
Bosnian	Austria, Germany	0	0	0	0	1	2	Victory
Bosnian	Serbia, Romania, Turkey	0	0	0	1	1	2	Submit
Agadir	France	0	1	1	0	0	2	Compromise
Agadir	Germany	0	1	0	0	1	0	Compromise
Pre-WWI	Entente	1	8	1	0	0	0	War
Teschen	Czechoslovakia	0	1	0	0	0	0	Compromise
Chaco Dispute	Paraguay	1	0	0	0	0	0	Compromise
Rhineland	France, Britain, Belgium	1	0	0	0	0	3	Submit
Rhineland	Germany	0	0	1	0	0	0	Victory
Polish–Lithuanian	Poland	0	0	0	0	0	0	Compromise
Danzig	Britain, Poland	1	2	2	0	1	0	War
French–Italian	France	0	1	0	0	1	0	Stalemate
Berlin Blockade	US, Britain, France	0	1	5	0	1	1	Victory
Trieste	Italy	0	1	2	1	0	4	Compromise
Honduran B.	Honduras	0	0	0	0	0	0	Compromise
Sino-Indian	China	0	1	2	1	1	2	Compromise
Bizerte	France	1	0	1	0	1	2	Submit
Cyprus	Turkey	0	1	2	0	1	0	Stalemate
Rann of Kutch	Pakistan	0	1	0	0	0	0	War
Cod War	Britain	0	0	1	1	0	4	Compromise
Beagle Channel	Argentina	0	1	1	0	0	0	Compromise
Beagle Channel	Chile	0	1	2	0	0	0	Compromise
	Total	5	27	24	5	10	27	98

to high levels of coercion. The reasoning behind this approach is that the overreaction communicates the gravity which the defender attaches to the seemingly minor challenge, while the underreaction to more serious threats emphasizes the gravity of the danger of escalating mutual coercion. Some empirical support for the effectiveness of this approach in Soviet–American crises has been reported by James and Harvey (1989).

Table 8.2 lists the responses, of states in the sample employing Reciprocating strategies, to negative influence attempts (threats and punishments). To gain a sense of how those states respond to different levels of coercive inducements, a distinction is made based on whether or not the negative inducements include the threat or use of force. The responses are classified according to whether they exceed, match, or fall short of, the degree of coercion to which they are responding.

Table 8.2 indicates that the sides employing Reciprocating strategies in our sample were more likely to underreact (52 percent), than to respond at the same level of coercion (38 percent), or to overreact (10 percent). Moreover, there is no evidence that those states that did underreact more often were more likely to suffer undesirable outcomes. An interesting distinction emerges when the coercive influence attempts are classified according to their severity, that is, according to whether or not military force was threatened or used. The states were most likely (48 percent) to match the coercion of the other side when responding to more severe threats, and to respond at a lower level of coercion than the other side (63 percent), when responding to milder threats.

Most often, the responses at lower levels of coercion consist of carrot-and-stick responses to negative influence attempts, a reaction that would be consistent with the intent of a Reciprocating strategy. That is, the party indicates its firmness by responding in kind to the threat, but it includes an accommodative offer to indicate its flexibility. When the Soviet Union initiated its blockade of West Berlin in 1948, for example, the Western powers responded in kind with a blockade of East Berlin, but, at the same time, they offered to begin negotiations for a settlement of outstanding issues as soon as the Soviet blockade was lifted.

The use of carrot-and-stick responses to coercive influence attempts suggests a mode of eliciting cooperation that has not been explored in game theoretic models. It would appear to be a particularly appropriate tactic to use in situations like militarized crises, in which a party wishes to combine a firm demonstration of its resolve with a signal that it is willing to work toward a cooperative settlement. This seems to have been the case in American–Soviet Cold War crises, in which carrot-and-stick inducements appeared to be particularly effective (Leng, 1984). One could argue, in fact, that carrot-and-stick responses represent the essence of what is meant by a "firm-but-flexible" response strategy.

These mixed reactions occur less often, however, when the other party threatens the use of force. In these instances, there is almost an even balance between responding at a lower level, or at the same level.[5] It is not difficult to speculate on reasons why the parties in the sample were less likely to leaven their responses with accompanying

173

carrots when faced with the threat or use of force: increased hostility generated by psychological reactance to threats to the security of the state, domestic pressures on the government to take an uncompromising position, the dynamics of escalating conflict, or simply a greater tendency on the part of national decision-makers to view crisis bargaining in power politics terms when the national security is threatened directly. But, regardless of which of these factors, or combination of factors, offers the best explanation for the behavior, the behavior itself suggests that, when military force is threatened or used, the opportunities for moving to a cooperative settlement diminish.

Forgiveness: accommodative responses to cooperative initiatives

Another of the presumed strengths of a TFT strategy in eliciting cooperation from the other side, is its "forgiving" quality. TFT requires that all cooperative initiatives from the other side be reciprocated, regardless of the actions that preceded them. This quality provides an important distinguishing difference between Reciprocating and Bullying influence strategies. Reciprocating strategies treat accommodative moves by the other party as opportunities for moving to a settlement; the same moves are viewed by Bullying strategies as signs of weakness to be exploited through intensified coercion.

Experiment with PD games have suggested that the forgiving quality of TFT is important in eliciting cooperation because it inhibits the repetition of negative inducements, which would encourage the two sides to become deadlocked in mutual coercive exchanges. Recent PD experiments by Komorita, Hilty, and Parks (1991), in fact, suggest that responding positively to cooperative moves is more important, in eliciting cooperation from the other side, than responding in kind to negative moves.

To test the extent to which the forgiving criterion is met by the sides employing Reciprocating strategies in our sample, we will examine how those parties respond to positive, or carrot-and-stick, initiatives[6] *that immediately follow negative influence attempts* (threats and punishments). The responses to positive and carrot-and-stick initiatives are divided into three categories, representing three degrees of reciprocation: (1) responses at the same, or a higher level of accommodation, that is, positive responses to positive inducements and carrot-and-stick, or positive, responses to carrot-and-stick inducements; (2) guardedly positive responses in the form of carrot-and-stick responses to positive inducements; and (3) negative responses to positive or

174

Table 8.3. *Reciprocating strategies: forgiving responses*

Crisis	Actor	Matching	C&S to positive	Negative to C&S or positive	Outcome
		Type of response			
Spanish–American	Spain	1	0	0	War
Fashoda	Britain	2	0	1	Victory
1st Moroccan	France	3	1	1	Victory
Bosnian	Austria, Germany	2	0	0	Victory
Bosnian	Serbia, Romania, Turkey	1	1	1	Submit
Agadir	France	1	0	1	Compromise
Agadir	Germany	1	1	0	Compromise
Pre-WWI	Entente	1	0	0	War
Teschen	Czechoslovakia	0	0	0	Compromise
Chaco Dispute	Paraguay	0	0	1	Compromise
Rhineland	France, Britain, Belgium	1	0	0	Submit
Rhineland	Germany	0	1	1	Victory
Polish–Lithuanian	Poland	0	0	0	Compromise
Danzig	Britain, Poland	1	0	0	War
French–Italian	France	0	0	0	Stalemate
Berlin Blockade	US, Britain, France	2	0	2	Victory
Trieste	Italy	3	0	1	Compromise
Honduran B.	Honduras	0	0	0	Compromise
Sino-Indian	China	1	0	0	Compromise
Bizerte	France	1	0	0	Submit
Cyprus	Turkey	1	0	0	Stalemate
Rann of Kutch	Pakistan	0	0	0	War
Cod War	Britain	0	0	0	Compromise
Beagle Channel	Argentina	0	0	0	Compromise
Beagle Channel	Chile	0	1	0	Compromise
	Total	22	5	9	36

Notes: C&S = Carrot-and-Stick. The negative inducement component of a "matching" response to a carrot-and-stick initiative must be at a level of coercion either equal to, or lower than, the negative component of the cooperative initiative.

There are instances where the opportunity to "forgive" does not arise, because there are no positive initiatives immediately following negative inducements.

carrot-and-stick inducements. Table 8.3 employs these categories to present the record of "forgiveness' among the states employing Reciprocating strategies.

Table 8.3 indicates that the Reciprocating states in the sample crises generally met the TFT criterion of forgiveness. Seventy-five percent of the time, the parties immediately responded either in kind to positive or carrot-and-stick initiatives, or with carrot-and-stick responses to positive initiatives, that followed on the heels of purely negative

175

inducements. Although our examination is limited by the relatively small number of observations, the distribution of responses is skewed in favor of the forgiveness criterion.

Clarity: communicating the strategy

The last of the four attributes of TFT that Axelrod (1984) identified as contributing to its effectiveness is its clarity. Axelrod assumed that a TFT strategy would be easily recognized by the other side. The Komorita, Hilty, and Parks (1991) experiments, in which human subjects played PD games against a stooge programmed to play TFT, cast doubt on that hypothesis. The experimenters found that subjects were more likely to think that their TFT-playing opponent was either selecting its moves randomly, or was attempting to seduce them into playing a cooperative strategy and then exploit them. These findings were consistent with those reported in similar studies by Bendor (1987) and Bendor *et al.* (1991).

If TFT's clarity is suspect in the simply structured, controlled, and non-hostile environment of laboratory experiments, it would appear to be far more difficult to recognize the use of a Reciprocating strategy in an interstate crisis, where the signal to noise ratio encourages misperception, and the highly charged atmosphere encourages both sides to distrust the intentions of the other. National leaders embroiled in an escalating crisis with their nations' security at stake, would appear to be more likely than graduate students, who are participating in an academic experiment for pocket money, to take a conservative view of their opponents' motives. There are also a number of reasons to expect a higher degree of ambiguity in signaling a Reciprocating strategy in the more complex and less perfectly programmed atmosphere of real world crises: (1) there may be more than one party on a side, and some of the parties may not be employing Reciprocating strategies; (2) actors may switch strategies during the course of a crisis so that, even though the predominant strategy is Reciprocating, its recognition is distorted by the noise associated with preceding strategies; (3) as we noted in Chapter 7, a side's influence attempt strategy may not be consistent with its response strategy; and (4) there may be inconsistency in the application of the influence strategy itself. The extent to which these potential sources of ambiguity occur among the cases in the sample in which at least one side is employing a predominantly Reciprocating strategy is illustrated in Table 8.4.

The X's in the columns in Table 8.4 indicate instances in which the communication of the Reciprocating influence strategy is distorted by

Table 8.4. *Ambiguity in reciprocating strategies*

Crisis	Actor	Multiple parties and strategies	Strategy switch	Different IA and response strategy	TFT not con- sistent	Total noise	Outcome
Spanish–American	Spain	0	X	0	X	2	War
Fashoda	Britain	0	0	0	0	0	Victory
1st Moroccan	France	X	X	0	0	2	Compromise
Bosnian	Austria, Germany	X	X	X	0	3	Victory
Bosnian	Serbia, Russia, Turkey	X	X	X	X	4	Submit
Agadir	France, Britain	X	0	0	X	2	Compromise
Agadir	Germany	0	0	0	X	1	Compromise
Pre-WWI	Entente	X	X	0	X	3	War
Teschen	Czechoslovakia	0	0	X	0	1	Compromise
Chaco Dispute	Paraguay	0	0	0	0	0	Compromise
Rhineland	France, Britain, Belgium	X	X	X	X	4	Submit
Rhineland	Germany	0	0	X	0	1	Victory
Polish–Lithuanian	Poland	0	X	X	X	3	Compromise
Danzig	Britain, Poland	X	X	X	X	4	War
French–Italian	France	0	0	X	X	2	Stalemate
Berlin Blockade	US, Britain, France	X	X	X	X	4	Victory
Trieste	Italy	0	X	0	X	2	Compromise
Honduran B.	Honduras	0	X	X	X	3	Compromise
Sino-Indian	China	0	X	0	0	1	Compromise
Bizerte	France	0	X	0	X	2	Submit
Cyprus	Turkey	X	0	X	0	2	Stalemate
Rann of Kutch	Pakistan	0	0	X	X	2	War
Cod War	Britain	0	X	0	X	2	Compromise
Beagle Channel	Argentina	0	0	0	X	1	Compromise
Beagle Channel	Chile	0	0	X	X	2	Compromise

one of the categories of noise listed above. At least two of the four categories are present in eighteen of the twenty-five cases. There also is some suggestion that the degree of distortion may be inversely related to successful outcomes. All seven of the cases in which there was none, or just one, of the categories of noise present ended in diplomatic victories or compromises for the side employing a predominantly Reciprocating strategy; whereas only half (nine of eighteen) of the other cases achieved successful outcomes. But the most striking finding in Table 8.4 is the degree of potential ambiguity that is associated with the communication of Reciprocating strategies in real world disputes, particularly when the degree of ambiguity is compared to TFT strategies in PD games, which are more easily recognized to begin with, and which are programmed to be perfectly consistent. If the TFT strategies in PD game experiments are not easily recognized by subjects, as the experiments by Komorita, Hilty, and Parks (1991) suggest, why do we find such a high degree of success in Reciprocating strategy in real world disputes, which are much harder to recognize?[7]

A possible explanation is that statesmen, unlike subjects playing PD games, are able to communicate directly with the other side and explain what is intended by their moves. The moves themselves may be ambiguous, but an interpretation of their intended effects is aided by the actor's accompanying explanation. The verbal explanation is a form of redundancy that aids in overcoming the noise accompanying the signal. This is not to say that the actor is offering an entirely honest explanation of its intentions, but the redundancy that the verbal explanation provides helps to clarify the signal that the actor wants the target to receive. When Hitler marched German troops into the Rhineland in March of 1936 and then assured the world that his intentions were completely defensive, not all statesmen believed him, but they did *hear* him; they had a clear understanding of the signal that he was trying to send to them. By the same token, when President Kennedy announced the US quarantine of Cuba during the Missile crisis of 1962, he told the Soviets that any attempt to breach it would be resisted militarily. The Soviets wondered if he actually would carry out the threat, or if he might be bluffing, but they had a clear understanding of the message that Kennedy was sending to them. As an aside, it might be noted that in the two years following the Missile crisis, Kennedy offered a series of cooperative initiatives to the Soviet Union, which were followed by a significant reduction in tensions between the two sides. Etzioni (1967) has argued that Kennedy, in effect, was following a GRIT strategy.

In Osgood's (1962) formulation of his GRIT strategy for eliciting cooperation between the United States and the Soviet Union, which was described in Chapter 7, he stressed the importance of communication of the actor's motives and planned course of action. Studies comparing GRIT to TFT have found that, when explicit communication is included in the GRIT strategy, it outperforms TFT. The key to its success appears to be the redundancy afforded in a noise environment by the opportunity for explicit communication. (Betz, 1991).

The explanation that accompanies influence attempts in real world crises, of course, is not likely to state that the actor will be employing a particular type of influence strategy, but it is likely to convey the actor's intentions regarding reaching a cooperative settlement, resisting bullying by the other side, or escalating the level of coercion. The clarity issue with regard to the effectiveness of a Reciprocating strategy should not be directed at whether or not the other side is likely to recognize it as a Reciprocating strategy *per se*, but to whether or not the other side will recognize the firm-but-flexible character of the bargaining. How this can be done most effectively is likely to be dependent on the environment in which the strategy is pursued. In the highly charged and hostile environment of an international crisis, we have found that states employing predominantly Reciprocating strategies are likely to demonstrate their firmness *before* attempting any cooperative initiatives. The cooperative initiatives, moreover, tend to be carrot-and-stick inducements, which do not run the risk of indicating weakness. A willingness to cooperate also is signaled by reacting to low level threats with mixed responses, which demonstrate flexibility as well as firmness. The objective is not to signal that the actor is employing a Reciprocating strategy *per se*, but that it is bargaining, and will continued to bargain, in a firm-but-flexible manner.

When states choose reciprocating strategies

Besides the question of how the application of a Reciprocating strategy should be tailored to fit the situation, there is the question of what situations are most appropriate for the use of Reciprocating strategies. Some recent studies in game theory have indicated that the effectiveness of TFT strategies, for example, is dependent on the situation, with TFT ineffective in hostile situations (see Alexrod and Dion, 1988). Our findings suggest that Reciprocating strategies *are* effective in the hostile environment of a militarized crisis, but the states in our sample chose predominantly Reciprocating strategies in less than a third (29 percent) of the cases. Is there a pattern to when states in militarized crises are most likely to choose Reciprocating strategies? And, if there is, does that pattern suggest that the effectiveness of Reciprocating strategies is situationally specific within crises? Do statesmen employ Reciprocating strategies when the situation, within a militarized crisis, suggests that they will be most effective?

There are many situational variables that one could hypothesize as having a significant effect on influence strategy choices, but three which would appear to be particularly salient are: (1) the actor's perception of the crisis structure; (2) its role as challenger or defender of the status quo; and (3) the influence strategy employed by the other side.

179

The crisis structure

Game theory experiments in which carrot-and-stick strategies have been found to be effective have been limited to Prisoner's Dilemma. PD games have two structural characteristics that are of particular relevance to our inquiry. (1) They are symmetrical. That is, each side has the same preference ordering with regard to possible outcomes. (2) Each side prefers a victory over a compromise, a compromise over war, and war over a diplomatic defeat. An analogous situation occurs in the sample of real world crises when the two sides share the same combined motivation scores, and the side employing a Reciprocating strategy views itself as evenly matched in the event of war.

The reader may remember that the motivation score consists of the sum of that side's rank scores on two variables: the perceived security interests at stake, and its perceived war-fighting capabilities. The structure of the crisis is viewed as symmetrical when the summed motivation scores for each of the two sides are equal. It is not necessary that they be the same on both measures. For example, side A may have nonvital security interests at stake (2), and view itself as roughly even to side B in war-fighting capabilities (2) for a motivation score of 4, whereas side B may have vital interests at stake (3), but view itself as over-matched militarily by side A (1), which also would yield a motivation score of 4. From what we have seen in Chapter 3, the utility of going to war may well be the same for both sides in this instance, because of the vital interests at stake for B. If B did not have vital interests at stake, however, the preference orderings would not be the same; B should prefer defeat to war. The second criterion is that the side employing a Reciprocating strategy not view itself as having such a large edge in war-fighting capabilities that it can win a war at low cost. If that were the case, it might prefer to go to war rather than to settle for a compromise outcome.

In Chapter 7, we found fairly strong associations between motivation scores and the choice of either Bullying or Trial-and-Error strategies, but none between motivation and the choice of Reciprocating strategies. Nor is there an observable pattern between structural configurations that are most consistent with Prisoner's Dilemma and the choice of Reciprocating strategies. States choose Reciprocating strategies 31 percent of the time in the overall sample, and 39 percent of the time when the structure is consistent with Prisoner's Dilemma. On the other hand, Reciprocating strategies do appear to be more effective than other strategies which fit the PD criteria. Reciprocating

180

strategies achieve successful outcomes in nine of twelve instances (75 percent) in crises with PD-like structures, as opposed to successes in just seven of nineteen (37 percent) successes when other strategies are used in PD-like crises.

Challenging or defending the status quo

One would expect states to be more likely to choose Reciprocating influence strategies when they are defending, rather than challenging, the status quo. The logic of a Reciprocating strategy – to demonstrate firmness without initiating coercive action – is defensive, rather than offensive. We would expect those states that are challenging the status quo to be more likely to adopt Bullying, or even Trial-and-Error, strategies. These expectations are realized to a moderate degree when we compare the sides initiating the crisis, or defending the status quo in Appendix 5.2 with those choosing Reciprocating strategies. In sixteen of the twenty-five cases, or 64 percent of the time, the party employing a predominantly Reciprocating influence strategy was defending, rather than challenging, the status quo. These cases range from Spain defending its colony in Cuba against the American challenge in 1898, to Chile defending its acquisition of the Beagle Channel Islands[8] against an Argentine challenge in 1977.

Fait accompli. These results become more interesting when we take a close look at the remaining nine cases, all of which, of course, are cases in which the party employing a Reciprocating influence strategy initiated the precipitant action that challenged the status quo. Challenges to the status quo most often come from coercive influence attempts, that is, demands accompanied by verbal threats, or physical demonstrations designed to serve as threats. Less often they represent *fait accompli*, that is, diplomatic or military initiatives by the challenger that effectively change the status quo in its favor. The interesting attribute to the nine cases in which a party employing a Reciprocating strategy precipitated the crisis is that, in all but one of the nine cases,[9] the precipitant action was a *fait accompli*. Table 8.5 lists present the categorization of those sides using Reciprocating strategies according to whether they are defending the status quo, defending a recent *fait accompli*, or neither.

States that precipitate the onset of a crisis with a *fait accompli* find themselves defending a new status quo, that is, the status quo created by the *fait accompli*. This places them in a deterrent position, the situation in which a Reciprocating influence strategy would appear to be most effective. To mention a notorious example, when Hitler

Table 8.5. *Defending or challenging the status quo and reciprocating strategies*

Crisis	Actor	Defending status quo	After *fait accompli*	Other	Outcome
Spanish–American	Spain	X			War
Fashoda	Britain	X			Compromise
Bosnian	Serbia, Russia, Turkey	X			Submit
Agadir	Germany	X			Compromise
Teschen	Czechoslovakia	X			Compromise
Chaco Dispute	Paraguay	X			Compromise
Rhineland	Britain, France	X			Submit
Polish–Lithuanian	Poland	X			Compromise
Danzig	Britain, Poland	X			Compromise
Italo–French	France	X			Stalemate
Trieste	Italy	X			Compromise
Bizerte	France	X			Submit
Cyprus	Turkey	X			Stalemate
Rann of Kutch	Pakistan	X			War
Cod War	Britain	X			Compromise
Beagle Channel	Argentina	X			Compromise
1st Moroccan	France		X		Victory
Bosnian	Austria, Germany		X		Victory
Agadir	France		X		Compromise
Rhineland	Germany		X		Victory
Berlin Blockade	US, Britain, France		X		Victory
Honduran B.	Honduras		X		Compromise
Sino-Indian	China		X		Compromise
Beagle Channel	Chile		X		Compromise
Pre-WWI	Entente			X	War

marched his troops into the Rhineland in 1936, his immediate objective was to solidify his control of the territory by gaining Western acceptance of the new status quo. He pursued this tactic through a Reciprocating strategy by indicating that he would defend his new territorial position militarily if necessary, but that he was ready to negotiate a new twenty-five-year nonaggression pact with France and Belgium. Whatever we may think of the initial action, or of Hitler's long-term intentions, Germany's behavior following the *fait accompli* represents an effective use of a firm-but-flexible bargaining strategy. In fact, the results from our small sample of instances of the use of Reciprocating strategies suggest that the dispute following a *fait accompli* may provide an ideal situation for the use of a Reciprocating influence strategy. The sides employing a Reciprocating strategy following a *fait accompli* obtain successful outcomes in all eight cases. Among the other seventeen cases, the sides employing Reciprocating strategies are successful 53 percent of the time. Four of the eight successes for parties using a Reciprocating strategy to defend a *fait accompli* are diplomatic victories; whereas all the successes in instances in which the party is defending the status quo are compromises.

The *fait accompli* can create a situation in which both parties believe that they are defending that status quo and both adopt Reciprocating strategies. An interesting example occurs in the Bosnian crisis of 1908. Amidst the accelerating distintegration of the Ottoman Empire, the Austrian and Russian foreign ministers reached an agreement that would allow Austria to annex Bosnia and Herzegovina, without Russian objection, in return for Russian military access to the straits. When Austria formally announced the annexation, it was challenged by the Serbs, who demanded that their Russian allies support their challenge. The Russian government performed an about-face; it repudiated its foreign minister's action and joined in the Serbian challenge to the Austrian annexation. Now both sides viewed themselves as on the defensive, and both sides employed Reciprocating influence strategies.

A defensive strategy. More generally, the association between the use of Reciprocating influence strategies and either the defense of the status quo ante, or the defense of a change in the status quo achieved through a *fait accompli*, suggests that the decision to employ a predominantly Reciprocating influence strategy is situationally dependent, that is, it is chosen by those states which find themselves in a defensive position. Reciprocating strategies, in fact, are the modal choices for states in such positions. They are employed in 48 percent of the cases in which states are either defending the status quo, or defending a *fait accompli*; whereas a Reciprocating strategy is employed in only one of the remaining twenty-eight cases. The choice appears to make sense, given the logic of the strategy. The flexible and unaggressive character of a Reciprocating strategy is consistent with a defensive position. The communication of resolve in the face of attempts at coercion by the other side is consistent with experimental findings indicating that individuals are likely to be more risk-acceptant when they are defending against losses than when they are seeking to obtain gains (see Kahneman and Tversky, 1979).

The selection of a Reciprocating strategy under these circumstances appears to be a good choice. If we define a successful outcome as one that results in either a diplomatic victory or a compromise, those sides that were defending the status quo, and were employing Reciprocating influence strategies, were successful 56 percent of the time, as opposed to a success rate of 12 percent for status quo defenders who chose other influence strategies. The success rate is even more impressive for states defending a *fait accompli*. There were twelve of these cases, and the states defending the *fait accompli* chose Reciprocating strategies in eight of the twelve cases. All eight of those sides that chose Reciprocating strategies were successful; all four of those that did not were unsuccessful.[10]

Do these results tell us that Reciprocating strategies are effective only when states are defending the status quo? We cannot begin to answer that question, because we have only one case in which the party employing a Reciprocating influence strategy was not either defending the pre-dispute status quo, or resisting a challenge to a new status quo created by a *fait accompli*. Clearly, Reciprocating strategies are effective in these conditions. What we do not know, is how successful Reciprocating strategies would have been had the states in the sample used them more often in other circumstances.

The other side's influence strategy

As the marginal frequency counts in Table 8.6 illustrate, the match-ups between Reciprocating strategies and other influence strategies in our sample are fairly evenly distributed among the three major types of strategies: Bullying, Reciprocating, and Trial-and-Error. When this distribution is compared to the overall sample, however, the number of match-ups between Reciprocating and Trial-and-Error strategies is a bit more impressive. Half of all instances of Trial-and-Error strategies appear in cases in which the other party employed a Reciprocating influence strategy. To put it another way, if one side employed a Reciprocating strategy, the other side employed a Trial-and-Error strategy in 40 percent of the cases, but if any strategy other than a Reciprocating strategy was employed, a Trial-and-Error strategy was used in only 18 percent of the cases. We only can speculate on whether states are more likely to choose Trial-and-Error strategies. when faced with the influence attempts and responses of parties employing Reciprocating strategies, whether it is the other way around, or if the combination is the result of other factors, such as the situational variables discussed above. What does seem clear, however, is that Reciprocating strategies do particularly well when the other side is employing a Trial-and-Error influence strategy.

Reciprocating versus Trial-and-Error strategies. As table 8.6 indicates, the parties employing Reciprocating strategies have been successful in eight of the ten crises in which they were matched against a side pursuing a Trial-and-Error influence strategy. The results are not surprising when one considers the decision rules for each of the two strategies. Reciprocating strategies reward cooperative moves and

184

Table 8.6. *Reciprocating strategies: match-ups with other strategies and outcomes*

Strategy Match-up	Crisis outcomes					
	Victory	Compromise	War	Submit	Stalemate	Total
Bullying	1 (0.14)	1 (0.14)	4 (0.57)	0 (0.0)	1 (0.14)	7
Trial & Error	2 (0.20)	6 (0.60)	0 (0.0)	1 (0.10)	1 (0.10)	10
Reciprocating	2 (0.25)	4 (0.50)	0 (0.0)	2 (0.25)	0 (0.0)	8
Total	5 (0.20)	11 (0.44)	4 (0.16)	3 (0.12)	2 (0.08)	25

Note: Numbers represent frequency counts with percentages in parentheses.

punish conflictive moves. Trial-and-Error strategies repeat those moves that achieve positive responses and change those that produce negative responses. Consequently, one would expect the intersection of these two influence strategies to move quickly to a compromise outcome. Finding its coercive moves punished by the Reciprocating player would encourage a Trial-and-Error player to attempt a cooperative move, which would be met with cooperation by the Reciprocating player and set in motion a sequence of cooperative moves by both parties. Should the Trial-and-Error player defect from cooperation, the Reciprocating player would respond immediately in kind, thus encouraging the Trial-and-Error player to return to cooperation, which would be rewarded immediately by the forgiving Reciprocating player. Obviously, we are not likely to find such a nicely synchronized movement to mutual cooperation in the real world, where the moves are more ambiguous, and the strategies are not pursued in a consistent manner. Nevertheless, the intersection of the decision rules that comprise these strategies offers a compelling explanation of why the success rate is so high when parties whose actions more closely approximate a Reciprocating strategy are matched against a party whose moves most closely approximate a Trial-and-Error influence strategy.

Reciprocating versus Bullying strategies. Reciprocating strategies are less successful when they are pitted against Bullying strategies. Although they are more effective in achieving successful outcomes against Bullying adversaries than any of the other strategies, four of the seven Reciprocating–Bullying match-ups end in war. An examination of the intersection of the decision rules for the two strategies indicates why there is a high risk of war. Bullying parties pursue a strategy of escalating coercion; Reciprocating strategies rely on firm responses to coercion, leavened by flexibility signalled through cooperative initiatives or carrot-and-stick responses. If the Bullying party does not respond in a positive manner to a cooperative initiative from the Reciprocating party – and the decision rules do not indicate that it should – then the two parties will become locked in a pattern of escalating coercion, as they did in four cases in our sample: the Spanish–American War, World War I, World War II, and the Rann of Kutch conflict between India and Pakistan. The three exceptions in our sample – Cyprus, the Cod War, and the Berlin Blockade – each have some interesting distinguishing characteristics. In the first two instances, the party employing a Reciprocating strategy had a clear military advantage over the other and, in the Cyprus dispute, there also was major power intervention to dampen the escalation.

The Berlin Blockade is a particularly interesting example of the use of a Reciprocating strategy, because of the dramatic success of a "circumventing" tactic, in the form of the Western powers' massive airlift to West Berlin, which circumvented Stalin's attempt to strangle the Western sectors of the city. Lockhart (1979:101–2) has suggested that circumventing tactics are particularly useful in situations where simple resistance, or "blocking tactics," are unlikely to be effective. The Western powers effectively changed the situation by rendering the blockade impotent, and shifting the initiative back to Stalin. Once Stalin was robbed of his ability to coerce the western powers into submission, the firm-but-flexible approach employed in subsequent Western actions led to a diplomatic victory for the West. The Berlin example suggests that the effective use of a Reciprocating strategy against a Bullying opponent may require imagination, as well as the proper mix of firmness and flexibility.

Reciprocating versus Reciprocating. If the effective use of Reciprocating strategies against Bullying opponents requires imagination, one would expect crises in which both parties are employing predominantly Reciprocating strategies to move naturally to compromise solutions. But this outcome occurred in only two of the four cases in our sample in which states pursuing Reciprocating strategies were pitted against each other. In the other two cases – the Bosnian crisis of 1908, and the Rhineland crisis of 1936 – one side achieved a diplomatic victory over the other. In both instances, one could argue that the outcome could be explained by the structure of the dispute. The leaders of the losing sides, Russia in 1908, and Britain in 1936, did not believe that they were ready for war.

Another potential explanation lies in the ambiguity of the Reciprocating strategies employed by Russia and its allies in the Bosnian crisis (1908), and by Britain and its allies in the Rhineland crisis (1936). The ambiguity scores for the losing sides in these two crises are among the four highest appearing in Table 8.4. In the Bosnian crisis, among the states on the losing side, Russia pursued a Reciprocating strategy, Serbia pursued a Bullying strategy, and Turkey pursued an Appeasing strategy. In the Rhineland crisis, while France and Belgium initially attempted to take a firm stand with Reciprocating strategies, Britain pursued an Appeasing influence strategy.

An intriguing third possibility lies in the nature of the situation. Both Austria in 1908, and Germany in 1936, were defending changes in the status quo brought about by *fait accompli*. It may be that Reciprocating strategies simply are not as effective when states are forced into compellent positions, that is, when they must dislodge the other side from a position that it has acquired through a *fait accompli*. The logic of an influence strategy based on initiating cooperation and using coercion only in response to the moves of the other side, would not appear to fit a situation in which a state is attempting to dislodge a determined adversary from a recently acquired *fait accompli*. In these compellent situations, a modified version of a Bullying strategy may be the only feasible choice.

Summary and conclusion

Attributes of an effective Reciprocating strategy

This chapter set out to take a closer look at the use and effectiveness of Reciprocating influence strategies, with effectiveness measured according to the actor's success in eliciting cooperation and achieving peaceful outcomes. Our examination began with an examination of the extent to which the actual practices of states employing predominantly Reciprocating strategies were consistent with what Axelrod (1984) has described as the four attributes of Tit-for-Tat strategies that contribute to their success: niceness, firmness, forgiveness, and clarity. This comparison allowed us to consider those similarities and differences between Reciprocating and TFT strategies that are likely to be most significant in achieving successful outcomes in the highly charged atmosphere of interstate crises. The findings for each of the four criteria can be summarized as follows.

(1) *Niceness*. Whereas TFT strategies begin with a cooperative initiative, the initial cooperative initiatives undertaken by states employing Reciprocating strategies in real world crises most often came only after the Reciprocating side had demonstrated its resolve through responses in kind to attempts at coercion by the other party. Moreover,

the actions signaling cooperation were most often in the form of carrot-and-stick initiatives that coupled offers to cooperate, which were usually offers to negotiate a settlement, with threats or warnings indicating the actor's continuing firmness. This suggests that "niceness," in real world crises, tends to be backed up by a prudent demonstration of firmness, both in the actions preceding the cooperative initiative and in the carrot-and-stick initiative itself. This approach also was the most effective in eliciting cooperative responses.

(2) *Firmness.* TFT requires that actors respond to coercive influence attempts in kind. In the real world crises, the sides employing Reciprocating strategies more often underreacted to threats, by employing carrot-and-stick inducements, which coupled a response in kind to the negative inducement with a positive offer. Carrot-and-stick responses were less likely to be used, however, when states were forced to respond to the threat or use of force. As in the case of cooperative initiatives, the states in the sample were inclined to mix firmness and flexibility within single moves.

(3) *Forgiveness.* The states employing Reciprocating strategies generally followed the TFT criterion of responding in kind to cooperative initiatives, even if they had been preceded by negative inducements.

(4) *Clarity.* The signal to noise ratio in the *predominantly* Reciprocating strategies in the sample suggested that there was too much ambiguity to recognize the application of the strategy through the influence attempt or response sequences employed by the actors. On the other hand, unlike in the computer games studied by Axelrod, real world statesmen have the advantage of verbally explaining the intentions behind their moves. Moreover, it can be argued that the clarity issue should not be directed toward the ability of the other side to recognize the presence of a particular type of influence strategy, but toward the ability of actors to communicate the firm-but-flexible character of their influence strategies.

When states choose Reciprocating influence strategies

The second half of the chapter examined when states were likely to choose Reciprocating influence strategies, and when Reciprocating strategies were most likely to be effective. Answers to these questions were sought in the crisis structure, the situation, and the influence strategy being employed by the other side. Although we found that Reciprocating strategies were avoided when states found themselves at a decided military disadvantage, in all other respects, the distribution of motivation scores for those sides choosing Reciprocating strategies parallels that for the full sample.

A strong association was found between states defending the status quo, and, especially, states defending a *fait accompli*, and the use of Reciprocating strategies. There was only one case of a side employing a Reciprocating strategy that did not fit into one of those two categories. The findings were consistent with both the defensive character of Reciprocating strategies, as well as the high level of risk acceptance required in demonstration of firmness in the face of challenges from the other side. We also found that Reciprocating strategies were relatively successful in these situations, with particularly impressive results for states defending a *fait accompli*.

With regard to the influence strategy of the other side, we found that states employing Reciprocating influence strategies were most often matched against states employing Trial-and-Error strategies, and that the states employing Reciprocating strategies enjoyed a high rate of success in those cases. The success rate is not surprising given the logic of the two strategies, which encourages reinforcing cooperative moves. The intersection of the decision rules when Reciprocating strategies were matched against Bullying strategies, on the other hand, would run a greater risk of war, and we did find that four of the seven cases in which these two strategies were matched against each other ended in war.

Conclusion

The manner in which states employing Reciprocating strategies in real world crises depart from a strict TFT strategy represents a prudent adjustment in the application of a firm-but-flexible strategy to fit a hostile and uncertain environment. The extensive use of carrot-and-stick initiatives and responses, in particular, offers a means of eliciting cooperation without running the risk of appearing irresolute. Reciprocating strategies also offer the advantage of more effectively communicating the dual intentions of a firm-but-flexible strategy. Studies indicating the superiority of GRIT strategies over TFT in PD games point to the explicit communication and redundancy of GRIT, which can be especially important in a noisy and contentious environment. An atmosphere of ambiguity, mixed with hostility and mistrust, which occurs in real world crises, places a heavy burden on effectively communicating intentions.

The use of Reciprocating strategies almost solely in defense of the status quo reflects a prudent understanding of the essentially deterrent, or defensive, nature of a firm-but-flexible influence strategy. The frequency with which Reciprocating strategies are chosen by states who have effectively changed the status quo through a *fait accompli*, and its effectiveness in preserving their recently acquired gains, is an unexpected finding, but it is consistent with the logic of the strategy. The underlying logic of a Reciprocating strategy and its relative effectiveness can be seen as well when Reciprocating strategies intersect with Trial-and-Error and Bullying strategies.

With regard to the larger issue of the role of realist and psychological perspectives on crisis bargaining, what we have observed in the modification of the rules of TFT to fit bargaining in an interstate crisis, and in the choice of situations in which Reciprocating strategies are used, represents an adaptation of a strategy, which is based on a psychological perspective, to fit a hostile environment. Those adaptations, however, reflect changes that mix psychological considerations, such as underreacting instead of overreacting to threats, with prudential realism, such as accompanying carrots with sticks to demonstrate continuing resolve. In the final analysis, the effectiveness of Reciprocating influence strategies may be a function of obtaining a proper balance between realist and psychological considerations in crisis bargaining.

9 SUMMARY AND CONCLUSION

This book began by raising the issue of the descriptive and prescriptive validity of a realist perspective on crisis behavior. The issue of realism's validity was placed at the forefront of this investigation because of the dominant position that realism continues to hold, not only in the study of interstate relations, but in the views of national leaders as well.

Thus, the investigation proceeded from the assumption that the prevailing view of interstate conflict from a realpolitik perspective finds its theoretical expression in classical political realism, both as a description of the nature of international politics and as a guide to successful behavior. Successful crisis bargaining is presumed by realists to be dependent on the state's military power and a convincing demonstration of its willingness to use it to achieve its objectives. The admonition to demonstrate power has been extended to a theory of manipulative bargaining by conflict strategists. Conflict strategists perceive effective crisis bargaining as being dependent on exploiting the other side's fear of war through the use of credible threats and punishments, that is, on demonstrating a willingness to accept the risk of war to achieve state objectives. Viewed from this perspective, interstate crisis bargaining is an essentially competitive activity in which success is achieved through the exploitation of the other side's fear of war coupled with a demonstration of resolve.

While the investigation began with the assumption that most statesmen view interstate crises from a classical realist perspective, it questioned whether they generally act in a manner consistent with the precepts of realism, and, when they do, whether they are likely to be successful. That is, we accepted the validity of realism as a description of how statesmen view crisis behavior, but we questioned its validity as a predictive theory of how states actually behave in crises, as well as its validity as a prescriptive guide to effective crisis behavior.

The realist perspective is challenged by the research of behavioral scientists, who have adopted a psychological approach to understanding conflict behavior. I have described these researchers as working

191

from a psychological perspective because the implied prescriptions in their work grow out of the confounding behavioral effects of psychological variables, in contradistinction to realist prescriptions based on assumptions of calculated rational behavior.[1] Their findings have suggested that the assumption that crisis bargaining must be viewed in competitive terms is overly pessimistic, and the assumption that foreign-policy-makers will respond to coercive influence attempts in a rational, calculating, manner is unrealistic. These researchers have pointed to a number of cognitive and emotional influences on crisis behavior that may exert a confounding effect on the behavior patterns predicted by realists and conflict strategists. Most of our attention was directed toward two of these factors: the potentially pathological effects of spiraling escalation, and evidence of patterns of reciprocating, or tit-for-tat behavior in the interactions of states in crises.

The competing perspectives raised the issue of whether the components of the crisis structure considered most salient by realists – the perceived interests at stake and comparative capabilities – exert the most potent influence on the behavior of the participants and the outcomes of crises, or whether the bargaining strategies and tactics chosen by the participants exert the strongest influence on the evolution and outcomes of crises. More specifically, do the coercive bargaining strategies and tactics prescribed by conflict strategists serve to clarify the dimensions of the crisis structure to the participants on each side, or do they engender psychopolitical reactions that encourage crises to escalate to war?

Summary of findings

Given the amount of ground that has been covered in the preceding chapters, it may be useful to summarize the key findings before offering some conclusions regarding the relative validity of the realist and psychological perspectives on crisis behavior.

Structure and behavior

Working from the classical realist assumption that relations among states are based on the pursuit of interests in terms of power, we identified two critical components to the crisis structure: each side's perception of the interests at stake and its comparative war-fighting capabilities.

Realists assume a hierarchy of interests, with security interests taking precedence over other concerns. Power is viewed in comparative terms, and, in a militarized crisis, its most salient component is the actor's perception of its comparative war-fighting capabilities. From this perspective, the crisis behavior of states can be viewed as a process of signaling and probing until each side is satisfied that it has an accurate perception of the crisis structure, defined as the intersection of the interests at stake and the perceived capabilities of the two sides. Classical realism would predict that states are more likely to accept the costs and risks of war when the security stakes are high and national leaders are relatively optimistic about the consequences of going to war. Conversely, they would be expected to compromise, or even to submit, when there are no security interests at stake and they are pessimistic regarding the consequences of a war.

Within the sample of forty crises, the observed correlation between operational indicators of the two structural variables (perceived interests and capabilities) and the likelihood that crises would end in war turned out to be consistent with realist predictions. The crises in our sample were most likely to end in war when one side perceived itself at a decided military advantage; the other side perceived the two sides to be relatively evenly matched; and both parties had security interests at stake. The interests at stake, however, appeared to be a more powerful predictor than capabilities. Crises in the sample were likely to end in war despite perceptions by both sides that one side enjoyed a significant military advantage, if the weaker side had vital security interests at stake. Moreover, war was avoided in all those cases in which neither side had security interests at stake, regardless of the perceived comparative war-fighting capabilities of the two sides. Predictions of the likelihood that a crisis would end in war based on the structural indicators employed in Chapter 3, yielded a 64 percent gain in accuracy over a simple random guess.

The predictions were most effective, however, in those cases where the indicators took on fairly extreme values, that is, when there was a strong imbalance in the perceived gravity of the interests at stake and the perceived comparative capabilities of the two sides. More than half of the cases in the sample fell into an intermediate category where the combination of interests and capabilities yielded moderate scores and weak predictions.

Behavioral patterns: escalation

From a realist perspective, the escalatory process of a crisis can be viewed as something akin to a learning curve. As the crisis escalates, each side obtains more and more information regarding the crisis structure, through a process of signaling its intentions and probing the resolve of its opponent. When each side is satisfied that it has an accurate perception of the crisis structure, in particular the resolve of the other side, the crisis reaches a turning-point, and moves to a settlement or war (see Snyder and Diesing, 1977).

Researchers adopting a psychological perspective focus their attention on what they see as the pathological consequences of conflict escalation: the physical and emotional effects of stress; the "competition in risk-taking" that results from competing adversaries intent on demonstrating their superior resolve; and the effects of psychological reactance, or of considerations of pride, reputation, or equity, all of which encourage the two sides to become locked in a pattern of escalating coercive exchanges. Where realists see a learning curve, those adopting a psychological perspective see a conflict spiraling out of control.

The investigation of the effects of crisis escalation in Chapter 4 began with the construction of a typology of behavioral types based on the combination of escalation and reciprocity exhibited in the interactions of the participants. A simple distinction between high and low levels of escalation and reciprocity yielded four basic types: a Fight (high escalation, high reciprocity), a Standoff (low escalation, high reciprocity), Resistance (high escalation, low reciprocity), and a Put-Down (low escalation, low reciprocity). The frequency of outcomes associated with each of the four behavioral types are listed in Table 9.1.

The greatest proportion (75 percent) of war outcomes occurs in the Fight category, which most closely models the high escalation and symmetry of a "conflict spiral." Only one of the twelve cases falling into the high reciprocity, low escalation, Standoff category ended in war; moreover, all but one of the nine crises with compromise outcomes occur in this category. The behaviorally symmetric crises falling into these categories are remarkably predictable, with war or compromise outcomes covarying with the degree of escalation. These patterns are consistent with the psychological perspective's emphasis on the dangers of coercive bargaining and the benefits of initiating cooperation.

The crises in the low reciprocity Resistance and Put-Down categories tend to end either in one-sided diplomatic settlements, or in war: none of the crises falling into these types end in compromises. The pattern of outcomes is consistent with the expectations associated with the "aggressor–defender" model of escalation described by these two types. On the other hand, within these two categories, we do not find a significant distinction between war and nonwar outcomes based

194

Table 9.1. *Behavioral types and outcomes*

Fight (R = High, E = Low)	Resistance (R = Low, E = High)
War = 6	War = 7
Nonwar: One-sided = 1	Nonwar: One-sided = 5
Nonwar: Compromise = 1	Nonwar: Stalemate = 1
Nonwar: Stalemate = 0	Nonwar: Compromise = 0
Standoff (R = High, E = Low)	Put-Down (R = Low, E = Low)
Compromise = 8	Nonwar: One-sided = 4
Nonwar: one-sided = 2	War = 3
War = 1	Nonwar: Compromise = 0
Nonwar: Stalemate = 1	Nonwar: Stalemate = 0

Note: R = Reciprocity, E = Escalation.

on the degree of escalation. The cases in the high escalation Resistance category are only marginally more likely to end in war than those in the low escalation Put-Down category. Overall, predicting crisis outcomes based on the behavioral types defined according to the degree of reciprocity and escalation, yields mixed results. The associations between high escalation and war, and between low escalation and compromise outcomes found among the high reciprocity cases, and the tendency of low reciprocity crises to end in either war or one-sided peaceful outcomes are consistent with a behavioral perspective, but the lack of any significant relationship between escalation and war in the low reciprocity cases indicates the insufficiency of predictions based on behavioral patterns alone.

Structure, behavior, and outcome

Structure and escalation. The crises in the sample were likely to escalate to higher levels of conflict when the combined structural scores (interests at stake and optimism regarding the consequences of fighting a war) for the two sides were higher. When this relationship is considered in light of the earlier findings indicating a positive association between high structural scores and war, we find a pattern that is consistent with classical realism as a predictive theory.

The behavior of the crisis participants does appear to have been driven by considerations of security interests and power. High security stakes and war-fighting optimism are associated with greater contentiousness and war outcomes. On the other hand, the strong association between high escalation and war outcomes observed in high reciprocity crises suggests the pathological effects of crisis escalation, a

195

finding that questions the wisdom of the bargaining prescriptions of conflict strategists. When the scores for the crisis structure and crisis escalation are in agreement in predicting whether or not the crisis will end in war, they are correct 92 percent of the time. High stakes and optimism on both sides, combined with high escalation, is the most dangerous mix.

Structure, reciprocity, and major power involvement. The degree of reciprocity in the interactions of the two sides is a good predictor of variations among peaceful outcomes in those crises that do not escalate to war. High reciprocity crises are more likely to end in compromises; low reciprocity cases tend to end in one-sided outcomes.

The degree of reciprocity appears to be unrelated to the crisis structure, but we did find that the involvement of major powers, either as participants on *both* sides, or as intervening third parties, was positively associated with peaceful outcomes, a finding consistent with the realist faith in the diplomacy of experienced major powers. On the other hand, there is no discernible association between major power involvement and high reciprocity scores, or between major power involvement and compromise outcomes. These findings suggest that crises are less likely to escalate to war when major powers are involved, which is consistent with classical realism, but that achieving compromise outcomes may be dependent on reciprocal cooperative exchanges that are independent of the presence, or absence, of major power involvement.

Structure and one-sided outcomes. The crisis structure appeared to be a good candidate to account for the variation between war and nonwar outcomes among crises with low reciprocity scores. While a conflict spiral of reinforcing symmetrical coercive exchanges might contribute to the outbreak of war in high reciprocity crises, the escalation of the low reciprocity Resistance and Put-Down crises would appear to be controlled by the stronger party, with the weaker party forced into a choice between war or submission. A realist perspective would suggest that the crisis is most likely to end in war when the stronger decides that the costs of war are so low that there is no need to moderate its demands and the weaker side has vital interests at stake; otherwise, the weaker side should submit. These patterns, however, fit only half of the twenty low reciprocity cases.

Initiators, escalation, and war. One of the implications in the bargaining prescriptions of conflict strategists is the notion that the escalation and outcome of an interstate crisis can be controlled through aggressive manipulative bargaining. In two-thirds of the crises in the sample, the side that is the first to threaten the use of force also exhibits

196

the higher mean level of escalation over the course of the crisis, and, between two-thirds and three-quarters of the time that side is victorious in those crises in which there is a peaceful outcome. It also turns out that the states exhibiting the higher level of belligerence over the course of a crisis are the most likely to prevail in war. But, if we judge success according to the effect on what realists would call the "national interest," only victories in relatively moderate wars could be considered successes. Based on that criterion, the more aggressive crisis bargainers achieved four military successes, while suffering five defects in moderate wars, and they become embroiled in severe wars in seven cases – hardly an enviable record.

In the sum, the findings from a macroscopic look at the crises in the sample offer some support for both the realists and their critics. The strong association between the crisis structure and war on nonwar crisis outcomes is consistent with classical realism's central precept: that the actions of states are governed by considerations of security interests and comparative capabilities. Added support for the validity of the classical realist perspective comes from the positive association between major power involvement and the avoidance of war. Some indirect support for the prescriptions of conflict strategists can be seen in the higher success rate enjoyed by the party leading the escalation in one-sided peaceful outcomes.

On the other hand, the high frequency with which high escalation, high reciprocity, Fights ended in war is consistent with the dangers of spiraling escalation emphasized by critics of the realists and conflict strategists. There also is an important warning in the high proportion of cases in which the side leading the escalation found itself in a costly war that, in some cases, also led to defeat.

That a macroscopic look at the crisis structure and crisis behavior can take us only so far can be seen from the gaps in what we were able to observe. The structural scores at the extreme ends of the continuum are excellent predictors of war or nonwar outcomes, but over half of the cases in the sample fall closer to the middle, where predictions cannot be made with any confidence. There is a strong relationship between escalation and war or nonwar outcomes in symmetrical crises, but the association does not obtain in that half of the sample that consists of asymmetrical, low reciprocity, cases. The reciprocity indicator is a good predictor of variations among peaceful outcomes, but the degree of reciprocity appears unrelated to either the crisis structure, or major power involvement. With these unexplained inconsistencies in mind, we turned to a more microscopic consideration of the influence tactics and strategies of the crisis participants.

197

Influence attempts and responses

The discussion of the psychological perspective, in Chapter 1, mentioned the role played by the norm of reciprocity in exchanges among states in an anarchical system. It also noted the observation, which was found in a number of studies, of the tendency of both individuals and states to respond in a tit-for-tat manner to both coercive and accommodative influence attempts. Brehm's (1966) theory of "psychological reactance," Esser and Komorita's (1975) and Axelrod's (1984) experiments with Prisoner's Dilemma games, and earlier empirical research on interstate crisis bargaining (Leng and Wheeler, 1979) all point to the pervasiveness of reciprocating reactions to influence attempts. The findings from these studies challenge the bargaining prescriptions of conflict strategies, with their strong emphasis on the use of credible threats of force to demonstrate greater resolve.

The microscopic examination of influence attempts (demands accompanied by accommodative and/or coercive inducements) and responses in Chapter 6, in fact, indicated a strong tendency on the part of crisis participants to respond in a tit-for-tat manner to *all* types of influence attempts. The strong reciprocating pattern also appeared in the association between the *degree* of coercion represented in inducements and responses. As the threats and punishments accompanying demands became more coercive, there was a consistent upward trend in the observed frequency of defiant responses.

We found only very weak associations between the target's perceived capabilities or interests at stake and its responses to influence attempts. And, when these predictions conflicted with those based on the expectation of reciprocating responses, the reciprocating hypothesis prevailed. We did find, however, that there was an association between the interests at stake for the target, and the *actor's* choice of inducement. The higher the stakes for the target, the more coercive the inducements chosen by the actor. This suggests the intriguing possibility, that, although policy-makers in crises do not respond to influence attempts in accordance with classical realist prudence, they may assume that their adversaries do so. The resulting combination is a particularly dangerous one: policy-makers responding to coercive inducements from the other side in a tit-for-tat manner, while relying upon escalating coercive inducements in their own influence attempts. The combination would lead to the two sides becoming locked in escalating coercive exchanges.

A multivariate analysis indicated that the type and degree of induce-

198

ments accompanyaing influence attempts are the keys to predicting target responses. A log-linear model indicated that these two variables interact with each other and with the specificity of inducements, as well as target responses. An important facet to this finding is its indication of what is *not* necessary to an adequate fit of the influence attempt–response model. Traditional realist considerations, such as the cost of compliance, the target's perception of its relative capability, of its interests, and of its interests and capability combined, are not significant predictors of how the target will respond to individual influence attempts. The strongest association lies in the bargaining techniques employed by the would-be influencer.

In addition to uncovering the structure of a remarkably parsimonious model, the analyses confirm the consistent superiority of the reciprocating hypothesis over realist assumptions. This model tells us that: (1) the states in the sample were overwhelmingly likely to respond in a tit-for-tat manner to positive, negative, or carrot-and-stick inducements from would-be-influencers; (2) as inducements became more coercive, there was a consistent trend toward more coercive responses; and (3) this pattern was not significantly affected by the relative capabilities of the disputants and/or the interests at stake for the target.

Influence strategies

Influence attempts represent the tactical components of a state's overall influence strategy. While the analysis of how states are likely to respond to different varieties of influence tactics can give us a sense of the prevalence of tit-for-tat exchanges in crisis bargaining, it could be a misleading way in which to judge the relative merits of coercive or accommodative approaches to bargaining. An immediate defiant response to an attempt at coercion, for example, may represent an initial "face-saving" reaction, from which the state later retreats. Moreover, responses in kind to accommodative influence attempts may come only after the accommodative move was preceded by a long train of escalating coercive inducements. A more complete image of the bargaining process can be obtained by focusing on the overall influence strategies employed by the participants over the evolution of the crisis.

The analyses of influence strategies, in fact, yielded results that were consistent with the findings for influence attempts and responses. The percentage of outcomes for each of the three major strategies employed – Bullying, Reciprocating, and Trial-and-Error – appear in Table 9.2.[2]

Table 9.2. *Influence strategies and outcomes*

| Strategy | Crisis outcomes (percentages) | | | |
	Victory	Compromise	War	Defeat
Bullying	23	4	65	4
Reciprocating	20	44	16	12
Trial and error	5	32	26	32

Note: Four cases with stalemate outcomes have not been included in the table.

Escalating coercive Bullying strategies led to war in nearly two-thirds of the crises in which they were employed, whereas modified Reciprocating influence strategies produced diplomatic victories or compromise outcomes in nearly two-thirds of the instances in which they were employed. The third major type of influence strategy, a Trial-and-Error approach, did slightly better than Bullying strategies in achieving diplomatic victories or compromises, but they also led either to war or diplomatic defeats in over half of the crises in which they were employed. Thus, the findings indicated that "firm-but-flexible" Reciprocating strategies produced the highest rate of success in allowing states to obtain diplomatic victories or compromise outcomes.

The association between the type of influence strategy employed and the crisis outcome is intriguing in light of the positive association observed between the crisis structure and crisis outcomes. The former is consistent with a reciprocating model of crisis bargaining, whereas the latter is more consistent with classical realism. Interestingly, we also observed some association between the crisis structure and the choice of influence strategy. Foreign policy-makers tend to choose Bullying strategies when the interests at stake and their war-fighting optimism are high, and they tend to choose Trial-and-Error strategies when the situation is reversed. That pattern fits the realist admonition to demonstrate power when it appears justified by the interests at stake and the military capability to prevail in war, and to exercise caution when the conditions do not justify taking large risks. On the other hand, the choice of Reciprocating strategies, which are the most effective influence strategic overall, appears independent of the crisis structure. Reciprocating strategies are the second most likely choice across all structural levels.

These findings returned us to a question, which was posed initially at the beginning of Chapter 3, regarding the relationship between the crisis structure, crisis behavior, and crisis outcomes. Is the crisis outcome primarily dependent on the crisis structure, as classical realism suggests? Or is the outcome of a crisis more dependent on the

200

behavior of the participants, as theorists working from a psychological perspective suggest? Or are variations in crisis outcomes a function of the combined influences of the crisis structure *and* the influence strategies of the participants? Although the constraints of the data make any conclusions tentative at best, the findings suggested that the most reasonable hypothesis is the third one. Although the choice of influence strategy is dependent to some extent on the crisis structure, the crisis outcome appears to be influenced by both the crisis structure and the influence strategies employed by the disputants.

In sum, the analysis of the relationships between the crisis structure, influence strategies, and crisis outcomes indicated that statesmen have been more likely to choose belligerent influence strategies when the stakes have been high and they have been relatively optimistic regarding the consequences of a war. In that respect, the findings are consistent with the views of classical realists, like Morgenthau (1960), or Blainey (1973). On the other hand, the association found between influence strategies and outcomes is more consistent with the views of realism's critics. The positive association found between Bullying influence strategies and war outcomes demonstrates the risks inherent in adopting a simple power politics approach. The positive association found between Reciprocating influence strategies and successful peaceful outcomes demonstrates the efficacy of adopting a firm-but-flexible approach, which reduces the psychological and political dangers associated with a strategy of escalating coercion. These findings are consistent with the psychological perspective of Esser and Komorita (1975), and Axelrod (1984), as well as my own previous work (Leng and Wheeler, 1979).

In essence, the findings related to influence strategies suggest that, while considerations of interests and capabilities play an important role in crisis decision-making, other factors, such as psychological reactance to threatening behavior, the symmetry of two sides determined to credibly demonstrate resolve, and the centrality of reciprocity in interstate exchanges, exert a strong influence on crisis behavior. The influence of these variables is suggested by both the immediate responses to influence attempts observed in Chapter 6 and the effectiveness of Reciprocating influence strategies observed in Chapter 7.

Reciprocating influence strategies

The firm-but-flexible approach associated with Reciprocating influence strategies is presumed to be effective in eliciting cooperation from the other side because it combines a credible demonstration of

201

the party's resolve to resist any attempts at coercion, while demonstrating a willingness to move to a cooperative settlement. Just how this is done, and when it works best, are important questions whose answers may help us better understand the relationship between the realpolitik and psychological dimensions of crisis behavior.

Reciprocating influence strategies are a more flexible version of the standard TFT strategy employed in Prisoner's Dilemma games, in which the TFT player begins with a cooperative opening move and then responds in a tit-for-tat manner to the moves of the other party for the remainder of the game. Axelrod (1984) has argued that TFT strategies are effective because they demonstrate *niceness*, through the opening cooperative initiative, *firmness* through the tit-for-tat responses to noncooperative moves, *forgiveness* in immediate tit-for-tat responses to any cooperative move, regardless of how many non-cooperative moves preceded it, and *clarity* in that the other side can easily recognize the tit-for-tat approach. With the exception of clarity, we found evidence of each of these qualities in the Reciprocating strategies employed by the states in the sample. Those qualities, however, appeared in more conservative variations, which seem to be better suited to the highly charged atmosphere of an interstate crisis, as well as being consistent with the classical realist admonition to exercise prudence.

Among the sides employing Reciprocating influence strategies in the real world crises, for example, the "niceness," represented by a cooperative initiative, was less likely to come at the outset of a crisis, than after the party exhibited its resolve through responses in kind to coercive moves by the other side. Moreover, those cooperative initiatives most often were conditional offers to negotiate that came in the form of carrot-and-stick influence attempts, rather than purely accommodative moves. The other side of this more conservative approach was apparent in the manner in which firmness was exhibited. Provided that the other side stopped short of threatening military force, the reciprocating states tended to underreact, rather than overreact to threats and punishments. The underreaction most often appeared in the form of a carrot-and-stick response, rather than in a tit-for-tat reaction to coercion. The "forgiveness" attribute noted by Axelrod was generally followed by the states employing Reciprocating strategies, with responses in kind to cooperative initiatives that followed on the heels of attempts at coercion. But, overall, the application of Reciprocating strategies in the real world crises exhibited a more cautious approach that would appear to be more effective than a simple TFT strategy in interstate crisis bargaining.

202

There was too much ambiguity in the implementation of the real world Reciprocating strategies to satisfy Axelrod's clarity criterion. On the other hand, real world statesmen, unlike players in Prisoner's Dilemma games, have the advantage of being able to explain their strategy to the other side. It can be argued too, that the clarity question, insofar as it has relevance to real world crises, lies not in recognizing the influence strategy *per se*, but in its firm-but-flexible character. The key is to communicate firmness in an unthreatening manner while also exhibiting a willingness to work toward a cooperative settlement.

Alongside the question of how states in real world crises employ Reciprocating strategies, there is the question of the situations in which they are most likely to be effective. I noted above that there was no apparent association between the choice of Reciprocating strategies and the parties' perceived interests and capabilities. There is, however, a remarkably strong positive association between the defense of the status quo, whether it is a long-standing status quo or the defense of a *fait accompli* resulting from the precipitant action of one of the sides to the dispute, and the choice of Reciprocating bargaining strategies. Moreover, Reciprocating strategies enjoy a remarkably high success rate (56 percent) compared to the use of other types of influence strategies in defensive situations (12 percent). It should not be surprising that exhibiting firmness in an unchallenging manner, while indicating a willingness to move to a cooperative settlement, should work best in a defensive position, but the linkage between the use of a *fait accompli*, and its successful defense through the use of a Reciprocating strategy, is revealing. As a bargaining tactic, the *fait accompli* is an effective means of shifting the initiative to the other side (see Schelling, 1966:43–49) and placing oneself in a stronger defensive position.

A third question concerns the relative effectiveness of Reciprocating strategies when they are paired against one, or another, of the types of influence strategies identified. Axelrod's (1984) experiments indicated that, although TFT strategies were the most effective prisoner's Dilemma strategies overall, they were less effective against parties employing essentially noncooperative strategies. Reciprocating strategies also have their greatest tendency to escalate to war in the real world crises in the sample when they are matched against Bullying strategies, although Reciprocating strategies are more effective against Bullying strategies than any of the other possible types of influence strategies, including Bullying pitted against Bullying strategies. The states in the sample were most likely to use Reciprocating strategies when they confronted other states who were employing Trial-and-Error influence strategies. These also were the match-ups in which

Reciprocating strategies were most effective. There were only four cases in the sample in which both sides employed Reciprocating strategies, and war was avoided in all four cases, with two of the crises ending in compromises.

One of the most interesting aspects to the findings regarding the pairings of Reciprocating strategies with other influence strategies in the real world crises is that the observed outcomes are consistent with what one would expect from the intersection of the decision rules of the two strategies. When a Reciprocating strategy is paired against a Bullying strategy, for example, the intersection of the decision rules of the two strategies should lead to escalating conflict. Bullying parties pursue a strategy of escalating coercion; Reciprocating strategies rely on firm responses to coercion, leavened by flexibility signaled through cooperative initiatives or carrot-and-stick responses. If the Bullying party does not respond in a positive manner to a cooperative initiative from the Reciprocating party – and the decision rules do not indicate that it should – then the two parties will become locked in a pattern of escalating coercion. On the other hand, when a Reciprocating strategy is matched against a Trial-and-Error strategy, a strategy that rewards cooperative moves and punishes conflictive moves intersects with a strategy that repeats those moves that achieve positive responses and changes those that produce negative responses. Consequently, one would expect the intersection of these two influence strategies to move quickly to a compromise outcome.

In sum, the closer look at Reciprocating strategies in Chapter 8 offers interesting insights on the variations in Tit-for-Tat that are necessary to the success of Reciprocating strategies, as well as the conditions under which they are most likely to be effective.

Conclusions

In the course of the methodological discussion in Chapter 2, it was argued that the best way to conduct a study of interstate crisis behavior is through the observation and description of the actual behavior of the crisis participants. At the same time, the reader was warned of the limits of findings based on correlational analyses of a limited set of variables within a limited sample of crises. Even with complete confidence in the validity of the observed associations, and of the representativeness of the sample, based on the correlational findings alone, it would not be possible to say *why* states do, or do not, act in a manner consistent with classical realist perspective, and why they are more, or less, successful when they follow the prescriptions of the conflict strategists. Given the nature of the research problem, the limited data available, and the research techniques employed, there can be no claim that this investigation is the last word on these questions. Nonetheless, the findings that we have been able to draw from the crises in the sample, support a middle ground explanation for the seeming contradictions between the views of classical realists and conflict strategists on the one hand, and the findings of researchers who have adopted a more psychological perspective, on the other hand.

I noted in the summary that the strong association found between the crisis structure and war or nonwar crisis outcomes is consistent with classical realism's core precept: that the actions of states are governed by considerations of interest, defined in terms of power. The security interests at stake and perceived war-fighting capabilities also were good predictors of the influence strategies and tactics chosen by crisis participants. Additional evidence in support of the prudential side of realism was found in the association between major power involvement and peaceful crisis outcomes. Morgenthau (1960, ch. 31), in particular, argues for the efficacy of traditional major power diplomacy as the most prudent way to manage interstate conflicts. We also found some evidence in support of the bargaining prescriptions of conflict strategists, who stress the importance of credibly demonstrating a willingness to risk war through the use of coercive bargaining tactics to achieve the state's objectives in a crisis. Those sides that initiate the threat or use of force, and behave in a more belligerent manner over the course of the crisis, are more likely to prevail in those crises with one-sided peaceful outcomes. Taken by themselves, these findings suggest support for classical realism as a predictive theory of crisis behavior, particularly with regard to the likelihood of crises escalating to war, as well as offering some support for the bargaining prescriptions of conflict strategists.

On the other hand, the positive association observed between symmetrically escalating Fights and war outcomes, suggests the dangerous consequences of two parties intent on following the prescriptions of conflict strategists, just as the strong association between high reciprocity, low escalation, Standoffs and compromise outcomes, suggests the rewards of moderation. The most serious challenge to the coercive bargaining prescriptions of conflict strategists, however, appears in the high degree of tit-for-tat found in the responses to both coercive, and cooperative influence attempts, and in the tendency of escalating coercive Bullying influence strategies to lead to war. The high degree of reciprocity in the crisis behavior of states generally, along with

205

evidence of a high rate of success enjoyed by states employing firm-but-flexible Reciprocating influence strategies, offer support for researchers working from a psychological perspective who stress the importance of psychological and political factors that encourage statesmen to respond to influence attempts in a tit-for-tat manner.

If there is another lesson to be learned from the relative effectiveness of Reciprocating influence strategies, it lies in the benefits that come from not attempting to be too clever. Besides the heavy reliance on the use of coercive bargaining techniques, the manipulative bargaining techniques of the conflict strategies create additional dangers by advocating bargaining strategems that create imprudent risks in order to achieve greater credibility in the eyes of the other side. Unwanted wars can occur because both sides are so intent on creating an inflated image of the ease with which they will enter into them. There is much to be said, in diplomacy as in other human affairs, for behaving in a straightforward and reasonable manner, for the choice of clarity over subtlety.

Overall, the evidence suggests that there is some validity to both the realist and psychological perspectives, but that neither can offer a sufficient description on its own. The structural variables identified as most important by realists appear to play a significant role in guiding the behavior of states in crises, but predictions based on the crisis structure alone can be confounded by the reactions of each side to the behavior of the other, as well as the dynamics of an escalating conflict. A credible demonstration of resolve is an important component of effective crisis bargaining, but overly aggressive behavior is likely to encourage escalation to war, and to an unwavering focus on the competitive side of crisis diplomacy that can cause statesmen to ignore opportunities to reach compromise settlements. In these respects, the findings are characterized most suitably as evidence of the limitations of a realist perspective, rather than a rejection of the validity of classical realism's basic tenets. The realists are correct in pointing to the variables that count in international conflicts, and in warning us that bargaining in a militarized crisis is not just a matter of "sitting down and reasoning together."[3]

The limitations of a realist perspective, however, lie in basing prescriptions for action on the assumption of rationality in crisis behavior. The realists appear to be correct in recognizing the salience of considerations of interest and power, but the behavior of the states in the crises examined in this investigation suggests that other psychological and political considerations exert a strong influence as well. The observed tendency of states to respond to both cooperative and coercive influence attempts in a reciprocating manner is consistent with psychological theories of reactance, as well as with the research on the role of reciprocity as a norm for social exchange.

The best approach to crisis bargaining is a prudential application of some of classical realism's basic precepts with a recognition of the dangers cited by its critics. Such an approach would include a recognition of the importance of considerations of security interests, power, and reputation for resolve for *both* sides, as well as the psychological and political factors encouraging states to respond to influence attempts in a tit-for-tat manner. The Reciprocating bargaining strategies, described in Chapters 7 and 8, offer a good illustration of an approach to crisis bargaining that takes both perspectives into account. In the form in which these strategies were most often employed by states in the sample, they represent a refinement of Tit-for-Tat that is more appropriate to the highly charged atmosphere of a real world crisis. The reciprocating party demonstrates its willingness to move to a cooperative settlement through accommodative initiatives, but only after demonstrating its resolve to the other side. The cooperative initiative itself is in the form of a carrot-and-stick inducement, in order to avoid communicating weakness.

On the other side of the coin, the reciprocating party does not initiate the threat of force, thus it avoids initiating threats to the security and independence of the other party. Resolve is demonstrated through responses in kind to threats and punishments, but these often are in the form of carrot-and-stick responses, which leave the door open for cooperation, rather than encouraging the two parties to become locked in to a pattern of spiraling conflict. When a Reciprocating influence strategy is employed in this manner, it indicates a willingness to move to a cooperative settlement without signaling weakness, and it exhibits resolve in a manner that does not threaten the other side's independence, or prestige.

In the sum, the answer to the descriptive and predictive questions regarding the validity of the classical realist perspective, which were posed at the outset of the book, is mixed. Classical realism does succeed in recognizing some of the most important variables influencing the crisis behavior of states, and in doing so, it improves our ability to predict the crisis behavior of the crisis participants and crisis outcomes. It also provides an important warning to recognize the limits of what can be attained by cooperative initiatives alone in "a world where power counts." The realist perspective, however, affords an incomplete picture, which undermines its predictive power. More important, ignoring those psychological and political variables that lie

207

outside of the realist perspective can lead to disastrous consequences for states following realist prescriptions, particularly as they are extended to manipulative bargaining by conflict strategists.

Policy implications

The broad policy implication behind all of these findings is that foreign-policy-makers need to adopt a middle ground that recognizes the role of both realpolitik and reciprocity in crisis bargaining. The findings suggest that, when states are in a defensive position, the best approach is embodied in what I have labeled a Reciprocating influence strategy, which allows states to exhibit resolve without adopting offensive coercive tactics, while, at the same time, indicating a willingness to move to a cooperative settlement through the use of carrot-and-stick inducements. As I noted in Chapter 7, an excellent example of the effective use of a Reciprocating strategy in defense of the status quo occurs in the bargaining of the Western powers in the Berlin blockade crisis of 1948–49, when a firm, but unthreatening, defense of Western access to the city was coupled with a willingness to negotiate on the issue of currency reform in the western zones of Berlin.

The policy prescription is more problematic for states that find themselves in disputes requiring that they challenge the current status quo, such as the situations confronting Great Britain in the Fashoda crisis of 1898, or the United States in the Cuban Missile crisis of 1962. In these instances, realism tells us that the challenger to the status quo must take the initiative in employing coercive threats in order to persuade the other side to abandon its position, that is, it may be necessary to adopt a modified version of a Bullying influence strategy. The role of reciprocity in interstate crisis behavior, as well as the frequency with which states in the sample who employed Bullying strategies found themselves in wars, suggests that such strategies must be applied with greater sensitivity and caution than is often found in interstate crisis bargaining. Unnecessary provocations must be avoided, and a way found for the other side to conduct a face-saving retreat in a negotiated settlement. That, in fact, is what Britain and the United States did in their successful influence strategies in the Fashoda and Cuban crises. The British managed to obtain a French withdrawal from Fashoda – ostensibly for reasons of health – via a predominantly Reciprocating strategy. The United States finally resorted to an ultimatum in the Cuban crisis, but it was accompanied by face-saving carrots in the form of a public pledge to refrain from any future invasion of the island, and a secret agreement to remove US missiles from Turkey.

After all of the frequency distributions, tables, and statistics in preceding chapters, these policy recommendations may seem like little more than common sense, or what classical realists would call "prudence." But it is a prudence that grows out of a recognition of psychological influences that are not part of the realist prescription particularly as it has been adapted to crisis bargaining by conflict strategists. By the same token, the works of those who prescribe bargaining based solely on cooperative initiatives too often neglect the role of considerations of power in interstate conflicts. Bargaining in a militarized crisis is not just a matter of "getting to yes."[4] Moreover, the policy prescriptions suggested by this study, however commonsensical, have not been applied as commonly as one might wish in real world crises. An instructive example appears in the case study of the Persian Gulf crisis that is presented in the Epilogue.

EPILOGUE:
THE 1990–1991 CRISIS IN THE
PERSIAN GULF

The research for this book was nearing completion in the summer of 1990, when Iraqi forces invaded Kuwait and precipitated the larger crisis that led to a larger war six months later. The analysis of a current crisis presents obvious data generation problems, but the opportunity to apply what we had been doing with the historical cases to escalating crisis in the Persian Gulf was too tempting to resist. Using only the daily *New York Times* as a source for the event data, we decided to undertake a "quick and dirty" analysis. The results, however tentative, offer an interesting perspective on the Gulf crisis, as well as underlining some of the more general findings regarding the descriptive and prescriptive validity of realist and psychological perspectives on crisis behavior.

Background: the key events

What began as an economic dispute over oil prices between Iraq and its Persian Gulf neighbors, escalated to a militarized crisis during the summer of 1990, when Iraq charged that the Gulf monarchies were engaged in a plot to keep prices down, and that Kuwait was stealing oil from the disputed Rumailia oil field that straddled the Iraqi–Kuwait border. By late July, Iraq had moved 100,000 troops to the border with Kuwait. Following a break-down in talks between the two states, Iraq invaded, conquered, and occupied Kuwait on August 2, 1990.

The Iraqi invasion was condemned as an act of aggression by the United States, the United Nations Security Council, and the Arab League. US President Bush declared that Saudi Arabia's security was of "vital interest" to the United States. On August 6, US paratroopers were dispatched to Saudi Arabia, as the United Nations Security Council was voting to impose mandatory economic sanctions against Iraq. Two days later, Iraq announced that it had annexed Kuwait, an action the Security Council quickly declared "null and void." Follow-

210

ing a call for a "holy war" against his adversaries, Saddam Hussein suggested, on August 12, that an Iraqi withdrawal from Kuwait was possible, dependent on an Israeli withdrawal from the occupied territories. Hussein seized Western civilians as hostages, and threatened to use them as "human shields" against a United States attack, by interning the hostages at military installations.

Iraq undertook new diplomatic initiatives in early September, by releasing some of the hostages, and renouncing the territorial claims that had been the basis of its war with Iran, in order to appease a potential adversary. Iraqi forces also raided Western embassies in Kuwait. The United States, and other members of the UN coalition, meanwhile, continued to add to the military build-up in Saudi Arabia, which now exceeded 100,000 troops.

At the beginning of October, President Bush suggested that an Iraqi withdrawal from Kuwait could be followed by efforts to resolve the Arab–Israeli conflict. There were unconfirmed Soviet reports, in mid-October, indicating that Iraq might withdraw from Kuwait in return for complete control over the Rumailia oil field and two strategically important small islands at the head of the Persian Gulf. Any compromise, however, was rejected by the United States, as President Bush reiterated his demand for nothing less than a total Iraqi withdrawal.

By early November, the UN coalition had assembled 200,000 troops in the Gulf region. Shortly after the US congressional elections, President Bush indicated that the force in Saudi Arabia would double by January, in order to provide for an offensive military option. Iraq responded by announcing that it would increase its forces in the area to 680,000. On November 29, the Security Council authorized the use of "all means necessary" to expel Iraqi forces from Kuwait, provided that Iraq did not withdraw voluntarily by January 15, 1991. On the next day, President Bush proposed a meeting between US Secretary of State Baker and Iraqi Foreign Minister Aziz. Several diplomatic efforts followed, including a fruitless one-day meeting in Geneva between Baker and Aziz, on January 9. As the January 15 deadline neared, a final trip to Iraq by Perez de Cuellar failed to break the deadlock. The fighting began with the bombing of Baghdad on January 16, 1991.[1]

Following over a month of intense bombing, the Iraqi forces were routed in a two-day land assault by the UN coalition. Iraq suffered up to 100,000 combatant fatalities, while the UN forces suffered fewer than 1,000 fatalities. There are no reliable estimates of civilian fatalities, but the war resulted in widespread human suffering and property damage in Kuwait and Iraq, and a regional environmental disaster of unprecedented proportions.

211

Analysis

The crisis structure

The indicators of the two sides' perceptions of the interests at stake and their comparative war-fighting capabilities, which are described in Chapter 3, have been the most subjective indicators employed in our investigation of crisis behavior. The application of the three level ranking to the two sides' estimates of their comparative war-fighting capabilities, however, is relatively straightforward. The United States, as the leader of the UN coalition, believed that, once sufficient forces were in place, the coalition could easily defeat Iraq. Saddam Hussein, on the other hand, appeared to have expected – or at least believed that he had good reason to hope for – a long war that would reach a stalemate that would lead to the withdrawal of the coalition forces.

President Bush and his advisors made it clear that they considered the security of Saudi Arabia, which was threatened so long as Iraq occupied Kuwait, to be important to United States security interests. Bush referred to Saudi security as a "vital" US interest, but his use of the term does not meet our more restrictive definition of vital interests, which requires a direct threat to the state's territorial integrity or political independence. Thus, for the United States, based on the rankings described in Chapter 5, the combined *motivation* score would be 5: the expectation of a decisive military victory (3), and nonvital security interests at stake (2).

Estimating the stakes for Iraq presents a more difficult problem. When Saddam Hussein announced that Iraq had annexed Kuwait as its nineteenth province, it technically made Iraqi control of Kuwait a vital security interest, that is, it became part of the territorial integrity of Iraq. It is doubtful, however, that Saddam saw it that way, as evidenced by his offers to withdraw from Kuwait, provided he were granted certain concessions. However insincere those offers may have been, the fact that they were made at all suggests that Saddam did not consider retention of Kuwait a vital interest for Iraq.

Prior to the Iraqi invasion of Kuwait on August 2, 1990, the dispute between Iraq and Kuwait that preceded the invasion was ostensibly over economic issues, although there have been some indications that Saddam Hussein viewed the actions of the other Gulf oil exporters as attempts to destabilize his regime. Whether or not Hussein perceived the pre-invasion dispute as related to Iraqi security interests, after Iraq occupied and annexed Kuwait, Hussein was not in a position to

212

withdraw without threatening the security of his regime. The issue then becomes one of whether it is reasonable to say that security was at stake, if the issue of security refers to the security of Saddam's regime, as opposed to the Iraqi state in a larger sense. Because we have defined our indicators in terms of the perceptions of those who are making foreign-policy decisions, the answer is yes. Saddam Hussein perceived his personal political security threatened by an unconditional withdrawal from Kuwait; therefore, how Iraq responded to the events over the course of the crisis, and any decision to go to war, or to accept one or another peaceful settlement, would involve considerations of security. Thus, the motivation score for Iraq would be 4. The Iraqi regime perceived that it had nonvital security interests at stake (2), and that, if it went to war, Iraq would have a reasonable chance of emerging from a protracted war without being defeated (2).

Based on what we found in the investigation of the sample of forty interstate crises, the 5–4 combined structural score is a dangerous pairing. Nine of the eleven (82 percent) cases in the sample with 5–4 pairings ended in war. In the other two instances, one side yielded to the demands of the other; there were no compromises. The predicted relationship between the intersection of the perceptions of the crisis structure held by the two sides and crisis outcomes is derived from the classical realist assumption that statesmen act rationally, according to considerations of interest, defined in terms of power. In the preceding chapters we found the crisis structure to be the best realist predictor of crisis outcomes, and the outcome of the Gulf crisis is consistent with those findings.

It is possible to carry the implications of the two sides' perceptions of the crisis structure one step further in a game theoretic model. Working from the perspective of Snyder and Diesing (1977), we can rank the preference orderings of the two sides with regard to possible outcomes. For the United States, which had nonvital security interests at stake and believed that it could win a war at low cost, the order of preferences were: (1) a voluntary, unconditional Iraqi withdrawal; (2) war to force an Iraqi withdrawal; (3) a compromise settlement; and (4) acceptance of the Iraqi seizure of Kuwait. For Iraq, which also had nonvital security interests at stake, but which viewed a war as likely to be protracted, with an uncertain outcome, the preference ordering was: (1) retention of Kuwait without war; (2) a compromise settlement; (3) war; and (4) a voluntary withdrawal from Kuwait. The preferences of the two sides can be depicted in the two-by-two game matrix in Table E.1.

The rank ordering of preferences for each side appears in the cells,

Table E.1. *Gulf War crisis game*

		Iraq strategies	
		Compromise	Resist
US/UN strategies	Compromise	Compromise settlement (2,3)	UN Coalition accepts Iraqi annexation of Kuwait (1,4)
	Escalate	Unconditional Iraqi withdrawal from Kuwait (4,1)	War (3,2)

with 4 indicating a player's most preferred outcome and 1 indicating its least preferred outcome. In this game, each player has a dominant strategy – Escalate for the United States, and Resist for Iraq – and the game has a strong equilibrium at the (3,2) war outcome.[2] Provided that the preference orderings of the two sides do not change, the outcome is unavoidable. In other words, Iraq can avoid war or a diplomatic defeat only by convincing the United States that a compromise is preferable to war, and the United States can avoid going to war, or accepting a compromise settlement, only by persuading Iraq that an unconditional withdrawal is preferable to war. If war is to be avoided, the two sides must bargain with an understanding of the outcome matrix in mind.

Escalation: the behavioral type

Time series of the actions of the two sides, categorized and weighted according to the procedures described in Chapter 4, appear in Figure E.1. The overall pattern in Figure E.1 is most consistent with the high escalation, low reciprocity, Resistance behavioral type. The low reciprocity score for the Gulf War crisis results from the growing distance between the escalation scores, starting in the sixth week of the crisis, that is, the second week of September 1990. During the first five weeks of the crisis, the behavioral pattern resembles the conflict spiral of a Fight. By mid-September, however, Iraq begins to moderate the degree of escalation on its side, with a variety of diplomatic initiatives, while the members of the UN coalition continue to increase the size of their military build-up, so that the behavioral pattern takes on the appearance of the aggressor-defender model of crisis escalation associ-

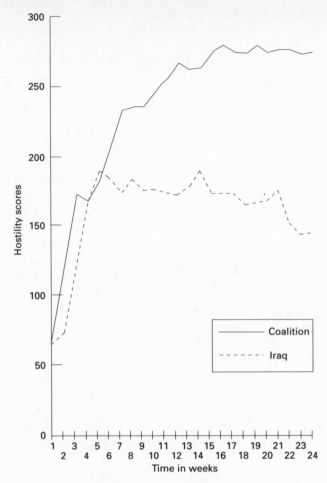

Figure E.1   Gulf War crisis, 1990–1991

ated with the Resistance and Put-Down behavioral types. A somewhat similar pattern can be seen in Figure 4.6 in Chapter 4, which exhibits the time series for the crisis over Fashoda between Britain and France at the end of the nineteenth century. The Fashoda crisis, which ended with France yielding in the face of carefully crafted British threats, never reached the level of escalation exhibited by the Gulf War crisis, however, largely due to the careful diplomacy of the British, who exhibited firmness, while avoiding inflammatory rhetoric and excessive coercion.

Twelve of the thirteen crises in the sample that fell into the Resistance category ended either in a war, or in one side submitting to the

215

demands of the other.[3] Given the structural pairing noted above, along with the high level of escalation, the more likely outcome was war. That was the fate of 92 percent of the crises in the sample that had a similar combination of high structural scores and high escalation.

Influence tactics

The Persian Gulf crisis began with a *fait accompli* – Iraq's seizure of Kuwait. The United States, and, ultimately, a large coalition of nations acting under the umbrella of the United Nations, challenged the action, and Iraq resisted the challenge. The overall pattern of influence attempts consisted primarily of escalating coercive attempts at compellence by the United States, which yielded tit-for-tat responses from Iraq.

The tit-for-tat responses by Iraq to efforts at coercion, whether to verbal threats or to military preparations for war, are consistent with the behavior patterns observed in the sample, which exhibited responses in kind to a variety of influence attempts under different circumstances. The situation in the Gulf War crisis would seem to be particularly conducive to this pattern. Following the *fait accompli*, Iraq was able to maneuver itself into a defensive position, with the initiative thrown to the United States and its partners in the UN coalition, who now were faced with a difficult effort in compellence. On the other hand, the seizure of Kuwait committed Saddam Hussein both politically and psychologically. It could be argued, from a manipulative bargaining perspective, that the inflexibility engendered by the commitment strengthened his bargaining position, but it also made it more difficult to retreat when the conditions demanded it. Saddam's *fait accompli* raised the stakes for Iraq. Retreat was made even more difficult by President Bush's rejection of any face-saving way out for Iraq.

Influence strategies

As the leader of the UN coalition, the United States employed an escalating coercive Bullying influence strategy throughout the crisis. The consistency of the US strategy is reflected in its identification as the predominant US influence strategy on all three of the operational indicators employed in Chapter 7: the pattern of escalation, the predominant influence attempt strategy, and the predominant response strategy. Iraq's predominant influence strategy is most consistent with a Reciprocating strategy. Although the predominant influence *attempt* strategy most closely resembles a Trial-and-Error approach, the other two indicators – Iraq's response strategy and the time series of its behavior over the course of the crisis – are more consistent with a Reciprocating influence strategy.[4]

These strategy choices are consistent with what was observed in the larger sample. States are most likely to choose Bullying strategies when their motivation scores are high, that is, when security interests are at stake and they are optimistic regarding the consequences of a war – the position in which American policy-makers saw themselves. Among the crises in the sample, the choice of Reciprocating strategies, on the other hand, was largely unrelated to the structural score. There was, however, a strong association between states defending the status quo, including a new status quo created by a *fait accompli*, and the use of Reciprocating influence strategies – the situation that Saddam Hussein had created for Iraq.

Within the larger sample, match-ups between Bullying and Reciprocating strategies ended in war in four of seven instances. The intersection of the decision-rules for the two strategies, in fact, encourages escalation. The Reciprocating party responds in kind to efforts at coercion and the Bullying party follows any response short of compliance with more coercion. If the Bullying party does not respond in a positive manner to cooperative initiatives from the Reciprocating party, then the two sides become locked in a pattern of rising escalation led by the Bullying party. That, in fact, is what happened in the Gulf War crisis.

On the other hand, Reciprocating strategies were found to be more successful against Bullying strategies than any of the other four types, and they were particularly successful when employed in the defense of a *fait accompli*. Thus, it appears that Iraq chose the best influence strategy available under the circumstances. The issue would appear to be whether it employed that strategy in the most effective manner.

Iraq's Reciprocating strategy. One of the most interesting findings in Chapter 8 concerns the difference between the successful application of Reciprocating strategies in real world interstate crises as opposed to strict Tit-for-Tat (TFT) bargaining strategies. There were three major differences. (1) Whereas TFT strategies begin with a cooperative initiative, the initial cooperative initiatives undertaken by states employing Reciprocating strategies in real world crises most often come after the Reciprocating side had demonstrated its resolve through responses in kind to attempts at coercion by the other side. (2) Cooperative initiatives generally were in the form of carrot-and-stick offers, so that the offer from the Reciprocating party would not suggest weakness. The most common initiatives, and those that were the most effective in eliciting cooperation, were offers to negotiate. (3) In exhibiting firmness in responses to coercive influence attempts by the other side, the sides employing Reciprocating strategies often underreacted, by employing carrot-and-stick responses that mixed firmness with flexibility in the same move, rather than reacting purely in kind.

In employing carrot-and-stick cooperative initiatives, Iraq suffered from its weak position. The threats that Iraq could employ – encouraging terrorism or mistreating hostages – increased the hostility and inflexibility of the other side, thus they had the effect of weakening, rather than strengthening the impact of any cooperative initiatives. As the weaker party facing a Bullying adversary, Iraq should have been the first to propose ongoing negotiations – the most common form of positive initiative among the states in the sample that employed Reciprocating strategies. Iraq took the opposite tack, and its intransigence only encouraged an image of inflexibility. The few cooperative initiatives from Iraq[5] either appeared to be propaganda efforts, such as the offer to withdraw from Kuwait in return for Israeli withdrawal from the occupied territories, or surfaced only as unsubstantiated hints through third parties, such as the Soviet report in mid-October indicating that Saddam might be willing to withdraw from Kuwait in return for a share of the Rumailia oil field and control of Warba and Bubiyan islands. Despite efforts by several interested parties, including the Soviets, the United Nations Secretary General, and the French, at no time did Saddam Hussein's government indicate that it was willing to consider anything resembling a realistic way out of the dilemma it had created for itself.[6]

As the party in a deterrent position, Iraq responded in a tit-for-tat manner to coercive American influence attempts. Verbal threats were met with counter-threats; increases in coalition troop deployments in Saudi Arabia were met with comparable increases in Iraqi forces in Kuwait. There was no attempt to signal flexibility with carrot-and-stick responses to negative influence attempts. In addition, any hint of Iraqi flexibility was drowned out by the noise from its bellicose propaganda statements, the seizure and mistreatment of Western hostages, and reports of Iraqi atrocities committed within Kuwait.

United States' Bullying Strategy. The American objective in the Gulf War crisis was stated on several occasions by President Bush: the "unconditional, and complete withdrawal of all Iraqi forces from Kuwait" (August 8, 1990). To achieve that objective, the United States employed a Bullying influence strategy that was a textbook example of the classical realist admonition to demonstrate power and of its extension to crisis bargaining by conflict strategists. The credibility of the US threat to go to war, if necessary, to achieve its objectives was demonstrated through its public statements, diplomatic activities, and, above all, the continuing military build-up. What Schelling (1966:ch. 2) has called the "art of commitment" was exemplified by the situation that the US government had created by the beginning of 1991: authorization to use force from both the Congress and the UN Security Council, the UNSC ultimatum, the President's repeated public commitments to accept nothing less than an unconditional Iraqi withdrawal, and over 443,000 US and other coalition troops in the area at combat readiness.

As the crisis escalated, the United States's Bullying strategy narrowed the path of retreat for Iraq. There was a modest positive cooperative US initiative in late August, when President Bush expressed a "willingness to open a dialogue," and another in early October when Bush indicated his willingness to follow an Iraqi withdrawal with efforts to resolve the Arab–Israeli crisis. The Iraqis responded indirectly to the second initiative via the compromise proposal reported by the Soviet Union in mid-October, but a compromise was not what Bush had in mind. The US position hardened as the crisis escalated and the balance of forces in the region shifted in its favor.

The prudential side of classical realism urges the avoidance of unnecessary wars, and conflict strategists, however much they may emphasize the importance of a credible demonstration of resolve, recognize the need to provide a means for the other side to save face (see Schelling, 1966:124). In the critical last month of the crisis, however, the US offered no line of retreat for Iraq. In conjunction with the Security Council ultimatum, President Bush stated his willingness to have Secretary Baker meet with Iraqi Foreign Minister Tariq Aziz, but solely to convince Saddam Hussein that "we are not bluffing" (*New York Times*, November 30, 1990). Then, when a date for the meeting finally had been agreed upon, Bush publicly declared that there would be "no negotiations, no compromises, no attempts at face-saving, and no rewards for aggression" (January 3, 1991). Bush's message to Iraq was clear: choose between submission or war.

In sum, to a large extent, the situation dictated the influence strategies chosen by the two sides. Given the deterrent situation that Iraq created for itself, a Reciprocating strategy represented the best approach to either retaining Kuwait, or to obtaining some concessions in return for withdrawing. Finding themselves in a compellent position against an adversary intent on defending its *fait accompli*, the

219

United States and its allies could achieve their objectives only through a coercive strategy. Thus, the fault, if there is one, in the bargaining of the two sides lies not in the choice of influence strategies, but in the inflexibility with which they were implemented. On both sides, an unwavering focus on the need to demonstrate resolve excluded the consideration of potential peaceful solutions.

Conclusion

The attributes of the Gulf War crisis are consistent with those observed in several cases within the sample of forty historical crises. The intersection of each side's ranking on the two structural indicators drawn from classical realism – perceived security interests and war-fighting capabilities – was highly associated with war outcomes in the larger sample. The pattern of behavior observed in the time series of the mix of weighted cooperative and conflictive actions for the two sides is consistent with the high escalation, low reciprocity, behavioral type that I have labelled Resistance. With just one exception, crises in the sample whose behavioral patterns fit the Resistance type, ended either in war or in one side yielding to the demands of the other. None ended in compromises. The intersection of Bullying and Reciprocating strategies runs a high risk of having the two sides become locked in a pattern of escalating conflict, led by the coercive influence attempts of the Bullying side. That was the pattern observed in the Gulf War crisis. In short, the Gulf War crisis is a very typical representative of a type appearing in the larger sample, a type that usually ends in war.

It is also representative of what we have found with regard to the issue of the descriptive and prescriptive validity of the realist perspective. The influence strategies chosen by the two sides, and the crisis outcome, are consistent with the structural attributes of the crisis. If there is an issue, it is not with the influence strategies chosen by the two sides. Based on what we have seen among the crises in the sample, the Bullying and Reciprocating strategies employed by the US and Iraq respectively, were the most appropriate choices under the circumstances. The issue concerns the manner in which those strategies were implemented, that is, the influence *tactics* employed by the two sides.

From a realist perspective, it could be argued that the bargaining of each side represented an overly crude and inflexible version of the prescriptions of the conflict strategists. On the other hand, critics of the approach of the conflict strategists would argue that those consequences are inherent in the focus on crisis bargaining as a strictly competitive activity. Iraq's inflexibility and bellicosity could be criticized from both perspectives. Realists would note that Iraq's bargaining represented a poor understanding of the realities of its comparative war-fighting capabilities; theorists working from a psychological perspective would note that many of Saddam Hussein's tactics – the inflammatory rhetoric, the seizure and mistreatment of hostages, the atrocities in Kuwait – unnecessarily encouraged the hostility and inflexibility of the other side. There were ample amounts of both in Bush's bargaining. Once the coalition had sufficient forces in place to withstand any attack from Iraq, he publicly committed himself to reject consideration of a face-saving retreat for Iraq. Bush also personalized the dispute between himself and Saddam Hussein, an approach that could only add to the psychological and political pressure on Saddam Hussein to adopt an inflexible approach as well.

It is easy to criticize the influence tactics of Saddam Hussein from either a realist or a psychological perspective. He woefully misjudged Iraq's power and the motivation of his adversaries, and his application of a Reciprocating influence strategy was devoid of the demonstration of flexibility necessary to elicit cooperation from the other side. The only reasonable way out of the trap into which Saddam Hussein had led his country was through a face-saving retreat. His refusal to make a serious diplomatic effort to do so is an inexcusable diplomatic failure. That refusal could have been related to Saddam's perception of the threat to his personal power that any retreat would entail. Thus, one could argue that for Saddam, there were "vital" interests, of a most personal sort, at stake. On the other hand, given the realities of his comparative military capabilities, even his personal power would have been better served by a face-saving withdrawal, with his military capabilities intact and the economic embargo lifted.[7]

If one assumes that, for the United States, a face-saving retreat by Iraq was a preferable outcome to the war, then President Bush's approach to bargaining can be criticized for its lack of flexibility and unnecessary bellicosity as well. By publicly committing himself to reject any face-saving way out for Iraq, Bush may have thrown away the only feasible possibility of achieving their stated objectives without war. On the other hand, as the crisis evolved, the Bush administration added new American objectives – elimination of Iraq's nuclear and chemical weapons capabilities, a severe reduction in Iraq's conventional forces, the removal of Saddam Hussein – which Iraq would be considerably less likely to accept in any peaceful settlement. Moreover, the Bush administration may have seen domestic advantages to going to war. When the cease-fire was announced on February 28, 1991, President Bush triumphantly declared that the United States had "exorcised the ghost of Vietnam." It is possible, in other words, that the preference ordering for the United States changed as the crisis escalated, so the White House came to prefer war over any other outcome, including Iraq's acceptance of the United Nations demands. This writer knows of no hard evidence to support that hypothesis, but there is no doubt that the American objectives grew with the escalation of the crisis, much in the manner described in Chapter 4, and that the new objectives made the achievement of a peaceful outcome considerably more difficult.

There is no way of knowing whether Saddam Hussein would have accepted a face-saving way out of the crisis had the United States offered it. Certainly, his actions signaled otherwise. Nor is there any way of knowing if the United States would have been willing to consider such a possibility had Iraq bargained in a more flexible, less provocative, manner. President Bush's public statements indicate that he saw no intermediate ground between unconditional acceptance of his demands and rewarding aggression.

Beyond the issue of whether a face-saving peaceful solution to the Gulf War crisis was possible, there is the issue of whether, from the perspective of the United States, and the larger international community, it would have been desirable. As a matter of principle, should the international community reject offering any concessions whatever to aggressors? Is the principle worth the deaths and suffering of hundreds of thousands of victims of its implementation? Such questions go well beyond the scope of this investigation. What it does tell us is that, in a situation fraught with a high probability of war, the bargaining of the two sides contributed nothing to its avoidance.

Appendix 1
CRISES: STANDARDIZED SCORES ON BEHAVIORAL DIMENSIONS

Crisis	Reciprocity			Escalation		
	Distance	Direction	Combined	Rate	Magnitude	Combined
Pastry	-0.186	0.219	0.033	-0.3841	-0.156	-0.540
Crimean	-0.501	-0.487	-0.987	-0.3606	0.115	-0.245
Schleswig–Holstein	0.595	-0.215	0.380	0.3689	-0.812	-0.443
Russo–Turkish	-0.522	0.219	-0.303	-0.3485	-0.386	-0.734
British–Russian	-0.844	0.813	-0.031	-0.3803	-0.233	-0.613
British–Portuguese	0.719	0.554	1.273	-0.2023	-0.892	-1.095
Spanish–American	-0.208	-0.838	-1.046	1.4515	0.584	2.035
Fashoda	-0.270	-0.229	-0.500	0.3242	-0.006	0.318
1st Moroccan	0.505	0.811	1.316	-0.4447	-0.967	-1.421
2nd Central American	0.510	0.600	1.200	0.3311	-0.684	-0.353
Bosnian	0.414	-1.057	-0.642	-0.3455	0.738	0.393
Agadir	0.777	0.629	1.405	-0.3682	-0.823	-1.191
1st Balkan	0.743	0.535	1.278	0.4674	-0.591	-0.123

Appendix 1 (*cont.*)

Crisis	Reciprocity			Escalation		
	Distance	Direction	Combined	Rate	Magnitude	Combined
2nd Balkan	0.631	0.446	1.077	-0.3189	0.275	-0.043
Pre WWI	0.066	-3.866	-3.800	4.8485	0.397	5.245
Teschen	0.250	1.024	1.274	-0.4152	-0.359	-0.774
Chaco Dispute	0.493	1.100	1.593	-0.4514	-1.019	-1.470
Chaco War	-0.619	0.744	0.125	-0.3425	-0.320	-0.662
Manchurian	0.587	-0.229	0.358	-0.0985	-0.653	-0.752
Italo–Ethiopian	-4.027	-0.580	-4.601	0.4826	1.803	2.285
Rhineland	0.630	0.673	1.304	-0.3803	0.496	0.116
Anschluss	0.576	-0.600	-0.024	0.7585	-0.897	-0.803
Munich	-1.139	-0.596	-1.735	0.3682	0.642	1.010
Polish–Lithuanian	0.617	0.231	0.848	-2.2652	-0.927	-3.192
Danzig	-0.386	0.458	0.072	-0.0530	0.138	0.085
Italo–French	0.657	0.345	1.002	-0.3712	-0.496	-0.867
1st Kashmir	0.092	0.442	0.534	-0.1235	2.022	1.898
Berlin Blockade	-0.145	-0.740	-0.886	-0.4386	2.758	2.320
Suez	-3.410	-3.041	-6.451	1.9265	2.098	4.025
Honduran Border	0.724	0.880	1.605	-0.4500	-0.974	-1.424
Sino–Indian	0.456	0.759	1.214	-0.4015	-0.433	-0.835
Bizerte	0.042	-0.132	-0.090	-0.7167	-1.319	-2.036
Cuban Missile	-0.342	-1.134	-1.476	0.4000	0.231	0.631
Cyprus	0.687	-0.391	0.295	0.3106	2.404	2.715
Rann of Kutch	0.252	-0.022	0.230	-0.0212	0.066	0.045
Cod War	0.587	0.560	1.146	-0.3129	-0.511	-0.824
Beagle Channel	-0.160	0.544	0.384	-0.2871	-0.250	-0.037
Sino Vietnamese	0.108	0.744	0.852	-0.3311	-0.653	-0.984

Appendix 2
STRUCTURAL VARIABLES AND PREDICTED BEHAVIORAL TYPES

War-fighting capability perception	Scores	Behavioral type
1 Both sides = easy victory.	3–3	Fight
2 A = easy victory, B = even.	3–2	Resistance
3 Both sides = evenly matched.	2–2	Standoff (Fight)
4 A = easy victory, B = lose.	3–1	Put-Down
5 A = even, B = lose.	2–1	Put-Down
6 Both sides = lose.	1–1	Standoff

Interests	Scores	Behavioral Type
1 Both sides = vital security.	3–3	Fight
2 A = vital, B = nonvital security.	3–2	Resistance
3 Both sides = nonvital security.	2–2	Fight (Standoff)
4 A = vital, B = nonsecurity.	3–1	Put-Down
5 A = security, B = nonsecurity.	2–1	Put-Down
6 Both sides = nonsecurity.	1–1	Standoff

Motivation score and behavioral type

6–6 = Fight	5–4 = Resistance	4–1 = Put-Down
6–5 = Fight	5–3 = Put-Down	3–3 = Standoff
6–4 = Resistance	5–2 = Put-Down	3–2 = Put-Down
6–3 = Put-Down	5–1 = Put-Down	3–1 = Put-Down
6–2 = Put-Down	4–4 = Standoff (Fight)	2–2 = Standoff
6–1 = Put-Down	4–3 = Put-Down	
5–5 = Fight	4–2 = Put-Down	

Appendix 3
CRISIS PRECIPITANT, FIRST THREAT OF FORCE, ESCALATION, AND OUTCOME

Crises	Precip- itant Act by:	1st threat of force by:	Escal- ation Score	Wars: Battle deaths/ 1,000	Outcome
Pastry War					
France	X	X	0.021		Diplomatic Victory
Mexico			0.005		Diplomatic Defeat
Crimean War				15.8	
Russia	X	X	0.008	14.4	War (Severe)
Turkey, Britain, France			0.026	16.7	War (Severe)
Schleswig-Holstein				0.8	
Prussia, Austria- Hungary		X	0.040	0.3	War (Victory)
Denmark	X		0.017	11.1	War (Defeat)
Russo-Turkish				23.1	
Russia	X	X	0.016	12.6	War (Severe)
Turkey			0.001	58.5	War (Severe)
British–Russian					
Britain	X	X	0.025		Diplomatic Victory
Russia			0.001		Diplomatic Defeat
British Portuguese					
Britain	X	X	0.011		Diplomatic Victory
Portugal			0.001		Diplomatic Defeat
Spanish–American				1.1	
Spain			0.068	2.7	War (Defeat)
United States	X	X	0.094	0.7	War (Victory)
Fashoda Crisis					
Britain		X	0.058		Diplomatic Victory
France	X		0.018		Diplomatic Defeat
1st Moroccan Crisis					
France	X		0.003		Diplomatic Victory
Germany		X	0.002		Diplomatic Defeat
2nd Central American				4.3	
Hondruas, Salvador	X	X	0.022	4.0	War (Defeat)
Nicaragua			0.036	5.0	War (Victory)
Bosnian Crisis					
Austro-Hungarian Germany	X		0.022		Diplomatic Victory
Serbia, Russia, Turkey		X	0.029		Diplomatic Defeat

Appendix 3 *(cont.)*

Crises	Precip- itant Act by:	1st threat of force by:	Escal- ation Score	Wars: Battle deaths/ 1,000	Outcome
2nd Moroccan Crisis					
France, Britain	X		0.005		Compromise
Germany		X	0.005		Compromise
1st Balkan War				25.5	
Serbia, Bulgaria, Greece	X		0.035	51.5	War (Severe)
Turkey		X	0.035	9.4	War (Severe)
2nd Balkan War				15.6	
Bulgaria			0.017	40.0	War (Severe)
Romania, Greece, Serbia, Turkey	X	X	0.024	12.4	War (Severe)
Pre-World War I				141.5	
Austria-Hungary, Germany		X	0.088	250.8	War (Severe)
Russia, Britain, France, Serbia	X		0.147	157.9	War (Severe)
Teschen Crisis					
Czechoslovakia			0.013		Compromise
Poland	X	X	0.005		Compromise
Chaco Dispute					
Bolivia	X		0.002		Compromise
Paraguay		X	0.002		Compromise
Chaco War				382.4	
Bolivia			0.023	320.0	War (Severe)
Paraguay	X	X	0.002	555.6	War (Severe)
Manchurian War				1.1	
Japan		X	0.014	1.5	War (Victory)
China	X		0.002	1.0	War (Defeat)
Italo-Ethiopian War				3.6	
Ethiopia		X	0.019	13.1	War (Defeat)
Italy	X	X	0.112	0.9	War (Victory)
Rhineland Crisis					
France, Belgium, Britain			0.018		Diplomatic Defeat
Germany	X	X	0.025		Diplomatic Victory
Anschluss Crisis					
Austria			0.006		Diplomatic Defeat
Germany	X	X	0.031		Diplomatic Victory
Munich Crisis					
Czechoslovakia, Britain, France			0.071		Diplomatic Defeat
Germany	X	X	0.023		Diplomatic Victory
Polish-Lithuanian Crisis					
Lithuania	X	X	−0.044		Compromise
Poland			−0.070		Compromise
Danzig (Pre-WW II)				106.3	
Germany	X		0.011	502.2	War (Severe)
Poland, Britain		X	0.041	61.6	War (Severe)

Appendix 3 (*cont.*)

Crises	Precip- itant Act by:	1st threat of force by:	Escal- ation Score	Wars: Battle deaths/ 1,000	Outcome
Italo-French Crisis					
Italy, Germany	X	X	0.012		Stalemate
France		X	0.006		Stalemate
1st Kashmir War					
India		X	0.044	[a]	War (Victory)
Pakistan	X	X	0.054	[a]	War (Defeat)
Berlin Blockade					
Britain, France, US	X		0.041		Diplomatic Victory
USSR		X	0.057		Diplomatic Defeat
Trieste Crisis					
Italy		X	0.001		Compromise
Yugoslavia	X		−0.003		Compromise
Suez Crisis				0.3	
Egypt	X	X	0.042	1.3	War (Defeat)
Britain, France, Israel			0.189	1.3	War (Victory)
Honduran Border					
Honduras	X		−0.000		Compromise
Nicaragua		X	0.001		Compromise
Sino-Indian Border					
China		X	0.011		Compromise
India	X		0.007		Compromise
Bizerte Dispute					
France			−0.026		Diplomatic Defeat
Tunisia	X	X	−0.001		Diplomatic Victory
Cuban Missile Crisis					
United States		X	0.064		Diplomatic Victory
USSR, Cuba	X		0.022		Diplomatic Defeat
Cyprus Crisis					
Greece, Greek Cypriots	X		0.067		Compromise
Turkey, Turkish Cypriots		X	0.062		Compromise
2nd Kashmir War				0.1	
India	X	X	0.019	0.1	War (Compro)
Pakistan		X	0.014	0.3	War (Compro)
Rann of Kutch					
India	X	X	0.032	[a]	War (Defeat)
Pakistan		X	0.023	[a]	War (Victory)
Cod War					
Britain			0.013		Compromise
Iceland	X	X	0.009		Compromise
Beagle Channel Dispute					
Argentina	X		0.029		Compromise
Chile		X	0.014		Compromise
Sino-Vietnam War				0.2	
China	X	X	0.015	0.1	War (Victory)
Vietnam	X	X	0.002	1.6	War (Defeat)

[a] Statistics not available from the Small and Singer (1982) data.

Appendix 4
IDENTIFYING INFLUENCE STRATEGIES BY TIME SERIES

Bullying
1 Consistent upward trend in the escalation of conflictive action.
2 Escalation level is consistently higher than, or equal to, that of other side.
3 Leads the other party in escalatory movement.
4 No deviations in the form of unilateral deescalation or accommodation, except for modest spikes following an extended period of escalation.

Reciprocating
1 Behavior matches other party's pattern of escalation and deescalation.
2 Level of escalation, or deescalation equal to, or close to, that of the other side.
3 Lags the other party in escalation.
4 If the reciprocator takes the lead in deescalation, the moves will appear as short downward spikes, unless matched by the other side.

Appeasing
1 Consistent pattern of increasing deescalation.
2 Escalation level lower and leading other party in deescalation.
3 Deescalation as the other side's escalation level remains constant or moves upward.

Trial-and-Error
1 Low reciprocity.
2 Switching direction between escalation and deescalation.

Stonewalling
1 Very low level of activity for long periods.
2 Moves are strictly conflictive, lagging those of the other party.

Appendix 5
DETERMINING THE PREDOMINANT INFLUENCE ATTEMPT STRATEGY

Last inducement (Actor) Response (Target)	Change in inducement for next influence attempt								
	Less Positive	More Positive	More Positive, More Negative	More Positive, Less Negative	Less Positive, Less Negative	Less Positive, More Negative	Less Negative	More Negative	Repeat
POSITIVE									
Comply	B	R,A	–			B		B	T,R,A
Placate	B	R,A,T	T			B		B	T,R
Ignore	R	A,T	T,A			B,T		T,B	A
Defy	T	A	T			R,B,T		R,T,B	A
Mixed	B,R	A	R			B		R,T,B	A
NEGATIVE									
Comply	R	R		R			R	B	T,B,R
Placate	R	R		R			R	B,T	B,T
Ignore	T	T		A,T			A,T	R,B,T	B,R

Defy	R,T	R	A,T			A,T	R,B	R
Mixed		R	R,A			R	B	B
CARROT & STICK								
Comply	R,T	–	R,T	B	R	B	B	B,A,T,R
Placate	A,R,T	–	R,A	B	T,A	B	R,B	R,T
Ignore	A,R,T	T,R	A,T	B,R	T,A	B,R	R,B,T	R
Defy	A,T	R	A,T	B,R	T,A	B,R	R,B	A
Mixed	A,T,R	T,R	A,T	B	T,A	B	R,T,B	R
NONE								
Comply	R	–					B	B,A,T,R
Placate	A,R,T	T					B,T	T
Ignore	A,T	T,R					B,T	–
Defy	A,T	T					B,R,T	–
Mixed	A,R,T	T,R					B,T	–

Notes: B = Bully, R = Reciprocating, A = Appeasing, T = Trial-and-Error influence strategies.

"–" indicates that the choice does not fit any of the strategies.

The table in Appendix 7.2 is read in the following manner:

(1) In attempting to influence the target, the actor chooses an inducement from one of the upper case categories in the first column: Positive, Negative, Carrot & Stick, or None.

(2) The target responds to that inducement with one of the five responses listed under the inducement type in the first column. For example, the actor may have employed a Negative inducement and the target responds with "Placate."

(3) Then the inducement employed in actor's *next* influence attempt is identified compared with that employed in the influence attempt in (1) above. The headings for columns 2 through 9 contain the possible comparisons.

Example: The actor, after having employed a negative influence attempt in the form of a warning, with no threat of force, to which the target responds in a placating manner, decides to move to a threat of force on the next influence attempt. The initial Negative inducement would be identified in column 1, along with the target's Placate response. Then, since the threat of force inducement chosen by the actor for its next inducement is "more negative" than the preceding inducement, we look for influence strategies which fit the type in the intersection of column 9 and row 7. The possibilities are Bully (B), or Trial-and-Error (T).

Appendix 6
DECISION RULES FOR IDENTIFYING RESPONSE STRATEGIES

Influence attempt	Response type								
Inducement	Comply	Placate	Ignore	Defy	Defy-TF	Defy-MF	Mixed	Mixed-TF	Mixed-MF
Positive	A,R	R	SW	B	B	B	B	B	B
None	A	A	SW	B	B	B	B,R	B	B
Negative	A	A	SW	R	B	B	R	R	R
Neg.-TF	A	A	SW	R	R	B	A	R	R
Neg.-MF	A	A	SW	R	R	R	A	R	R
C&S	A	A	SW	B	B	B	R	B	B
C&S-TF	A	A	SW	SW	B	B	A	R	B
C&S-MF	A	A	SW	SW	R	B	A	A	R

Notes: TF = Threat of Force, MF = Use of Force. A = Appeasing, B = Bullying, R = Reciprocating, SW = Stonewalling strategies. Trial and Error response strategies are a special case. They are identified according to the sequence of responses following influence attempts in a manner similar to determining the strategies for influence attempts. For example, if state A responds to a negative influence attempt with a Placate response, and then, when confronted with another negative influence attempt, A switches to a Defy response, the pattern would be consistent with a Trial-and-Error strategy.

Appendix 7
INFLUENCE STRATEGIES

Crisis	Actor	Influence strategy indicators				Final choice
		Time Series	Predominant Influence Attempt	Predominant Response	Qualitative Judgment	Influence Strategy
Pastry	France	R,T	B	B	B	Bully
	Mexico	T	A	T	T	T & E
Crimean	Russia	A,T	B,T	B,R	T	T & E
	Britain et al.	B	B,A	R,SW	B	Bully
Schleswig-Holstein	Germany, Austria	B	B	B	B	Bully
	Denmark	A,T	–	SW	SW	Stone-wall
Russo-Turkish	Russia	B	B,R,T	B	B	Bully
	Turkey	A	–	SW	SW	Stone-wall
British–	Britain	B	B,R,T	SW	B	Bully
Russian	Russia	A	T	A	A	Appease
British–	Britain	B	B	B	B	Bully

Appendix 7 (cont.)

| Crisis | Actor | Influence strategy indicators | | | | Final choice |
		Time Series	Predominant Influence Attempt	Predominant Response	Qualitative Judgment	Influence Strategy
Portuguese	Portugal	R	–	T,A	T	T & E
Spanish–American	US	B,T	B	R	B	Bully
	Spain	R,T	R,B	R	R	Reciprocate
Fashoda	Britain	B,T	R,T	R,SW	R	Reciprocate
	France	T	T,A	R	T	T & E
1st Moroccan	France	T,R	R,T	SW,A	R	Reciprocate
	Germany	T,A	R,T	SW,A	T	T & E
Central American	Nicaragua	B	–	B	B	Bully
	Honduras	B	–	R	B	Bully
Bosnian	Austria-Germany	T	R	SW	R	Reciprocate
	Serbia, Russia, Turkey	T	R	SW	R	Reciprocate
Agadir	France, Britain	R	R,T	R,T	R,T	Reciprocate
	Germany	R,	R,T	R,T	R,T	Reciprocate
1st Balkan	Serbia, Bulgaria, Greece	B	–	SW	B	Bully
	Turkey	B	–	SW	B	Bully
2nd Balkan	Bulgaria	R	–	B	SW	SW
	Serbia, Greece, Romania	B	–	B,SW	B	Bully
Pre-WWI	Germany, Austria	B	B,R	R	B	Bully
	Serbia, Russia, Britain, France	R	R	R	R	Reciprocate
Teschen	Poland	T	–	B	T	T & E
	Czechoslovakia	R	–	R	R	Reciprocate
Chaco Dispute	Bolivia	T	R,T	R	t	T & E
	Paraguay	T,R	R,T	R,B	R	Reciprocate

Crisis	Actor					Outcome
Chaco War	Bolivia	B	–	–	B	Bully
	Paraguay	A,T	–	SW	T	T & E
Manchurian	Japan	B	B,R	B	B	Bully
	China	R,T	T	R	T	T & E
Italo-Ethiopian	Italy	B	B,T	B	B	Bully
	Ethiopia	R,T	T	SW,T	T	T & E
Rhineland	France, Britain, Belgium	R,T	R,A	SW	R	Reciprocate
	Germany	R,B	R,B	SW	R	Reciprocate
Anschluss	Austria	A,T	–	R,A	A	Appease
	Germany	B	R,B	B,R	B	Bully
Munich	Czechoslovakia, Britain	B,T	T	A,T	T	T & E
	France	B	B	SW,A	B	Bully
	Germany	R	–	–	R	Reciprocate
Polish–Lithuanian	Poland	T,A	–	–	T	T & E
	Lithuania	R	B	SW	B	Bully
Danzig	Germany	B,R	B,T	R	R	Reciprocate
	Britain, Poland	T	–	SW	T	T & E
French–Italian	Italy	R	–	B,R	R	Reciprocate
	France	B,R	B,R	–	B	Bully
1st Kashmir	India	B	B,R	SW	B	Bully
	Pakistan	T,R	T	R,SW	R	Reciprocate
Berlin Blockade	US, Britain, France	B	B,R,T	B,SW	B	Bully
	USSR	R	R	SW,R	R	Reciprocate
Trieste	Italy	R,T	R,T	R	T	T & E
	Yugoslavia	T	T	B,R	T	T & E
Suez	Egypt	B	B	B,SW	B	Bully
	Britain, France, Israel	T,B	T,B	–	R	Reciprocate
Honduran Border	Honduras	R	–	–	T	T & E
	Nicaragua	B,T	–	–	T	T & E
Sino-Indian	India	T	R,T	B	R	Reciprocate
	China	B,R	T,R	SW,R	R	Reciprocate

Appendix 7 (*cont.*)

Crisis	Actor	Influence strategy indicators				Final choice
		Time Series	Predominant Influence Attempt	Predominant Response	Qualitative Judgment	Influence Strategy
Bizerte	France	A	R	R	R	Reciprocate
	Tunisia	T	–	B	T	T & E
Cuban Missile	US	B	B,R	B	B	Bully
	USSR, Cuba	R,A	T,A	R,T	T	T & E
Cyprus	Greece	B,R	B	B,SW	B	Bully
	Turkey	B,R	T	R	B	Reciprocate
Rann of Kutch	India	B	–	B	B	Bully
	Pakistan	R,T	R	B	R	Reciprocate
2nd Kashmir	India	B	–	B	B	Bully
	Pakistan	R	–	B	B	Bully
Cod War	Iceland	R,B	B	B	B	Bully
	Britain	B,R	R	T,R	B	Bully
Beagle Channel	Argentina	B	R,T	R,SW	R	Reciprocate
	Chile	R	R	B,SW	R	Reciprocate
Sino-	China	B	B,T	SW	B	Bully
Vietnamese	Vietnam	A,T	R	SW	T	T & E

Notes: B = Bully, R = Reciprocate, A = Appeasing, T = Trial & Error, SW = Stonewall.
"–" = Insufficient information to determine a predominant strategy.

NOTES

1 Realist and psychological perspectives

1 For a more formal and detailed discussion of the role of political belief systems in foreign-policy-making, see George (1969). George makes a useful distinction between the more general, or philosophical view of the nature of international politics, which he calls the "master belief," and the "instrumental" component, which deals with how a state should act under given circumstances.

2 Realism also has served as the dominant research paradigm for international relations scholars in the period since World War II (see Vasquez, 1983).

3 The more commonly used term for these writers is "deterrence theorists." The work of conflict strategists, however, extends beyond deterrence *per se*.

4 For a concise discussion of variants of realism, see Levy, 1989:224–25. A more extended discussion appears in Vasquez, 1977.

5 Ashley (1981) refers to this as "practical realism," a shared informal perspective that makes it possible to orient action within a common tradition, as opposed to a more deterministic view of realism as a set of objective laws governing interstate behavior.

6 Morgenthau's views changed to some extent in latter years, so I have used the 1960 edition of *Politics Among Nations* to provide a reference closer to his original theoretical perspective.

7 Not all classical realists agree on the role of different elements in the power drive. Machiavelli, for example, would consider the pursuit of personal glory to be one of the purposes of ruling; whereas Hobbes decries its deleterious effects.

8 For Waltz the unit of analysis shifts from the state to the international system, with the behavior of individual states a reflection of the structure of the system (see Waltz, 1979). Waltz's systemic perspective is less appropriate to an understanding of crisis behavior, which is primarily a dyadic relationship between the contending parties. A systemic perspective might represent a more appropriate approach to examining the occurrence of interstate crises, and, as in the case of the work of Small and Singer (1982), the amount of war underway in the system at a given time.

9 Schelling (1960:4–5) emphasizes that interstate conflicts contain elements of common, as well as competing interests. The prescriptive advice, however, deals primarily with coercion strategies.

10 It is important to distinguish an integrative solution from a mere compromise. Realists recognize the need for accommodation to avoid wars when the costs will outstrip the benefits, but, in these instances, the assumption is that each side sacrifices some portion of the interests it would like to maintain or obtain. An integrative settlement enables both sides to achieve their interests without any significant sacrifice.

11 An excellent summary of this work appears in Holsti (1989). For a contrary view, see Oneal (1988).

12 One could argue, from a realist perspective, as Thucydides had the Athenian ambassadors argue to the Melians, that weak states should expect to be coerced by stronger states. But even Thucydides' Athenians were quick to admit that their behavior was not legitimate.

13 Recent research on the largely ritualized escalation of fights between lower animals suggests that there may well be bluffing in animal displays of aggressiveness as well (see Archer and Huntingford, 1991).

14 In a social trap, the actor expends more than would be justified by the original stakes because the perceived potential proximity of success encourages the actor to commit more and more resources, rather than cut her losses. A simple example would be that of a long distance caller whose call has been placed on hold. The cost grow as the caller waits for the other party to come to the phone, but if she hangs up the receiver, then redialing will incur a high initial cost. Should she continue to wait just a bit longer? The other party could pick up the line at any second. The possibility of imminent success encourages the continued commitment of resources.

2 Methodology

1 An explicit effort at bridging the gap between qualitative and quantitative studies appears in a comparison of a study by the author (Leng and Wheeler, 1979) with the comparative qualitative study of Snyder and Diesing (1977). See Leng and Walker (1982).

2 The MID figures are tentative estimates, as new cases continue to be added to the data set.

3 The concepts "precipitant" and "challenge" have been taken from Snyder and Diesing (1977:11–12).

4 In the discussion of particular cases, I have tried to keep this clear by referring to the two "sides" to the disputes, although, in some instances, I may refer to those participants on one or another side as a "party" to the dispute, or a "target" of the actions of the other side.

5 Coverage in Langer (1968) becomes sparse after 1945, especially in the case of newly independent states. Butterworth (1976) includes many cases that fall short of the criteria for MICs.

6 Cases used in preliminary studies, which were not selected randomly, have been removed from the sample for the purpose of this study.

7 The count of 593 reciprocated threats, displays, or uses of force from the MID data, however, is considerably larger than the population of MICs. This is because the MID data represent counts of individual incidents of the threat, display, or use of force. There may be several such incidents within a single MIC.

8 A list of the source used in each case appears in Leng (1987a).

9 These scores may overstate the reliability of the data, as lower scores have been obtained for the more complex descriptors in the coding process, particularly the tempo of physical actions, which has yielded a score of 0.84.

10 The week was chosen as the appropriate time interval to obtain a manageable number of observations that would not be distorted by weekends, when diplomatic activity may be lower than usual, falling irregularly into different time intervals.

11 A systematic examination of the possible effects of variations in the structure of the international system on the behavior of states in crises occurring between 1928 and 1980 appears in Brecher and Wilkenfeld (1989).

3 The crisis structure and war

1 One could use indirect indicators based on presumed outside influences that would increase or decrease the psychological and political pressures on decision-makers; however, the most prominent choices would be those tangible elements of interests and relative power that we already are employing as predictors in their own right.

2 Snyder and Diesing (1977:188) suggest that the evidence that they have been able to find indicates that national leaders are overly concerned about the salience of their resolve reputations.

3 The distinction between major and minor power began coterminously with the modern state system, when Britain, Austria, Russia, and Prussia decided, prior to the opening of the Congress of Vienna, to exclude less powerful European states from participation in setting the boundaries of post-Napoleonic Europe (see Nicolson, 1946:137).

4 This does not necessarily require a defensive alliance. For example, Britain's "blank check" to Poland during the Polish–Danzig crisis of 1939 would meet the criterion for a formal commitment to come to Poland's aid, although it would not qualify as a defensive alliance *per se*.

5 For a more extended discussion of contemporary theorizing and research on capability preponderance as a necessary or sufficient cause for war initiation, see Levy (1989:241–55).

6 The most problematic of these is Buena de Mesquita's (1981) measure of utilities (interests) based on formal alliance commitments. The rationale is that the objective in fighting a war is to bring the foreign policy of the adversary more into line with one's own policies; therefore the degree of current congruence, or lack of it, can be measured by comparing formal alliance commitments. The method employed is discussed in detail in Buena de Mesquita and Lalman (1986).

4 Patterns of behavior

1 Missing from the repertoire of the lower animals is the possibility of compromise, which requires higher communication skills.

2 The scale was designed by Rubin and Hill (1973) for use with WEIS data and

239

modified for use with the BCOW data. Actions are weighted according to a simple six-point scale ranging from most hostile (3) to most cooperative (−3).

3 Keohane (1986:4) makes a distinction between "specific reciprocity," that is, returning good for good and ill for ill in relatively equal measure, and "diffuse reciprocity," which refers more to a set of reciprocal obligations, or shared commitments and values. This investigation focuses on the former.

4 The combined reciprocity measure is chosen over correlations in light of the nonlinearity of the time series of weighted actions, as well as the need to obtain a direct measure of the distance dimension of reciprocity. Taking first differences could relieve the linear dependence on time, but not quadratic dependence, which can occur if there are large changes in the last quarter of the time series, a fairly common occurrence in crises.

5 The initial intent was to use three categories of escalation – high, medium, and low – to obtain six behavioral types (reciprocity would remain high, low); however, the break-points for the three escalation types became even more arbitrary. That is, the boundaries would have required placing cases with very similar scores in different categories. The median has been chosen over the mean primarily because the break-points appeared to be more consistent with an intuitive reading of the degree of escalation and reciprocity in the crises in the sample.

6 The categorization is essentially the same as that used in Gochman and Leng (1983); however, different indicators of reciprocity and escalation are used.

7 In our sample, the Pre-World War I crisis falls into the Resistance category because of a fairly low level of reciprocity in the early stages of the crisis. This is largely because I have included the interactions between Austria and Serbia, which dominated the early phase. The North, Brody, and Holsti (1964) study confined itself to interactions among the major powers.

8 A compound resistant smoother has been employed to remove the effects of outliers and exhibit the trend line for each of the cases presented in Figures 1–10. See Velleman (1980:609–15).

5 Structure, behavior, and outcomes

1 Given the borderline ambiguity of the cases in which the combined structural scores are 4–4, those nine cases are not included in Tables 5.2 and 5.3

2 Morgenthau (1960:ch. 31) excludes the United States and the Soviet Union on the grounds that they are too inexperienced and ideological to meet his criteria. I have followed Small and Singer (1982) in including them among the major powers.

3 In a seventh case, independent mediation efforts by the United States and Great Britain, in conjunction with the mediation efforts of the UN Security Council, led to an agreement in the Cyprus crisis of 1963–64, that is best characterized as a stalemate.

4 A militarized dispute is an interstate conflict in which *either* party explicitly threatens, demonstrates, or uses military force. Thus, it is one step below a crisis on the ladder of escalation from a dispute to war.

5 The derivation of the escalation measure is described in Chapter 4.

240

6 Although it has been a fact of modern war that the largest number of fatalities occur among civilians, we will employ the Small and Singer indicator here because of its availability and the authors' reputation for reliability.

7 When the two sides are tied for the first threat or use of force, I have used the precipitant action to determine the initiator. This is one case, the Sino-Vietnam crisis of 1978, in which there is a tie for both the first threat or use of force and the precipitant action. That case is not included in these tests, so that there are sixteen, rather than seventeen, wars included.

8 There are, of course, those situations in which a state finds that the threat to vital interests, such as its political survival, requires accepting higher risks. In those instances, a willingness to fight a severe war to preserve those interests might be considered acceptable. It is hard to imagine instances in which the state defending those interests would also be the initiator of the dispute and the leader in the use of aggressive tactics. In any event, there are no such cases in our sample.

9 The United States was less confident than the other three. The build-up of the Spanish navy in the early months of 1898 worried even that "bully" adventurist Theodore Roosevelt (see Gould, 1982:38).

6 Influence tactics

1 The reasoning behind this exception to the coding rules is based on the assumption that demands for "promises" to make large sacrifices are not of the same seriousness and immediacy as simple demands that those sacrifices be made.

2 Snyder and Diesing (1977:188) note that the evidence suggests that statesmen are overly concerned about the effect of reputation for resolve on their bargaining power. See Jervis (1984:216) on the relationship between perceptions and interests in crises.

3 Schelling (1960:37–43), in fact, argues for the advantages of acquiring a reputation for being stubbornly inflexible, even irrational.

4 In the analysis of game theoretic models, a simple distinction is made between the target's perception of the actor's willingness to carry out its threats or promises and its capability to do so (Zagare, 1987:33–37), but the line between the two is not as easily drawn in the real world.

5 If the target is behaving in accordance with realist precepts, its perception of the comparative war-fighting capabilities should be the same, since the realist prescription is to calculate capabilities in an objective manner and to assume that the other side is acting in the same manner.

6 This category combines two response categories (comply and placate) used in earlier studies (Leng, 1980, 1988). This was done because of the small number of cases of outright compliance with an explicit demand, and in order to reduce the number of categories in the multivariate analysis described below.

7 The associations predicted by the realists are consistent with the views of some social psychologists who view threats as more effective than promises in eliciting compliant responses (see Pruitt and Rubin, 1986:55). These researchers argue that threateners seem more powerful than promisers,

and that threats are more consistent with the sense of aggrieved justice that accompanies interstate disputes.

8 In this and other instances where the cross-tabular results are not significant, I have not included the tables, in order to save space.

9 The Leng (1980) study employed a stratified sample of fourteen militarized crises.

10 Levy (1988:507–508) notes a possible selection bias that suggests caution in interpreting these results, a caution that applies to this study as well. The states being considered in militarized crises are only those states where both parties have resisted the military threats of the other; otherwise there would not be a crisis. Consequently, it would be a mistake to generalize about the limited role of capability considerations beyond militarized crises. A consideration of relative capabilities may well keep states from becoming involved in crises in the first place.

11 An easily accessible summary of the technique appears in Reynolds (1977). A fuller description and discussion appears in Feinberg (1977).

12 Maximum likelihood estimation was used in this case because of the presence of some zero cell entries.

7 Influence strategies

1 GRIT stands for graduated reciprocation in tension reduction, a process of calculated unilateral concessionary moves designed to reduce tension in the Cold War conflict between the United States and the Soviet Union.

2 Those cases in which one of the parties did not enter into serious negotiations, but planned on war from the outset, have been dropped from tests of the association between influence strategies and outcomes.

3 The fifth type, a Stonewalling strategy, is characterized by the absence of any influence attempts, thus there are no accompanying decision rules.

4 The procedure is a bit more complicated in the case of trial-and-error response strategies. See the explanation in Appendix 7.3.

5 The cases are: The Schleswig-Holstein War crisis of 1864, in which Bismarck was bent on war, the First Balkan War crisis of 1912, in which Serbia, Bulgaria, and Greece planned war against Turkey, and the Italo-Ethiopian crisis preceding Mussolini's invasion of Ethiopia in 1935.

6 The motivation scores for each of actors appear in column 6 of Table 3.1.

7 Chi square = 20.99, with four degrees of freedom for columns 2–3, with rows 3 and 4 collapsed. $p = 0.001$.

8 As in Table 7.3, the crises in which war was the objective of one side from the beginning of the crisis have not been included in the table.

9 Chi square = 27.07 with 6 degrees of freedom, with rows 3 and 4 combined and column 3 (stalemate) removed to eliminate cells with expected zero entries.

8 Reciprocating influence strategies

1 GRIT strategies continue the unilateral initiatives for an extended period of time, even in the face of negative responses.

2 Open communication is a feature that is presumed to be critical to the success of GRIT strategies.

3 Harford and Solomon's (1967) influence strategy would include ignoring early positive moves from the other party, which would violate the tit-for-tat rules of a Reciprocating strategy in cases where a Reciprocating player was confronting an opponent employing an exclusively coercive strategy.

4 In Chicken, the worst outcome for each player comes at the intersection of strategies of defect by both players, for example, the outbreak of war in a nuclear crisis. The ordinal pay-offs for Chicken at each strategy intersection are: Cooperate/Cooperate = (3,3), Cooperate/Defect = (2,4) or Defect/Cooperate (4,2) and Defect/Defect = (1,1), with 4 as the most preferred outcome and 1 as the least desired outcome.

5 The reader may remember that, in Chapter 6, we also found no association between threats of force and defiant responses.

6 A "positive initiative" consists of an influence attempt that is accompanied by either positive inducements, or carrot-and-stick inducements.

7 Some experiments with PD games have suggested that TFT strategies are significantly less effective in "noisy" environments. Mueller (1987) found the most effective strategy in a noisy environment to be an unforgiving approach that he calls "GRIM" – begin with a cooperative opening move and, if the other party defects, never cooperate again.

8 The territorial dispute had been submitted to the Queen of England for arbitration. She awarded the islands to Chile, and Argentina challenged the decision.

9 The one exception is the precipitant that touched off the pre-World War I crisis, the assassination of the Austrian Archduke Francis Ferdinand by a Serbian terrorist. The action is difficult to categorize, and one could argue that it is the Austrian ultimatum that should be properly considered the challenge in this crisis and that Serbia and its allies should be considered the defenders of the status quo.

10 The four other cases were: Denmark in the Schleswig-Holstein crisis, Egypt in the Suez crisis, the Soviet Union in the Cuban Missile crisis, and India in the Second Kashmir War crisis.

9 Summary and conclusions

1 As I noted in Chapter 1, classical realism does not deny the influence of certain psychological variables on human behavior, but its predictions and prescriptions for policy are based on assumptions of rationality in decision-making.

2 Table 9.2 is a simplified version of Table 7.3. Four stalemate outcomes are not included; consequently, the percentages do not total 100 percent.

3 A phrase ruefully employed by US President Lyndon Johnson when musing about meeting with the North Vietnamese to bring an end to the Vietnam War.

4 The title of a national bestseller by Fisher and Ury (1981).

Epilogue

1 The Persian Gulf War, in fact, began on August 2, 1990, with the Iraqi invasion of Kuwait. The reference to the beginning of war on January 16, 1992 more properly refers to the entry of the United States and its UN allies.

2 The equilibrium at (3,2) obtains regardless of whether the game is played with a single simultaneous move, or is played sequentially starting at any initial outcome, and regardless of whether the players play myopically or nonmyopically.

3 The exception is the Cyprus crisis of 1963–64, which ended in a stalemate.

4 See Chapter 7 for a discussion of the method employed in determining the predominant influence strategy.

5 The reader is reminded that the data for the examination of the Gulf War crisis are limited solely to what was reported in the *New York Times*. It is possible that there were private initiatives that were not reported.

6 A potential opportunity for Saddam Hussein to find a face-saving way out of the crisis came in early October, when President Bush declared the US's willingness to consider a general solution of Middle East problems if Iraq withdrew from Kuwait.

7 In describing Saddam Hussein's behavior, it could be argued that the most appropriate realist theorist to cite is not Morgenthau (1960), but Machiavelli ([1513] 1964). The Iraqi leader appears to have been motivated more by a concern for his personal power, than by a consideration of the national interest of his country.

REFERENCES

Allison, G. (1971). *Essence of Decision: Explaining the Cuban Missiles Crisis*. Boston: Little, Brown.

Archer, J. and Huntingford, F. (1993). "Game Theory Models and Escalation of Animal Fights," in *Escalation of Aggression*, M. Potegal and J. Knutson (eds.) (forthcoming).

Aron, R. (1966). *Peace and War: A Theory of International Relations*. Garden City: Doubleday and Co., Inc.

Ashley, R. K. (1981). "Political Realism and Human Interests," *International Studies Quarterly*, 25:204–36.

(1984). "The Poverty of Neo-Realism," *International Organization*, 38:225–86.

Axelrod, R. (1984). *The Evolution of Cooperation*. New York: Basic Books.

Axelrod, R. and Dion, D. (1988). "The Further Evolution of Cooperation," *Science*, 242:1385–89.

Bales, R. F. (1951). *Interaction Process Analysis: A Method for the Study of Small Groups*. Reading: MA: Addison-Wesley.

Bartos, O. (1970). "Determinants and Consequences of Toughness," in *The Structure of Conflict*, P. Swingle (ed.). New York: Academic Press.

Bell, C. (1971). *The Conventions of Crisis*. London: Oxford University Press.

Bendor, J. (1987). "In Good Times and Bad: Reciprocity in an Uncertain World," *American Journal of Political Science*, 31:531–58.

Bendor, J., Kramer, R. and Stout, S. (1991). "Cooperation in a Noisy Prisoner's Dilemma," *Journal of Conflict Resolution*, 35:691–719.

Betz, B. (1991). "Strategy and Communication in an Arms Race–Disarmament Dilemma," *Journal of Conflict Resolution*, 35:678–90.

Blainey, G. (1973). *The Causes of War*. New York: Free Press.

Blau, P. M. (1964). *Exchange of Power in Social Life*. New York; Wiley.

Brams, S. J. (1985). *Superpower Games: Applying Game Theory to Superpower Conflict*. New Haven, CT: Yale University Press.

Brams, S. J., and Kilgour, D. M. (1988), *Game Theory and National Security*. New York: Basil Blackwell.

Brams, S. J. and Wittman, D. (1981). "Nonmyopic Equilibria in 2×2 Games," *Conflict Management and Peace Science*, 6:39–62.

Braver, S. L. and Rohrer, V. (1978). "Superiority of Vicarious over Direct Experience in Interpersonal Conflict Resolution," *Journal of Conflict Resolution*, 22:143–54.

Brecher, M. (1977). "Toward a Theory of International Crisis Behavior," *International Studies Quarterly*, 21:39–74.
   (forthcoming). *Crises in World Politics*.
Brecher, M. and James, P. (1986). *Crisis and Change in World Politics*. Boulder: Westview Press.
Brecher, M. and Wilkenfeld, J. (1989). *Crisis, Conflict and Instability*. Oxford: Pergamon Press.
Brehm, J. W. (1966). *A Theory of Psychological Reactance*. New York: Academic Press.
Brehm, S. S. and Brehm, J. W. (1981). *Psychological Reactance: A Theory of Freedom and Control*. New York: Academic Press.
Bremer, S. A. (1992). "Dangerous Dyads: Conditions Affecting the Likelihood of Interstate War, 1816–1965," *Journal of Conflict Resolution*, 36.
Brockner, J. and Rubin, J. Z. (1985). *The Social Psychology of Conflict Escalation and Entrapment*. New York: Spring-Verlag.
Bueno de Mesquita, B. (1981). *The War Trap*. New Haven, CN: Yale University Press.
Buena de Mesquita, B. and Lalman, D. (1986). "Reason and War," *American Political Science Review*, 80:1113–29.
Burns, A. L. (1961). "Prospects for a General Theory of International Relations," in *The International System*. Princeton, NJ: Princeton University Press.
Butterworth, R. (1976). *Managing Interstate Conflict, 1945–1974*. Pittsburgh: University Center for International Studies.
Carr, E. H. (1939). *The Twenty Years Crisis*. London: Macmillan.
Clausewitz, K. von [1832] (1966). *On War*, F. N. Maude (ed.). New York: Barnes and Noble.
Corson, W. (1971). *Measuring Conflict and Cooperation Intensity in East–West Relations: A Manual and Codebook*. Ann Arbor, MI: University of Michigan (mimeo).
Crankshaw, E. (1981). *Bismarck*. New York: Viking.
Dollard, J., Miller, N., Doob, L., Mowrer, O. and Sears, R. (1939). *Frustration and Aggression*. New Haven: Yale University.
Esser, J. K. and Komorita, S. S. (1975). "Reciprocity and Concession Making in Bargaining," *Journal of Personality and Social Psychology*, 31:864–72.
Etzioni, A. (1967). "The Kennedy Experiment," *Western Political Science Quarterly*, 20:316–80.
Feinberg, S. E. (1977). *The Analysis of Cross-Classified Categorical Data*. Cambridge: MIT Press.
Fisher, R. and Ury, W. (1981). *Getting to Yes: Negotiating Agreement without Giving In*. New York: Houghton Mifflin.
French, J. R. P., Jr. and Raven, B. (1959). "The Bases of Social Power," in *Studies in Social Power*, D. Cartwright (ed.). Ann Arbor, MI: University of Michigan Press.
Gamson, W. A., and Modigliani, A. (1971). *Untangling the Cold War: A Strategy for Testing Rival Theories*. Boston: Little Brown.
George, A. L. (1969). "The Operational Code," *International Studies Quarterly* 13:190–222.
   (1979). "Case Studies and Theory Development: The Method of Structured,

246

Focused Comparison," in *Diplomacy*, P. G. Lauren (ed.). New York: Free Press.

George, A. L. and Smoke, R. (1974). *Deterrence in American Foreign Policy: Theory and Practice*. New York: Columbia University Press.

Gochman, C. S. (1990). "Capability-Driven Disputes," in *Prisoners of War? Nation-States in the Modern Era*, C. S. Gochman and A. N. Sabrosky (eds.). Lexington, MA: Lexington Books.

Gochman, C. S. and Leng, R. J. (1983). "Realpolitik and the Road to War: An Analysis of Attributes and Behavior," *International Studies Quarterly*, 27:97–120.

Gochman, C. S. and Maoz, Z. (1984). "Militarized Interstate Disputes, 1816–1976: Procedures, Patterns, Insights," *Journal of Conflict Resolution*, 28:585–615.

Goldstein, J. S. and Freeman, J. R. (1990). *Three-Way Street: Strategic Reciprocity in World Politics*. Chicago: University of Chicago.

Goodman, L. A. and Kruskal, W. H. (1954). "Measures of Association for Cross-classifications," *Journal of American Statistical Association*, 58:310–64.

Gould, L. L. (1982). *The Spanish–American War and President McKinley*. Lawrence, KS: University of Kansas Press.

Gouldner, A. W. (1960). "The Norm of Reciprocity: A Preliminary Statement," *American Sociological Review*, 25:161–78.

Harford, T. and Solomon, L. (1967). "'Reformed Sinner' and 'Lapsed Saint' Strategies in the Prisoner's Dilemma Game," *Journal of Conflict Resolution*, 11:104–9.

Hermann, C. F. (1972). *International Crises: Insights from Behavioral Research*. New York: Free Press.

Hobbes, T. ([1651]1958), *Leviathan*. Indianapolis: Bobbs-Merrill.

Holsti, O. (1969). *Content Analysis for the Social Sciences and the Humanities*. Reading, MA: Addison-Wesley.

(1989). "Crisis Decision Making," in *Behavior, Society, and Nuclear War*, P. E. Tetlock, *et al.* (eds.). New York: Oxford University Press.

Holsti, O., Brody, R. and North, R. (1964). "Affect and Action in International Reaction Models," *Journal of Peace Research*, 1:170–90.

Holsti, O., North, R. and Brody, R. (1968). "Perception and Action in the 1914 Crisis," in *Quantitative International Politics*, J. D. Singer (ed.), New York: Free Press.

Homans, G. C. (1961). *Social Behavior: Its Elementary Forms*. New York: Harcourt, Brace.

Howell, L. (1983). "A Comparative Study of the WEIS and COPDAB Data Sets," *International Studies Quarterly*, 27:149–59.

Huth, P. (1988). *Deterrence and War*. New Haven: Yale University Press.

Huth, P. and Russett, B. (1984). "What Makes Deterrence Work? Cases from 1900 to 1980," *World Politics*, 36:496–526.

(1988). "Deterrence Failure and Crisis Escalation," *International Studies Quarterly*, 32:29–45.

James, P. and Harvey, F. (1989). "Optimal Threats: An Assessment of Super-power Rivalry in International Crises, 1948–1985," A paper presented at the Annual Meeting of the International Studies Association, Atlanta, GA.

Jervis, R. (1976). *Perception and Misperception in International Politics*. Princeton: Princeton University Press.

(1984). *The Illogic of American Nuclear Strategy*. Ithaca: Cornell University Press.

Kahn, H. (1962). *Thinking About the Unthinkable*. New York: Horizon Press.

(1965). *On Escalation; Metaphors and Scenarios*. New York: F. A. Praeger, Inc.

Kahneman, D. and Tversky, A. (1979). "Prospect Theory: An Analysis of Decision Under Risk," *Econometrica*, 47:263–91.

Karsten, P., Howell, P. D. and Allen, A. F. (1984). *Military Threats: A Systemic Historical Analysis of the Determinants of Success*. Westport, CT: Greenwood Press.

Keohane, R. O. (1986). "Reciprocity in International Relations," *International Organization*, 40:1–27.

(1989). *International Institutions and State Power*. Boulder, CO: Westview Press.

Kissinger, H. A. (1957). *Nuclear Weapons and Foreign Policy*. New York: Harper.

(1964). *A World Restored: Metternich, Castlereagh and the Problems of Peace, 1812–1822*. Boston: Houghton Mifflin Company.

(1982). *Years of Upheaval*. Boston: Little, Brown.

Komorita, S. S. and Esser, J. K. (1975). "Frequency of Reciprocated Concessions in Bargaining," *Journal of Personality and Social Psychology*, 32:699–705.

Komorita, S. S., Hilty, J. A. and Parks, C. D. (1991). "Reciprocity and Cooperation in Social Dilemmas," *Journal of Conflict Resolution*, 35:594–618.

Langer, W. L. (1968). *An Encyclopedia of World History*. Boston: Houghton, Mifflin Company.

Lebow, R. N. (1981). *Between War and Peace*. Baltimore: Johns Hopkins University Press.

Leng, R. J. (1980). "Influence Strategies and Interstate Conflict," in *The Correlates of War II: Testing Some Realpolitik Models*, J. D. Singer (ed.). New York: Free Press.

(1984). "Reagan and the Russians: Crisis Bargaining Beliefs and the Historical Record," *American Political Science Review*, 78:338–55.

(1987a). *Behavioral Correlates of War, 1816–1975: A User's Manual*. Ann Arbor: Inter-University Consortium for Political and Social Research.

(1987b). "The Future of Event Data: A Backward Glance," Paper presented at the Annual Meeting of the American Political Science Association, Chicago, IL (September 3–6).

(1991). *Behavioral Correlates of War: Coders Manual for Describing International Actions* (7th revised ed.). Middlebury, VT: Middlebury College (Mimeo.).

Leng, R. J. and Gochman, C. S. (1982). "Dangerous Disputes: A Study of Conflict Behavior and War," *American Journal of Political Science*, 26:664–87.

Leng, R. J. and Goodsell, R. (1974). "Behavioral Indicators of War Proneness in Bilateral Conflicts," in *Sage International Yearbook of Foreign Policy Studies*, II, P. McGowan (ed.). Beverly Hills: Sage.

Leng, R. J. and Singer, J. D. (1987). "Militarized Interstate Crises: The BCOW Typology and its Applications," *International Studies Quarterly*, 32:155–73.

Leng, R. J. and Walker, S. (1982). "Comparing Two Studies of Crisis Bargaining:

Confrontation, Coercion, and Reciprocity," *Journal of Conflict Resolution*, 26:571–91.

Leng, R. J. and Wheeler, H. (1979). "Influence Strategies, Success, and War," *Journal of Conflict Resolution*, 23:655–84.

Levy, J. S. (1988). "When do Deterrent Threats Work?" *British Journal of Political Science*, 18:485–612.

Levy, J. S. (1989). "The Causes of War: A Review of Theories and Evidence," in *Behavior, Society, and Nuclear War*, P. E. Tetlock, *et al.* (eds.). New York: Oxford University Press.

Lindskold, S., Betz, B. and Walters, P. (1986). "Transforming Competitive or Cooperative Climates," *Journal of Conflict Resolution*, 30:99–114.

Lindskold, S., Walters, P. and Koutsourais, H. (1983). "Cooperators, Competitors, and Response to GRIT," *Journal of Conflict Resolution*, 27:521–32.

Lockhart, C. (1979). *Bargaining in International Conflicts*. New York: Columbia University Press.

Machiavelli, N. ([1513]1964). *The Prince*. New York: St. Martin's Press.

Maoz, Z. (1982). *Paths to Conflict: International Dispute Initiation, 1816–1976*. Boulder, CO: Westview Press.

(1983). "Resolve, Capabilities, and the Outcomes of Interstate Disputes, 1816–1976," *Journal of Conflict Resolution*, 27:195–229.

Masters, R. (1969). "World Politics as a Primitive Political System," in *International Politics and Foreign Policy*, revised ed., J. N. Rosenau (ed.). Englewood Cliffs, NJ: Prentice-Hall.

McClelland, C. D. (1961). "The Acute International Crisis," *World Politics*, 14:182–204.

(1968). *International Interaction Analysis: Basic Research and Some Practical Implications: Technical Report* No. 2. Los Angeles, CA: University of Southern California (Mimeographed).

(1983). "Let the User Beware," *International Studies Quarterly*, 27:169–78.

Molander, P. (1985). "The Optimal Level of Generosity in a Selfish, Uncertain Environment," *Journal of Conflict Resolution*, 29:611–18.

Morgenthau, H. J. (1946). *Scientific Man Versus Power Politics*. Chicago: University of Chicago Press.

(1960). *Politics Among Nations: The Struggle for Power and Peace*, 3rd ed. New York: Alfred A. Knopf.

Mueller, U. (1987). "Optimal Retaliation for Optimal Cooperation," *Journal of Conflict Resolution*, 31:692–724.

Neustadt, R. E. (1970). *Alliance Politics*. New York: Columbia University.

Nicolson, H. (1946). *The Congress of Vienna: A Study in Allied Unity: 1812–1822*. London: Harcourt, Brace.

Niebuhr, R. (1944). *The Children of Light and the Children of Darkness*. New York: Charles Scribner's Sons.

North, R. (1967). "Perception and Action in the 1914 Crisis," *Journal of International Affairs*, 21:103–22.

North, R., Holsti, O. and Brody, R. (1964). "Some Empirical Data on the Conflict Spiral," *Peace Research Society (International) Papers*, 1:1–14.

Oneal, J. R. (1988). "The Rationality of Decision Making During International Crises," *Polity*, 20:598–622.

Osgood, C. (1962). *An Alternative to War or Surrender*. Urbana, IL: University of Illinois Press.

Osgood, R. E., and Tucker, R. W. (1967). *Force, Order, and Justice*. Baltimore: John Hopkins University Press.

Patchen, M. (1987). "Strategies for Eliciting Cooperation from an Adversary: Laboratory and International Findings," *Journal of Conflict Resolution*, 31:164–85.

Powell, R. (1988). "Nuclear Brinkmanship with Two-Sided Incomplete Information," *American Political Science Review*, 82:155–78.

Pruitt, D. G. (1969). "Stability and Sudden Change in Interpersonal and International Affairs," in *International Politics and Foreign Policy*, revised ed., J. N. Rosenau (ed.). New York: Free Press.

Pruitt, D. G. and Rubin, J. Z. (1986). *Social Conflict: Escalation, Stalemate, and Settlement*. New York: Random House.

Rapoport, A. (1960). *Fights, Games, and Debates*. Ann Arbor: University of Michigan Press.

(1968). *Clausewitz on War*. Middlesex, UK: Penguin.

(1974). "Prisoner's Dilemma: Recollections and Observations," in *Game Theory as a Theory of Conflict Resolution*, A. Rapoport (ed.). Dordrecht, Holland: D. Reidel Publishing.

Reynolds, H. T. (1977). *Analysis of Nominal Data*. Beverly Hills: Sage Publications.

Richardson, J. L. (1988). "New Perspectives on Appeasement: Some Implications for International Relations," *World Politics*, 40:289–315.

Richardson, L. F. (1960). *Arms and Insecurity: A Mathematical Study of the Causes and Origins of War*. Pittsburgh: Boxwood Press.

Riker, W. H. and Ordeshook, P. C. (1973). *An Introduction to Positive Political Theory*. Englewood Cliffs, NJ: Prentice-Hall.

Rubin, T., and Hill, G. (1973). *Experiments in the Scaling and Weighting of International Events Data*. Arlington, VA: Consolidated Analysis Centers.

Schelling, T. C. (1960). *Strategy of Conflict*. Cambridge, MA: Harvard University Press.

(1966). *Arms and Influence*. New Haven: Yale University Press.

Simon, H. (1957). *Models of Man*. New York: Wiley.

Singer, J. D. (1963). "Inter-Nation Influence: A Formal Model," *American Political Science Review*, 57:420–30.

(1969). "The Incompleat Theorist: Insight without Evidence," in *Contending Approaches to International Politics*, K. Knorr and J. N. Rosenau (eds.). Princeton, NJ: Princeton University Press.

(1976). "The Correlates of War Project: Continuity, Diversity, and Convergence," in *Quantitative International Politics: An Appraisal*, F. W. Holle and D. A. Zinnes (eds.). New York: F. A. Praeger.

Singer, J. D. and Small, M. (1966). "The Composition and Status Ordering of the International System, 1815–1940," *World Politics*, 18:236–82.

Siverson, R. M. and King, J. (1979). "Alliances and the Expansion of War," in *To*

Auger Well: Early Warning Indicators in World Politics, J. D. Singer and M. Wallace (eds.). Beverly Hills, CA: Sage Publications.

Small, M. and Singer, J. D. (1969). "Formal Alliances, 1816–1965: An Extension of the Basic Data," *Journal of Peace Research*, 3:257–82.

(1982). *Resort to Arms: International and Civil Wars, 1816–1980*. Beverly Hills, CA: Sage Publications.

Snyder, G. and Diesing, P. (1977). *Conflict Among Nations: Bargaining, Decision Making, and System Structure in International Crises*. Princeton: Princeton University Press.

Stephan, W. G. (1975). "Actor versus Observer: Attributions to Behavior with Positive or Negative Outcomes and Empathy for the Other Role," *Journal of Experimental Social Psychology*, 11:205–14.

Sullivan, M. P. (1990). *Power in Contemporary International Politics*. Columbia, SC: University of South Carolina Press.

Thucydides. (1975 [1625]). *Hobbes's Thucydides*. New Brunswick, NJ: Rutgers University Press.

Vasquez, J. A. (1983). *The Power of Power Politics: A Critique*. New Brunswick, NJ: Rutger University Press.

(1987). "The Steps to War: Toward a Scientific Explanation of Correlates of War Findings," *World Politics*, 38:80–117.

Velleman, P. (1980). "Definition and Comparison of Robust Nonlinear Data Smoothing Algorithms," *Journal of the American Statistical Association*, 75:690–15.

Waltz, K. N. (1959). *Man, the State, and War*. New York: Columbia University Press.

(1967). "International Structure, National Force, and the Balance of World Power," *Journal of International Affairs*, 21:220–28.

(1979). *Theory of International Politics*. Reading, MA: Addison-Wesley.

Walzer, M. (1977). *Just and Unjust Wars*. New York: Basic Books.

Ward, M. D. (1982). "Cooperation and Conflict in Foreign Policy Behavior," *International Studies Quarterly*, 26:87–126.

Wayman, F. W. (1991). "Alliances and War: A Time Series Analysis," in *Prisoners of War?*, C. S. Gochman and A. N. Sabrosky (eds.). Lexington, MA: Lexington Books.

Wayman, F. W., Singer, J. D. and Goertz, G. (1983). "Capability, Military Allocations, and Successes in Militarized Disputes," *International Studies Quarterly*, 27:497–515.

Weinberg, G. L. (1988). "Munich After 50 Years," *Foreign Affairs*, 67:165–78.

Worchal, S. (1974). "The Effects of Three Types of Arbitrary Thwarting on the Instigation to Aggression," *Journal of Personality*, 42:300–18.

Worchal, S. and Brehm, J. W. (1971). "Direct and implied Social Restoration of Freedom," *Journal of Personality and Social Psychology*, 18:294–304.

Yukl, G. A. (1974). "Effects of the Opponent's Initial Offer, Concession Magnitude, and Concession Frequency on Bargaining Behavior," *Journal of Personality and Social Psychology*, 30:322–35.

Zagare, F. C. (1987). *The Dynamics of Deterrence*. Chicago: University of Chicago.

Zartman, W. I. and Berman, M. R. (1982). *The Practical Negotiator*. New Haven: Yale University Press.

Zinnes, D. A., North, R. and Koch, H. (1961). "Capability, Threat and the Outbreak of War," in *International Politics and Foreign Policy*, revised ed., J. N. Rosenau (ed.). New York: Free Press.

Zinnes, D. A., Zinnes, J. L. and McClure, R. D. (1972). "Hostility in Diplomatic Communications," in *International Crises: Insights from Behavioral Research*, C. F. Hermann (ed.). New York: Free Press.

INDEX OF NAMES

INDEX OF SUBJECTS

inducements and, 127, 198
intangible, 48–49, 57–58, 62–64
power and, 4, 6, 7, 45
reputation for reliability, 51–55, 58–60
reputation for resolve, 49–51, 58–59
tangible, 48–49, 57–58, 62–64
vital, 15, 48–49, 58, 65, 193, 212, 221
war outcomes and, 57–59, 99–100, 193, 195
international system, *see* interstate system
interstate dispute, 25–26
interstate system, 5, 17, 40
Italo-Ethiopian war, 1914–35, 30, 62, 103, 109, 242n.5
Italo-French crisis, 1938–39, 30, 88

"lock-in" effect in escalation, 17, 166, 186, 194, 198, 217
log linear analysis, 129–31 *passim*, 199

major powers, 50–51, 58–59
definition of, 50–51, 239n.3
managing crises, 100–1, 110, 196
minor powers and, 50–51
realist perspective, 50–51, 196
war outcomes and, 58–59, 101, 110
Manchurian War, 1931, 30, 62, 81, 88, 103, 109, 157
Melian dialogue, 3, 57, 62, 128
methodology, 20–44
caveats, 39–44
militarized interstate crises (MICs)
BCOW sample, 28–29, 43, 238n.6, 238n.7
boundaries, 27
classical realism and, 6
defined, 1, 25–29
outcomes of, 45–46, 97–112
participants in, 27–28, 238n.4
stress in, 12–13
structure of, 45–65, 192–93
militarized interstate crises, behavioral types, 66–89, 111, 194–95
classification of, 66–67, 81–84
"cross-over" patterns, 78–80, 87
dimensions, 66
Fight, 74, 89–90, 157, 194
peaceful outcomes, 88–89, 111
Put-Down, 80–81, 90, 104, 156–57, 194–95
Resistance, 78–79, 87, 90, 104, 156–57, 194–95, 214–16
Standoff, 74–78, 89–90, 157, 194
war outcomes, 85–88, 111
militarized interstate disputes, 25–26, 240n.4
minor powers, 50–51
major powers and, 50–51

compromises and, 102–3
misperception, 12–13
in recognizing influence strategies, 176–79
motivation in militarized crises
in Persian Gulf crisis, 212–13
influence strategies and, 149, 152–55
operational indicator of, 94–95
Reciprocating influence strategies and, 180
responses to inducements, 128–29
war outcomes and, 154–55
Munich crisis, 1938, 30, 40, 47, 51, 88, 102, 142, 147–48

national interest, 6
neo-Clausewitzians, 7
neo-realists, 5
1914 crisis, *see* Pre-World War I crisis
noise to signal ratio, 12, 176

Pastry War, 1838–39, 30, 103
Pelopennesian Wars, 5
perceptions, 47
Persian Gulf crisis, 1990–91, 209–22, 244n.1
policy implications, 208–9
Polish–Lithuanian crisis, 1938, 30, 102
power
classical realism and, 4–6, 49
crisis bargaining and, 7–8, 141
definition, 45
interests and, 4, 6–7, 45
power politics, 55–56, 65, 92
Pre-World War I crisis, 1914, 27–28, 30, 51, 79, 81, 87, 186, 240n.7, 243n.9
Pre-World War II crisis, 1939, *see* Danzig crisis
precipitant action, 27
pride, 4
Prisoner's Dilemma (PD) games, 137–39, 198, 202–3
described, 137–38
findings from, 18, 22, 139, 164, 166–81 *passim*, 243n.7
structural attributes, 180
prudence, 5–6, 10, 113, 202
resolve and, 95–96, 209
psychological perspective, 10–18, 191–92, 197, 204–8
on bargaining, 114, 136–38, 159, 162, 194
on escalation, 68–69, 89–90, 194
on Persian Gulf crisis, 221
Reciprocating influence strategies and, 190
psychological reactance, 13–15, 19, 23, 68, 141, 162, 174, 198, 201

257

172

$$\begin{array}{r}86\\3\overline{)259}\\2\,4\\\hline 1\,9\end{array}$$

$$\begin{array}{r}36\\12\\\hline 72\end{array}$$

$$\begin{array}{r}36\\43,200\end{array}$$

T.W
FSS
TW

$$\begin{array}{r}458\\4\\\hline 1892\end{array}$$

$$\begin{array}{r}808\\42\\\hline 135\end{array}$$

2500
2000
570

$$\begin{array}{r}135\overline{)258}\\270\\\hline 180\quad 47\end{array}$$

$$\begin{array}{r}288\overline{)11520}\\858\\\hline 2080\\1616\end{array}$$